D1499288

ON STRIKE!
Capital Cities and
the Wilkes-Barre Newspaper Unions

ON STRIKE!

Capital Cities and the
Wilkes-Barre Newspaper
Unions

Thomas J. Keil

The University of Alabama Press
Tuscaloosa and London

Copyright © 1988 by
The University of Alabama Press
Tuscaloosa, Alabama 35487
All rights reserved
Manufactured in the United States of America

Library of Congress Cataloging-in-Publication Data

Keil, Thomas J.
    On strike! Capital Cities and the Wilkes-Barre unions

    Bibliography: p.
    Includes index.
    1. Strikes and lockouts—Newspapers—Pennsylvania—Wilkes-Barre. 2. American newspapers—Pennsylvania—Wilkes-Barre. 3. Capital Cities Communications, Inc. (U.S.) 4. Wilkes-Barre Publishing Company. I. Title. PN4899.W55C375
1988   071'.4833   86-30881   ISBN 0-8173-0360-X

British Library Cataloguing-in-Publication Data is available.

Dedication

To the memory of Mary Lillis
Hogan, whose deep sense of
local history and whose
personal commitments to and
interpretations of the anthracite
region's trade union culture
helped shape my own
understandings of that special
world of the working class

Contents

Acknowledgments

I would like to express my appreciation both to the College of Arts and Sciences and to the Office of Graduate Programs and Research, University of Louisville, for providing the financial support for this project. Also, I thank the following colleagues who, at one time or another, were willing to take the time to read and discuss various parts of this manuscript with me— Scott Cummings, Chuck Ekstrom, Pam Oliver, Jon Rieger, Joyce Rothschild, Bob Schulman, Wayne Usui, and Robert Wolensky—and the anonymous readers whose carefully considered comments on various drafts of the manuscript made this a much better work than it could possibly have been without their insights. My deep gratitude also goes to the men and women at the *Citizens' Voice* and the *Times Leader* who were willing to be interviewed for this project and to my other sources as well. Both newspapers provided photographs to illustrate this book, some of which are printed here in altered form to protect individual identities. Finally, I thank Lorraine, Jacqueline, and Deborah Ann, whose toleration of my periodic prolonged absences and the hours spent in front of my Apple IIe composing and revising allowed me to persist on this project without feeling too much guilt, and to my parents, Thomas L. and Mary Hogan Keil, whose assistance and encouragement helped in ways too numerous to mention.

ON STRIKE!
Capital Cities and the
Wilkes-Barre Newspaper Unions

Introduction

In October 1978 workers at the *Times Leader,* a subsidiary of
Capital Cities Communications, Inc., began a long, bitter, and
costly strike that still continues. The strike started within six
months of Capital Cities' purchase of the Wilkes-Barre Publishing Company from the local families who had owned it
since the company was formed in 1939.

The Wilkes-Barre Publishing Company produced an all-day,
Monday through Saturday, paper with a daily, monopoly circulation of around seventy thousand copies. The only other
daily paper in the county was published in Hazleton, a city
some thirty miles south of Wilkes-Barre. The Sunday market
was controlled by the locally owned, family-managed *Sunday
Independent.*

Two other daily papers carried county news. Both were published in Scranton, fifteen miles north of Wilkes-Barre. The
Scranton papers had large circulations in the small towns in
northern Luzerne County but few readers in the central part
of the county around Wilkes-Barre. Allegedly the owners of
the Scranton and Wilkes-Barre papers had an informal agreement that they would not invade each other's territories in
search of news, advertising, and circulation.

At the time of the sale, the Wilkes-Barre Publishing Company's main competition for advertising revenue came from

the *Sunday Independent* and other media. The regional market was served by three commercial television stations, one in Scranton, one in Wilkes-Barre, and one midway between the two cities. In addition, there was a fiercely competitive radio market.

Through the late 1970s the Wilkes-Barre Publishing Company faced heavy media competition, a stagnant if not declining local economy, heavy losses incurred in recovering from a major flood and from a failed effort to start a Sunday edition, the hyperinflation characteristic of the newspaper industry at the time, and the unions' unwillingness to grant contract concessions. These pressures resulted in the owners' decision to sell the publishing company. They quietly put it on the market. Several prospective buyers looked at the property, but none made an offer the owners found acceptable. Finally, Capital Cities' bid of $10.5 million was accepted. It seemed as though Capital Cities had gotten a bargain. Normally a monopoly paper with a circulation the size of Wilkes-Barre's should have sold for between $20 and $30 million.

When Capital Cities acquired the paper, it was undistinguished. Its graphics were outmoded, and its reporting and editing were lackluster. It held on to its circulation by default. Discriminating readers interested in more complete national and international news had to turn to New York or Philadelphia papers, but for local news they had no alternative to the paper published by the Wilkes-Barre Publishing Company.

Capital Cities had ambitious plans for its new property. It wanted to expand the local newsnet to include all of northeastern Pennsylvania. Capital Cities especially coveted the Scranton market. The company also had an interest in developing a Sunday edition. To expand circulation and the paper's advertising base, Capital Cities knew that the quality of the paper would have to be substantially improved, but changes of the desired scale would require not only significant capital investment but also the cooperation of employees.

At first, some of the workers seemed receptive to Capital Cities' plans. One reporter told me that after an early meeting with the new executives, "A lot of us came away . . . feeling good about the purchase. We felt that Capital Cities was a company that was interested in producing a first-rate newspaper, and we wanted to be a part of that effort." Initial enthusiasm soon soured when the workers came to believe that the new owners' desired improvements were going to come at a considerable cost to them and their unions.

The first sign of trouble between the new owners and the unions came in the contract negotiations between the company and the stereotypers' and pressmen's locals. These negotiations began shortly after Capital Cities assumed control of the paper. The pressmen and stereotypers had been working for quite some time without a contract. During the spring of 1978 their international representative had been trying to get them to sign an agreement with the old owners, telling them that the international had heard rumors that "something big was about to happen in Wilkes-Barre." Claiming that the international did not know what was about to take place, he urged them to sign their contract because there only were a few points of disagreement left between the company and the union. The locals did not heed his advice, and the paper was sold before they had a contract.

The unions realized negotiations would not be easy when the company told them that bargaining could not take place on the publishing company's premises and that the unions would be expected to share expenses for renting a room at a neutral site, which cost the unions $35 a day.

From that point on, relations between the company and the unions deteriorated. After failing to reach contract agreements, the unions called a strike on October 6, 1978. The vote in favor of a strike was 185 to 5. On October 9, the strikers started publishing their own paper, the *Citizens' Voice*. The company has continued publishing the *Times Leader*. Capital Cities admitted to having lost at least $20 million in the first eighteen months of the strike and reportedly has lost $2 million a year since then because of competition from *Citizens' Voice*. By 1986, the *Citizens' Voice* reported a circulation of close to forty-seven thousand papers per day, which was verified by the Audit Bureau of Circulation. Capital Cities does not report its paid circulation, but in early April 1986 it claimed that it finally had pulled even with the *Citizens' Voice*.

Although strike papers are common in the newspaper industry, there are few examples of papers produced by workers achieving the success the *Citizens' Voice* has, especially when locked into direct competition with the strikers' former employer. The strikers have been successful not only because of their militance, solidarity, and skills at putting together and running a newspaper but also because they have been able to mobilize broad-based grass-roots support for their efforts. Without such support, they would have had little chance of surviving in direct competition with such a resource-rich company as Capital Cities.

To understand why the Wilkes-Barre workers have been able to mobilize the bulk of the region's population on their behalf, it is necessary to understand the area's labor history and its current economic situation. The first chapter presents a brief overview of workers' attempts to respond to corporate exploitation during the years when anthracite mining was the region's main economic activity and an overview of what happened to the local economy when mining ceased. This chapter establishes the context of the strike and shows how traditions and practices built up by the mine workers during their almost continual struggles with the coal operators were put to use in the conflict between Capital Cities (and its local allies, principally the regional business elite) and the four unions at the Wilkes-Barre Publishing Company and their allies. The remaining chapters focus on Capital Cities and its contract demands, the response of the unions, the nature of the strikers' paper, and the ways in which the strikers were able to mobilize massive community support.

1

The Setting:

The Anthracite Mining Era

Wilkes-Barre, a city of some fifty thousand people, is located in northeastern Pennsylvania, roughly 110 miles west of New York City and about 100 miles northwest of Philadelphia. It is Luzerne County's seat of government. Between the 1840s and 1950s, Wilkes-Barre was a major financial center for the anthracite coal industry's Wyoming field. The region's experience with anthracite production has left indelible marks not only on its physical terrain but also on its demographics, social structure, social practices, and culture. To understand the region and its people's response to the strike at Capital Cities' *Times Leader*, one must understand the mining industry and its effects on Luzerne County.

Anthracite production began in the 1820s in the Schuylkill and Lehigh fields to the south of Wilkes-Barre. Using relatively primitive drift and slope mining techniques (Yearly, 1961), entrepreneurs competed to service the growing urban economies on the East Coast. Mining began on a large scale in Luzerne County in the 1840s. Almost from the first, the Wyoming field was dominated by corporate operators. The geomorphology of the Wyoming coal deposits and the lack of navigable rivers for transporting mined coal all but ruled out petty production. Operators could not get to the coal deposits with simple mining techniques. They had to use deep-mining

5

technologies. Deep mining raised the costs of opening and operating a mine to a point that few individuals had the resources to enter the business.

Under corporate domination, the Wyoming field's levels of production soon soared past those of other regions. By the end of the Civil War, Wyoming operators controlled the largest part of the market. The corporations' market position was helped because they reached informal trade agreements among themselves while operators in other fields had to contend with the effects of anarchistic competitive relations.

In the Schuylkill, for example, the large number of petty producers never were able to construct stable production agreements (Yearly, 1961). As a result, the entire anthracite industry was plagued with periodic depressions characterized by plunging coal prices and profits. In 1869 the Reading Railroad began buying up small producers, driving those who resisted out of business, and modernizing the Schuylkill's mines (Greene, 1968). With the Reading's move into production, the stage was set for creating effective interregional, industrywide trade agreements.

Between 1873 and 1892, the corporations tried on several occasions to build a stable cartel, but they never were able to do so (Wardell and Johnston, 1983). For various reasons, production agreements quickly broke down or the government took action against the trusts that were formed (von Halle, 1895; Roberts, 1901; Greene, 1968). Finally, in 1893, J. P. Morgan established a cartel that, despite a shaky start and government opposition, lasted well into the twentieth century. Through a variety of formal and informal arrangements, Morgan and his allies held the trust together until the corporations began abandoning the industry after World War I.

Because of its chronic instability, the coal industry never provided its workers with decent wages and working conditions or stable employment. Even in good times, the miner's lot was hard. Prosperity resulted in only small improvements in the miners' well-being. Given the economic plight of the mine workers when times were good, it is not surprising that the industry's history was marked by continual conflict between labor and capital.

The industry's first major strike occurred in 1842 in Schuylkill County. In 1849 there was a second major strike in the Schuylkill, led by a small group of mine workers in that county who had formed the Bates Union. The Bates Union—the first recorded formal mine workers' organization in the anthracite industry (Greene, 1968; Keil, 1982)—was never able to spread beyond a few production points, and it disappeared in 1850.

Between 1850 and 1868, mine workers continued their efforts to build a union. None of the unions lasted for more than a few months, and none spread beyond one or two production points. Lacking organization, the mine workers seldom won strikes during these years.

Unable to construct a viable union, mine workers had no way to protect themselves except the private and particularistic associations built around their households, kinship networks, neighborhoods, and ethnic groups. Although in the absence of an effective union or a public welfare system such associations were indispensable to the survival of a miner and his family, they were often a source of deep divisions and antagonistic relationships within the mining camps and settlements. For example, different ethnic groups and factions within ethnic groups struggled with each other for control over jobs and promotions. These struggles often led to violent attacks by one group or another. Gangs of Irish workers sometimes attacked other Irish immigrants whom they believed threatened to take their jobs.

Often violence was intercommunal, as in the case of the so-called Molly Maguire terrorism. The Mollies were a secret Irish terrorist group that operated in the coal fields from the late 1850s through the late 1870s (Bimba, 1932; Coleman, 1936; Lewis, 1964; Aurand, 1971; Keil, 1982). Until they were crushed by the combined forces of the Pinkertons, the Coal and Iron Police, and the state, the Mollies directed their attacks at both mine owners and Welsh, German, and native workers whom they believed were collaborating with employers to exploit the Irish (Keil, 1982). Such attacks only exacerbated already difficult and sometimes antagonistic relations between the Irish and other workers in the coal region.

In 1868 mine workers formed the Workingmen's Benevolent Association (WBA). It was the first mining union to unite workers from all of the anthracite fields, and it was the first U.S. union to be organized along industrial rather than craft lines. The WBA managed a successful strike in 1869 and succeeded in having a number of mine safety bills passed by the Pennsylvania legislature. It conducted less successful strikes in 1870 and 1871.

By 1875 the WBA had changed its name to the Miners' and Laborers' Benevolent Association (MLBA). It called a strike again in 1875 in response to a 20 percent wage cut. After six months, the workers returned to the mines, starved and beaten into submission. After its defeat in this strike, the MLBA disappeared. But though the union had lasted for only six years, the WBA-MLBA made several significant contributions to the workers' movement in the anthracite industry.

It showed the men that it was possible to overcome the internal cleavages of ethnicity, skill level, and field to forge an organization that could advance the economic, political, and social interests of all mine workers. It also showed them the advantages of organized political and economic action rather than "prepolitical" protest, which Eric Hobsbawm defines as reactive and defensive, relying on ad hoc organization, and with no specific program for political and social change. Political action, by contrast, has a more or less permanent organization, continues after the stimulus or threat that set the protest in motion has disappeared, and has a program for structural change (Hobsbawm, 1959).

When the MLBA collapsed, mine workers reverted to protecting themselves through their particularistic social networks, associations, and institutions. Old antagonisms and conflicts within the work force resurfaced, adding to the mine workers' political difficulties. Without the MLBA mine workers found it impossible to cooperate on an industrywide basis. Their disorganization led to defeat in an 1877 strike, when the Wyoming men walked out in support of striking railroad workers. The Reading Railroad's miners refused to honor the call for an industrywide walkout and continued to work while the Lehigh and Wyoming men were on strike.

In Scranton and northern Luzerne County, the 1877 strike was marked by massive public demonstrations and other acts of civil disobedience (Brecher, 1972). Six demonstrators in Scranton were killed and fifty-four were wounded when a group of vigilantes shot into a citizens' march. The militia was sent into the Wyoming field to restore order. On their way to Wilkes-Barre and Scranton troop trains were attacked as they wound their way through mountain passes. It was several weeks before military authorities reestablished order in the region. In the meantime, the Schuylkill miners kept producing and the Wyoming men felt betrayed because the Schuylkill workers had not joined them.

But it was not only interfield rivalries that came to the forefront once the MLBA was defeated. So, too, did interethnic and political-philosophical divisions within the work force. Sometimes these divisions overlapped and seriously weakened the workers' movement. Such an overlapping contributed to the eventual defeat of the Knights of Labor's attempt to unionize the coal fields. In the late 1870s, the Knights were successful in organizing the Wyoming miners, especially around the cities of Scranton, Carbondale, and Pittston. They had less success in penetrating the Schuylkill, where they encountered resistance from German, Welsh, and native miners who resented Irish dominance of the Knights and objected to several aspects of the Knights' political program.

Many of the Schuylkill miners rejected the Luzerne County Knights' political activism under the banner of the Greenback-Labor party (Keil, 1982). In addition, there was considerable resistance to parts of the Knights' political program, which called for the nationalization of the mines and municipal ownership of coal yards. They also were suspicious of the

Knights' call for the formation of cooperatives as a way to free workers from the wage system, which the Knights regarded as tantamount to slavery. Finally, many of the non-Irish miners in the Schuylkill rejected the Knights' pan-labor philosophy, preferring industrial unionism. A large number of the Schuylkill's non-Irish miners joined the Amalgamated Association of Miners and Mine Laborers of Pennsylvania. The result was dual unionism.

Competition between the Knights and the Amalgamated seriously weakened the workers' cause. Even when the two unions cooperated with each other, as they did in the strike of 1887–88, their combined force proved no match for the cartel controlling the industry at the time. The loss of this strike brought an end to both unions in the anthracite region, and once again disorganization reigned in the coal fields.

This situation lasted until the mid-1890s, when organizers from the small bituminous workers' union, the United Mine Workers of America (UMWA), entered the region. As had the Knights, the UMWA found its earliest success in the Wyoming field. Although the Schuylkill proved more difficult to organize, the UMWA eventually was as successful there as it was in the Wyoming.

Aside from corporate opposition, one of the most difficult problems that the UMWA organizers had to overcome was the animosity between English-speaking mine workers and newer immigrants from Russia, Poland, Hungary, Lithuania, Sicily, Moravia, Bohemia, the Ukraine, Slovenia, and Croatia. English-speaking workers saw the new immigrants as strikebreakers, cheap laborers who were undermining the wage rate, and potential competitors for the better jobs in the industry. The new immigrants saw the English-speaking workers, especially the Irish contract miners, as another group that was willing to exploit and abuse them.

UMWA organizers eventually convinced English-speaking miners that the new immigrants were indispensable to unionization because without their support it would be impossible to conduct a successful strike. The union also convinced the new immigrants that their only hope for improving their situation was to ally themselves with the English-speaking mine workers (Greene, 1968).

The UMWA's cause among the new immigrants was helped when a sheriff's posse gunned down a group of Slavic mine workers who were holding a peaceful protest march. The men were on their way to close down a mine owned by the Pardee family when they were met by a posse led by Luzerne County Sheriff James L. Martin. The posse opened fire on the marchers, who were armed only with American flags, killing nineteen and wounding thirty-two of them.

Martin and his deputies were tried for murder. They were defended by Henry Palmer, who had been Pennsylvania's attorney general. Palmer denounced the marchers as "socialists, anarchists, and haters of organized government" (Novak, 1978:232). The killers' acquittal further infuriated the new immigrants and strengthened their resolve to put an end to their brutalization and exploitation.

By 1900 the UMWA was able to carry out a successful six-week strike, at the end of which workers gained several major concessions from the operators. The terms of the settlement were to remain in effect until April 1901 (Roberts, 1901; Greene, 1968). When the agreement expired, the operators refused to meet with the UMWA or to recognize its right to bargain for the entire industry. Relations between the workers and the corporations were at a low. In 1901, there reportedly were more than one hundred localized conflicts between the men and their employers (Greene, 1968). In 1902, the men asked for an eight-hour day, a 20 percent wage increase, and adjustments in the dockage rates for waste materials in the coal brought to the surface. J. P. Morgan and the other operators refused to negotiate, and the UMWA called a strike that lasted from May 12 until October 20, 1902, a total of 165 days. The strike was settled only after the federal government intervened and convinced the operators to accept binding arbitration of their differences with the union.

Mine workers endured unbelievable economic hardships

during the strike. As in the past, support for and participation in the strike knew no age or sex boundaries in a mine household. Everyone was expected to contribute in all ways possible, including marching and picketing along with the mine workers and sharing in the misery that prevailed until the strike was concluded. Miners, their wives, and their children presented a united front against the corporations. The mine patches and settlements displayed incredible solidarity and self-discipline. Men, women, and children policed the community to ensure against scabbing. Scabs were often beaten and driven out of the coal fields. When the strike ended in October and the men returned to the mines, they had achieved only limited economic gains, the biggest of which was that the companies were finally forced to recognize the UMWA as the de facto bargaining agent for the industry.

Recognition did not put an end to the operators' resistance to the union. The companies continued to do everything in their power to break the UMWA. These pressures eased only with the onset of World War I. The war brought government-sponsored cooperation between labor and capital to the region and unparalleled prosperity for workers and corporations alike. Production soared to all-time highs. In 1917 anthracite production reached the staggering total of 100.69 million tons, more than one-third of it (37 million tons) from Luzerne County. This was more anthracite than had been produced in any one year since the industry had begun, and it would be one of the best years in the industry's history. Even with record production levels, relatively full employment, and labor peace, however, mine workers were still poorly paid in comparison to other workers. W. J. Lauck and Edgar Sydenstriker (1917) found that miners had one of the lowest annual incomes of any blue-collar male heads of household and miners' wages made up a smaller proportion of total family income than was the case for other male blue-collar workers. Total family income of miners' households was lower than that for most other occupations. If this condition prevailed during the prosperity of the war years, one can imagine the deprivation miners experienced during hard times.

After the war, anthracite production virtually collapsed, as Table 1.1 shows.

Table 1.1. Decline of Anthracite Production

Year	Millions of Tons
1895	53.0
1917	100.7
1929	73.8
1931	59.6
1933	49.4
1934	57.4
1935	51.0
1936	54.8

Source: Ernst, 1937.

The drop in production between 1917 and 1929 resulted only in part from declining demand for anthracite. Corporate disinvestment was another cause. Corporations increasingly found it more profitable to invest in the nonorganized bituminous mines in Kentucky and West Virginia, where wage rates were lower, safety standards minimal, and union work rules nonexistent.

As economic conditions deteriorated in the mining industry, operators took advantage of hard times to increase their pressure on the union. Membership dropped throughout the coal fields. To preserve the union's organizational integrity, John L. Lewis made a number of concessions to the operators (Aronowitz, 1983). Lewis's willingness to compromise generated a good deal of discontent within the anthracite region. In 1928 members of a Pittston local rebelled against their leadership and elected a new slate of officers. The district president declared the election illegal. The rank and file refused to accept the president's ruling. The insurrection led to the brutal murder of two of the dissidents' leaders, Tom Lillis and Alex Campbell; Campbell reportedly was shot while his young daughter looked on. Both Lillis and Campbell had been longtime union activists, and both had held a number of offices in their local. One of the district president's loyalists also was killed. Following Lillis's and Campbell's murder, Pittston erupted in violence. There were bombings, assaults, and riots. John L. Lewis backed the district president and dismissed the insurrection as the work of communists (Miller and Sharpless, 1985). The union establishment eventually prevailed by making several compromises with the dissidents, but many of the fundamental grievances that had led to the internal rebellion were left unresolved and would lead to even more widespread rebellion and killings in the 1930s. Thomas Maloney and his son and Michael Gallagher, a union official, were killed by a letter bomb on April 10, 1936.

The depressed conditions in the anthracite fields deteriorated further with the onset of the Great Depression. Operators enacted deep wage cuts, and men lost their jobs or were put on short time. As the Depression wore on, miners and their families experienced increasing destitution and misery. Reporters who went into the coal fields during these years noted signs not only of hunger but malnutrition and associated diseases. The want was staggering, and private charities were overwhelmed by the demands for assistance.

Seeing no other way to relieve their destitution, many miners took matters into their own hands. They entered company property and opened abandoned shafts or sank drift and slope mines. The scope of these operations ranged from one- or two-man diggings to works involving a hundred or more miners. The miners also organized their own system for distributing and marketing coal (Brecher, 1972).

Try as they might, the companies were unable to eradicate bootleg operations. Local authorities refused to act against the expropriators. The police would not make arrests, prosecutors would not press charges, juries would not convict mine workers, and judges would not sentence them. The operators had to deploy their own private police forces against the bootleggers. Miners and guards fought pitched battles for control of the land, which the guards normally won. When they lost control of one site, the miners would move somewhere else and begin again.

Finally, the operators took their case to the state, and Pennsylvania's governor set up a "blue-ribbon" commission to investigate. Like many such organizations, the committee met, deliberated, and issued a report stating that the grievances of both miners and operators were legitimate (Ernst, 1937). Few of the commission's recommendations were put into effect.

Mass expropriation by the workers ended with economic recovery. Expropriation was an example of prepolitical action. The workers had not seized coal fields because they had become radicalized, as some charged and others hoped. They had acted merely out of expediency—they and their families were starving; and seizure of the coal lands was a way to help alleviate misery.

World War II brought prosperity back to the coal fields. Demand was high, and surplus labor was siphoned from the labor market. But when the war ended, hard times returned to the anthracite region. Production fell, unemployment rose, and the corporations accelerated their withdrawal of capital from the industry. Between 1950 and 1955, 20,600 jobs in anthracite mining were lost. From 1956 to 1978, another 12,500 were eliminated, most of them between 1956 and 1960 (Pennsylvania Bureau of Statistics and Planning, 1974). As jobs disappeared, people replaced coal as the region's principal export.

On a balmy January night in 1959, deep mining was brought to a fitting, bloody close in the Wilkes-Barre area when the Susquehanna River broke through the roof of the Knox Mine just south of Pittston. Twelve men were killed. Before the damage could be repaired, millions of gallons of water flooded all of the deep mines in the Wyoming Valley that lay to the south of the breakthrough. The mines never reopened.

By the time of the Knox disaster, as it came to be called, the industry was a shell of what it once had been. Few mines were working and fewer still provided full-time employment. Most of the corporations had ceased mining operations and had sold their assets to undercapitalized entrepreneurs. These small-scale producers sold to an ever-shrinking market. To make profits, owners frequently resorted to unsafe mining practices such as robbing pillars—the large columns of coal left behind to provide support for mine roofs and, hence, the ground surface—and mining too close to the ground surface. The Knox disaster was the result of just such practices.

Presently, although the Wyoming field still contains vast coal deposits, little mining is taking place there. Only a few strip mines operate on the mountainsides. In 1980–81, Luzerne County was averaging a million tons of anthracite per year, and only 646 employees were listed as working in the industry (Pennsylvania Department of Environmental Resources, 1981).

During the century when it was the dominant industry in Luzerne County, anthracite mining never achieved the stable production that would have permitted operators to integrate their workers into a smoothly functioning "social structure of accumulation," which David Gordon and colleagues define as "the specific institutional environment within which the capitalist accumulation process is organized" (1982:10). Operators were plagued by competitive economic relationships, first among the petty producers in the Schuylkill and Lehigh fields, then between the petty producers and the corporations in the Wyoming field, and finally between the Reading and the Wyoming corporations. When the corporations finally managed to reach industrywide agreements in the 1880s, they found their markets being eroded by cheaper, nonunion, bituminous coal. Never able to secure a monopoly for themselves, the corporations victimized the workers so as to maintain profits.

The result was that mine workers and their families had to endure and struggle against some of the worst forms of exploitation imaginable. Not only were the workers paid low wages and subjected to labor practices that ensured a large reserve of surplus workers trained and ready to work at a moment's notice, but they also were under attack in countless other ways.

Companies deployed private armies such as the Reading's hated Coal and Iron Police, which in the mid-1860s had been granted sweeping powers of arrest anywhere in the Commonwealth of Pennsylvania by the state legislature. They used private detective agencies and informers to spy on the men and their families. They encouraged and deployed vigilante groups to suppress organization and rebellion among the workers. The courts, the public police, and the militia attacked workers and their families. Companies fanned ethnic animosities and encouraged interethnic conflicts. Dissident workers were blacklisted.

Miners who had to live in the company towns were the worst off. They were exploited both as producers and as consumers. As elsewhere in the coal industry (Corbin, 1981), mine workers often were paid in scrip, which was redeemable only at company stores. At these stores, miners and their families had to pay inflated prices for their goods. But this was not the only problem that faced company town residents. Housing was poorly constructed, sanitary facilities were almost nonexistent, and diseases were pandemic. In addition, residents of these towns were subject to far more elaborate social control systems than were miners and their families who lived in public municipalities. In the company towns, there was little room for an autonomus private life. Workers and their families who were unable to meet company production standards and standards of personal and domestic comportment faced the threat not only of job loss but also of eviction. The company towns and their institutional structures almost seemed planned to build a massive system of social scrutiny and social control that worked on behalf of company interests to maintain a well-disciplined, orderly, obedient, and compliant work force.

In this situation of repression, economic deprivation, political powerlessness, and daily humiliation it is small wonder that anthracite workers and their families continued to struggle to build a union, despite the numerous defeats unionism suffered between 1842 and 1902. As a result, the region was marked by almost continual labor conflict as the mine workers dreamed of and struggled to develop some means to defend themselves, advance their economic and political interests, and live free of constant degradation and humiliation. Their struggles ranged from mundane, day-to-day displays of resistance in the pits and company towns to more dramatic mass strikes that drew entire families, including women and children, and communities into the fray. The mine workers had learned through practical experience that if they could mobilize community institutions and private associations to work on their behalf they stood a far better chance of winning than if they tried to fight on their own. The mine workers' drive to achieve economic and social justice brought them into confrontation not only with the corporations but also with the local upper class.

Although few members of the local upper class were directly engaged in mining, their economic well-being was inextricably bound up with the health of the mining industry. Many upper-class families held coal leases from which they received revenues only when mines were producing; they had investments in companies that sold mining equipment and supplies and professional services to the mining companies; and many of their fortunes were based in real estate development, finance, and related activities that were tied directly and indirectly to the continued growth and prosperity of the mining industry (Keil, 1987). Realizing that their own economic fortunes and destinies were bound up with the investment activities of the mining companies, the local upper class naturally sided with the corporations in their struggles with the workers.

From the early 1800s until well into the twentieth century, the local upper class ruled politically. Edward J. Davies (1983) has shown, for example, that between 1865 and 1875, members of the upper class held forty-two of the fifty-two elected offices in the city of Wilkes-Barre. They also held a number of county offices, including most judicial posts and most of the seats in the county's state legislative delegation, and had a monopoly on the county's congressional seat.

First through the MLBA, and later through the UMWA, the mine workers and their allies in other industries mounted continuing challenges to the political rule of the local upper class. In the early decades of the twentieth century, the local working classes, in alliance with professional and ethnic politicians in the Democratic party, began to achieve some success in displacing the upper class from office, especially outside of Wilkes-Barre city.

Thomas D. Nicholls, a militant president of District 1 of the UMWA, won election to Congress as a Democrat in 1906 and served three consecutive terms (1907–12). In 1912, John J. Casey, an officer of the plumbers' and steamfitters' union, also running as a Democrat, was elected to Nicholls's old seat. Between 1913 and 1930, Casey served six terms in Congress. In 1944, this seat was won by Daniel J. Flood, a grandson of one of the UMWA lawyers who had helped negotiate an end to the 1902 coal strike. Flood lost in the next election but was reelected in 1948 and 1950. In 1952 he was defeated, only to run again and win in 1954. Flood held the seat until shortly after the strike against Capital Cities. Throughout his career, Flood maintained a close working relationship with the county's unions. He won his last political victory in 1978. Before this election he had been indicted by a federal grand jury for alleged corruption in office. Flood's trial ended in a hung jury. Rather than undergo a second trial, he resigned from office and was replaced by state Representative Rafael Musto. Like Flood, Musto had close ties to organized labor, particularly to the International Ladies' Garment Workers Union (ILGWU). Musto lost the 1980 election to a Republican, James Nelligan. Nelligan served one term and was defeated by Frank Harrison, a Democrat. Harrison lost in the next Democratic primary. His opponent, attorney Paul Kanjorski, went on to win the seat in the general election.

The Democratic-labor alliance was successful not only in winning congressional elections. Between 1900 and 1920, it succeeded in electing several Democrats sympathetic to labor's cause to the state general assembly. But in most of those years, the Republicans continued to dominate the county's state legislative delegation. Democratic and labor fortunes changed dramatically in the county in the 1920 elections. Democrats were swept out of a large number of offices, and Republicans returned to power. By the end of the decade, there were no Democrats in the county's state legislative delegation. In 1926, for example, there was only one Democrat from Luzerne County in the state House of Representatives and one state senator, Asa K. DeWitt, who had held his seat since 1911. Both men were out of office in 1927.

Between 1927 and 1936, the Democrats never held more than two of the county's eight seats in the state House of Representatives and did not win an election to the state senate. In the county's 1936 elections, the Democrats, again relying mainly on ethnic and working-class votes, managed to win a number of offices. In 1937 the county's state legislative delegation had an overwhelming majority of Democrats. The Democrats retained their political preeminence until their defeat in the 1942 elections. From 1942 to 1952, the Republicans dominated the county. In 1946, for example, the Republicans had approximately 135,000 registered voters in the county, while the Democrats had only about 52,000 (Wolensky, 1984). But despite this registration edge, the Democrats were able to revive their fortunes so that between 1953 and 1958, the two parties competed on fairly even terms.

A turning point in local politics came in 1959. The Democrats became the major party in the county and in Wilkes-Barre city. The party had a five-to-two advantage in the state House delegation and one of two state senators. It also took control of Wilkes-Barre city. The Democrats have retained their preeminence in the county ever since that date. By the time of the strike in 1978, they had 108,948 registered voters against the Republican registration of 65,334. The Democrats had sizable majorities not only in Wilkes-Barre (Democrats, 16,208; Republicans, 7,637) but also in the other major cities in the county. In Pittston, the Democrats had 4,966 registered voters and the Republicans had 744; in Hazleton the Democrats totaled 9,192, with the Republicans at 5,438; and in

Nanticoke the Democrats had 5,542 registered voters and the Republicans had 1,911 (*Pennsylvania Manual*, 1978–79: 776–77).

So complete was the domination of the county's Democrats that between 1961 and 1966 the Luzerne County Republicans had no one in the state House of Representatives, and between 1967 and 1971 only one Republican was elected to that body from the county (*Pennsylvania Manual*, 1978–79:288–315). There were only a few bright spots for the Republicans from 1959 to 1978. One was that they managed to retain control over a suburban-rural state senate seat, and the other was that they took control of Wilkes-Barre city government in 1967 (Wolensky, 1984). The Republicans held their majority on the city council for only a few years. By 1972, the Democrats were back in power in Wilkes-Barre city government.

At the time of the strike in 1978, the Democrats held the mayor's office and all seven council seats, as well as the city controller's post. In Pittston and Nanticoke, the mayor, all four council members, and the treasurer and controller were Democrats. In Hazleton, the mayor was a Republican, as was one of the city's four councilmen, but the treasurer and the controller were Democrats (*Pennsylvania Manual*, 1978–79: 645, 642–43, 639).

In the state House of Representatives, the county had four Democrats and two Republicans. One Republican state representative was an upwardly mobile Irish Catholic businessman who had started his work life as an unskilled blue collar worker and union member. In the state senate the county had one Democrat and one Republican. In the county government, there were two Democratic commissioners and one Republican, and the Democrats held ten of the other eleven elected posts (*Pennsylvania Manual*, 1978–79:603).

The Democrats could not have emerged as the major party in Luzerne County without the support and active involvement of the county's trade unions. At all levels of the political system trade unionists held office. In 1978, for example, one of the county's longtime state representatives had been a president of the stereotypers' union, one of the unions involved in the strike against the *Times Leader.* Another state representative had close ties to the county's teachers' union, and a Wilkes-Barre city councilman was connected to the teamsters. In addition, countless other trade unionists held offices in the county's small towns and posts in both the Democratic and Republican parties.

Direct union political activism is one of the mining era's legacies to Luzerne County. The Workingmen's Benevolent Association, the Miners' and Laborers' Benevolent Association, the Knights of Labor, and the United Mine Workers of America were all politically active trade unions in Luzerne County. All recognized that various forms of prepolitical protest such as short, violent strikes, riots, and terrorism would not be sufficient to advance their members' general interests. More important, they also recognized that trade unionism, pure and simple, would not win and guarantee their members' interests. In the view of the mine unions, direct economic action had to be coupled with direct and sustained political activism.

By combining economic and political action, mining unions, especially the UMWA, brought major improvements in miners' lives. Wages were advanced, gains were made in mine safety and working conditions, and the most brutal forms of state-sponsored and state-supported repression gradually were ended (even the Coal and Iron Police was disbanded in 1935, when most of its functions were taken over by the Pennsylvania State Police).

Political activism was not the only legacy that the mining era left to the county's workers. It also taught them the importance of, if not the necessity for, interunion cooperation and solidarity. Such unity was a major element of the Knights' philosophy and later of the UMWA. The latter helped the initial efforts of a number of Luzerne County's fledgling unions, including the Wilkes-Barre Newspaper Guild. In the late 1930s, the UMWA provided critical support to this group during its recognition strike. Had it not been for UMWA backing, the newspaper strike very well might have been defeated.

Mining also left the area with a distinctive social structure. Out of their encounter with one another and with the mining industry, the various individuals and social groups that immigrated into the region in search of work created a social structure that was, and continues to be, infused with the principles and practices of trade unionism, making Luzerne County a trade union community in the fullest sense of the term. Building this community was no easy task. It required forging bonds among disparate religio-ethnic groups, strata within classes, and social classes.

The various ethnic groups that came into the region had to overcome not only their rivalries with each other but also sharp internal differences. Contrary to what might be imagined, few of the immigrant groups arrived with a well-developed national consciousness and with high levels of internal structural unity already in place. In many critical respects, structural unity and ethnic consciousness emerged after the fact of immigration (Yancey, Erikson, and Juliani, 1976; Oppenheimer, 1974; Reich, 1977; Cox, 1948). The anthracite mining towns, even when made up mostly of residents from a particular national group, brought together people from different kin groups, villages, and provinces of the old country. Residents lacked a central bond of old village life—common history. Thus they lacked such traditional guides as in-depth knowledge of past behavior and knowledge of family background for determining who could and could not be trusted, who was and was not dependable, and so on. These qualities became possible only with the building of viable community institutions, including both formal and informal social networks.

Among the earliest of these institutions were taverns, churches, neighborhoods, and benevolent associations. These private, voluntary associations were indispensable to the survival of the workers and their families in an economy in which employers and the state took no responsibility for public welfare. The tavern was not merely a place where men gathered to drink before and after work. As in many other working-class communities (Cumbler, 1979), the tavern was a multifunction institution that stood at the hub of daily social life. Taverns served as places where workers and others could gather to exchange news and information about work, as labor exchanges, and as boardinghouses and information sources on housing for new arrivals or displaced persons. Taverns sponsored sports teams and served as informal banks for regular customers, and the tavern keeper sometimes also served as a scribe, writing letters for illiterate workers. Frequently taverns were at the center of ward politics. Tavern keepers could often get customers favors from local politicians. Playing these various roles, the tavern helped knit individuals and households into coherent neighborhoods and communities.

Like the taverns, churches were multifunction institutions, and their importance, too, extended far beyond their formal function as places of worship. The ethnic church was one of the first organizations built by immigrant groups in the coal fields. It was founded, perhaps, only after the ethnic tavern. According to Victor Greene (1968), the Catholic ethnic churches, especially those of the southern and eastern Europeans, were built largely through lay initiatives. Thus, as in the case of Protestant churches, they provided opportunities for social participation and served as a means for creating ties among those active in the organizing efforts. The churches of all creeds also provided various social services. Like the taverns, they were sources of information about jobs and housing and, in times of extreme need, a source of charity and possibly even a job. Bonds among church members were further strengthened in congregations that established elementary and high schools. The churches also played a critical role in helping to build the ethnic middle class. Church contracts for services, construction, and the like helped spawn and maintain many ethnic professionals and businesses.

Another major institution that contributed to the formation of group consciousness and solidarity within the various immigrant populations was the mutual benefit society, many of which continue to exist in Luzerne County. Scott Cummings (1980) suggests that such societies were a direct product of the United States's nineteenth-century laissez-faire political economy. The mutual benefit societies were far more than insurance funds or even centers of social activity. They also were a means for communal discipline. Because most benefit societies had rules providing for the suspension and expulsion of members whose behavior fell short of communal standards (Stolarik, 1980), the societies were important means for collective discipline within ethnic communities. With dismissal a member lost his or her benefits and was forced to make do without the support of the community. Mutual benefit societies were an important means for capital formation and circulation in the ethnic communities. They also had important political functions, not the least of which was their role as a training ground for ethnic political leaders. More than one of Luzerne County's ethnic politicians started his political career in these organizations in the early part of the century, and membership in mutual benefit societies continues to be mentioned prominently in politicians' campaign materials and biographical statements.

In sum, the tavern, the church, the ethnic school, the mutual benefit society, the fraternal organization, and other formal and informal social networks knit individuals, households, kin groups, class fractions, and strata into larger communities that provided their members with social acceptance and some degree of protection against the vicissitudes of economic life in the anthracite fields. Without even the minimal levels of protection and assistance afforded by the ethnic community, life was very difficult for the mine worker and his family.

The ethnic communities, however, were important not only for the personal assistance they provided their members. They also were fashioned into collective weapons that were harnessed to the mine workers' cause and that often figured prominently in mine workers' struggles against their employers (Greene, 1968; Keil, 1982; Miller and Sharpless, 1985). In these struggles ethnic communities blended non- or preindustrial traditions and practices with more modern strategies and tactics. For example, at the same time that Irish mine workers were active supporters of and participants in various trade union movements and actively engaged in specifically political actions to advance their interests, some Irish communities in the coal fields spawned and supported communal terrorism, the roots of which can be traced back to rural Ireland (Keil, 1982). Similarly, the Slavic mine workers relied on peasant and village social practices during times of labor turmoil to ensure that the community would act as a disciplined unit on their behalf (Greene, 1968).

Just as the ethnic groups were a source of unity at one level, however, they were a source of division at another, especially for the working classes. Before the emergence of the UMWA, ethnicity was a major cleavage within the mine work force. In the mines groups competed against each other for jobs and promotions; outside the production process, they competed for choice residential locations and political power. For example, Luzerne County's Irish politicians in the state legislature were strong supporters of legislation that required workers to pass an English literacy test to be licensed as miners. This law was designed to restrict eastern and southern European workers' access to skilled jobs in the mines.

Mine owners and the local upper class fanned interethnic rivalries and hostilities through the press and other means. It was a common practice during strikes for mine owners to circulate in the working-class communities handbills, printed in various languages, that accused one group or another of having betrayed the strike. The local media often ran stories that denounced one ethnic group or another and gave positive press coverage to nativist political movements and organizations. Henry M. Hoyt, a Luzerne County politician from a prominent local family, who served as a Republican governor of Pennsylvania from January 1879 to January 1883, had been backed for public office early in his career by the Know Nothing party.

Just as joint participation in the mining industry generated numerous instances of interethnic hostility, rivalry, and conflict, it also generated political and economic cooperation among the various ethnic groups. For example, in the late nineteenth century Terence Powderly, a skilled railroad worker active in Irish ethnic organizations who headed the Knights of Labor in Scranton and later became the Knights' national leader, was thrice elected mayor of Scranton on a Greenback-Labor ticket with the support of the city's normally Democratic Irish Catholic mine workers and its Protestant, normally Republican, Welsh mine workers. Greene (1968) has noted that despite the hostility that English-speaking mine workers expressed toward eastern and southern Europeans and the latter's exploitation at the hands of English-speaking contract miners, the eastern and southern Europeans invariably supported strikes when called on to do so, even though their behavior was not always reciprocated. But though the ethnic mine workers did show evidence of being able to cooperate on the basis of common grievances growing out of their class position, this cooperation never proved durable until the UMWA provided them with a "platform for collective action" (Wardell and Johnston, 1983). The UMWA made interethnic and, hence, intraclass antagonisms manageable within the mine work force, and all miners benefited from the attachment of the various ethnic communities to the workers' cause. The linkages between the mine workers' movement and the local ethnic communities left a lasting mark on both structures. The workers' movement adopted forms of protest that were characteristic of ethnic communal conflicts and synthesized them with more modern forms of class struggle and conflict and, as will be discussed later, adopted conceptions of economic and social justice that were heavily influenced by the moral economies of rural, peasant, ethnic societies. In turn, the ethnic communities, originating in the adaptive experience of immigrants to the mining industry, could not help but become infused with the social practices, politics, and culture of trade unionism.

The mining industry left Luzerne County not only with strong ethnic communities that were tied to the labor movement but also with vital neighborhoods and municipalities that, like the ethnic groups, were mobilized on behalf of the workers' cause. Luzerne County has seventy-five municipal governments that are empowered to provide a complete range of public services. Until recently, these towns even had their own school systems. Although this high degree of government fragmentation has resulted in gross inefficiencies in the provision of services, the public has continually resisted consolidation, preferring to maintain as much control as possible over the levels and quality of services.

Most of these municipalities sprang into being in the period between 1880 and 1910, when the region's population was mushrooming. The small towns in Luzerne County, like such towns elsewhere (Ashton, 1984), were and continue to be important devices for producing, maintaining, and reproducing specific forms of privilege in the metropolitan area. There have always been significant differences in the towns' class compositions. Some are largely composed of blue-collar workers, others have a more equal mix of production workers and white-collar workers, and still others are largely made up of white-collar workers, professionals, and businessmen (U.S. Bureau of the Census, 1980). The last groups are found mainly in the newer suburban settlements located outside of the Wyoming Valley and the densely settled urban core centered around Wilkes-Barre, whereas the more heavily working-class towns are found within the Wyoming Valley and in the former mining areas extending north and south of the valley.

The towns also reveal high levels of ethnic residential segregation (U.S. Bureau of the Census, 1980), in part because many of the older towns grew up around mining shafts and it once was common for companies to hire mostly men from one ethnic group to work at a particular production point, hoping that if men from one ethnic group struck a particular mine, workers from a different group at another site would continue producing.

There is a strong correlation between ethnicity and social class in the county. Towns largely made up of eastern and southern Europeans, including Italians, tend to be more highly working class, whereas those composed of Irish, German, or British stock tend to be less proletarian and more white collar. Partly as a result of the overlap between ethnic and occupational segregation, ethnicity, social class, and municipal patriotism became mutually reinforcing axes of social differentiation and solidarity. And because of the high levels of residential stability in the county this mutual reinforcement has persisted through time. Luzerne County has higher proportions of homeowners living in the same house since 1950 than elsewhere in the state. In Luzerne County 27.5 percent of owners have lived in the same residence since 1950; the statewide figure is 16.7 percent. For renters, the county has a similar pattern: 13.4 percent have lived in the same unit since 1960, compared to 7.1 percent for the state as a whole (U.S. Bureau of the Census, 1980).

High concentrations of working-class ethnics in a municipality and its constituent neighborhoods was no guarantee that the local state structures would support the mine workers or, even, remain neutral in their struggles against the corporations. Such outcomes came only when and where the working classes managed to gain a measure of direct political control over the local state. With such control, workers not only were able to mobilize a municipality's residents and its private institutions to work on their behalf, but they also could ensure, at the very least, that state structures, especially the local police and courts, would not be used against them in their fights against the mining companies. Results of this political leverage were seen as early as the mid-1930s, when local authorities refused to act against the popular, mass expropriation of coal deposits by mine workers.

In sum, because of the way in which local social networks, groups, formal and informal organizations, institutions, and the like either were developed or reshaped by the mine workers for use as defensive and offensive weapons in their struggles against the corporations and their local allies, Luzerne County has developed and maintained what might be called a "union culture." In this culture, the values, attitudes, and social practices of trade unionism are not merely abstract ideas to which people are willing to give lip service but little else. Rather, the principles and practices of trade unionism exist as a set of moral and practical precepts and guides to action, organizing not only how one ought to deal with employers but also with other workers.

Postanthracite Economic Reorganization

As corporate mine capital withdrew from the region, the local economy went into a steep decline. Few people were prepared for the industry's shutdown. When the mines closed, unemployment skyrocketed. Everything had hinged on the mines. When they closed, so, too, did many ancillary factories, shops, mills, and railroads.

Anthracite's "death" had such profound effects on Luzerne County because of the investment patterns of local capitalists during the mining era. During that time, the county's upper class, for the most part, had eschewed investments in productive activities that were not related in some way to the mining industry (Folsom, 1981) and the growth it generated. In 1810, Luzerne County had approximately 18,000 residents; in 1850, shortly after mining had begun in earnest in the county, the population had increased to over 56,000; by 1900 there were approximately 257,000 people in the county (U.S. Bureau of the Census, 1810, 1850, 1900). The population explosion created tremendous opportunities for profits in real estate, construction, sales of building materials, utility development, transportation, wholesale and retail trade and merchandising, banking, insurance, and professional services. Luzerne County's business elite invested its capital in such enterprises as well as in selected industries that provided the mining companies with supplies and equipment.

Because there was no alternative economic base, the loss of the anthracite industry plunged the county into a deep depression and set off a scramble to find new investors. The Greater Wilkes-Barre Chamber of Commerce took the leading role in trying to find companies willing to open production facilities in the county. Many firms were reluctant to locate production facilities in Luzerne County. According to a former official of the Chamber of Commerce, who was familiar with the county's industrial recruitment difficulties, the biggest problem in recruiting high-paying firms was the reputation of the work force. As an economic development official in the county told me, prospective employers often felt that the county's workers were "strike prone," that the former mine workers "would never be content with industrial wages," and that the mine workers did not have "the skills and discipline necessary for modern industrial work."

Between 1945 and about 1959, the Chamber of Commerce succeeded in attracting mainly low-wage, labor-intensive industries, among which garment manufacturers were typical. These companies came to the coal region to escape high taxes, unions, high wages, and government regulation in New York City and other East Coast cities. More important, they came to exploit the area's newest and greatest "natural" advantage: a large supply of cheap surplus labor.

It was not long before the low-wage employers encountered labor difficulties. Many of the new industries had to contend with union organizing drives within a year or two of their opening. The drives and the subsequent contract negotiations often led to strikes, further complicating attempts to attract new investors. The community's working classes were determined to maintain the unions that already existed and to unionize the new industries. And they did. Using the tactics and strategies they had learned during the mining era, local workers defended the unions that still survived and built a number of new ones, among the largest of which was the International Ladies' Garment Workers Union. In 1953 there were 75 American Federation of Labor (AFL) locals in the county; 22 railroad locals, 18 of which were affiliated with the AFL and 4 of which were independent; and 35 Congress of Industrial Organizations (CIO) locals, for a total of 132 locals (Wolensky, 1984). In 1977, despite a sharp drop in the number of railroad unions, the number of AFL-CIO locals in Luzerne County had grown to over 170 (Wolensky, 1984). To get some idea of the relative strength of unions in Luzerne County, the Committee for Economic Growth, a local development group, surveyed 516 local employers. It received responses from 184 (approximately 35.9 percent of the total to which surveys were sent). The study found that 39 percent of the work force was unionized (Committee for Economic Growth, 1985). Assuming that respondents are representative of county employers, this figure is roughly twice the current national level of unionization.

Because of the industrial strife that took place as new unions were being organized and older unions tried to maintain themselves and the erosion of upper-class political power in the county, it is small wonder that the chamber had a difficult time trying to rebuild the local economy. No longer having the power to organize the county into a "growth machine" (Molotch, 1976), the local upper class could not guarantee to outside investors conditions that are taken to be indicative of a good business climate: low taxes, stable government expenditures, governments committed to maintaining high profit levels, a police force committed to protecting business interests, and a relatively compliant and docile work force (Molotch, 1976; Block, 1977).

In the 1960s Luzerne County's economy had a brief spurt of expansion. The chamber succeeded in attracting a number of higher-paying manufacturing industries. Manufacturing growth in the 1960s resulted in part from national economic prosperity. But it is unlikely that Luzerne County would have benefited from national trends had not the local business elite begun to take steps to reach an accommodation with local labor unions and Democratic elected officials. Beginning in the late 1950s and continuing throughout the 1960s, labor, elected officials, and the local business elite, working through the Greater Wilkes-Barre Chamber of Commerce, the Wilkes-Barre Industrial Fund, the Economic Development Council of Northeastern Pennsylvania, and the Northeastern Pennsylvania Committee for Economic Development, began taking steps that led to the establishment of a coalition for growth.

Democratic officeholders were given positions on the chamber's economic development groups, members of the business elite were appointed to city and county economic development boards and commissions, labor was given what a former chamber official described as an honorary seat on the chamber's board of directors, and a citizens-labor-management committee was formed. To many business leaders this committee was a keystone of the county's economic development efforts. The committee had twenty-four members who were divided equally among labor leaders, businessmen, and supposedly neutral, third-party community representatives.

According to local sources familiar with the establishment of this committee and its operation, the initial impetus for its formation came from the chamber, which believed such an organization was essential for "turning the local labor situation around and improving the area's reputation" with respect to labor-management relations. The committee's primary function was to serve as an informal mediator between labor and capital. It also served as a means for labor and capital to communicate with each other outside of normal channels, free from the pressures of collective bargaining sessions and the glare of publicity.

Cooperation between capital, labor, and elected officials enabled Luzerne County to put together attractive incentive packages designed to draw manufacturing employers into the county. Between 1960 and 1965 there was an increase of more than six thousand manufacturing jobs. Between 1965 and 1968, another five thousand were added (Pennsylvania Bureau of Statistics and Planning, 1974). Many of these jobs were in higher-paying, unionized industries. No one is willing to talk about what wage concessions the county's unions made to help attract new employers. One individual who was closely connected with union-management groups in the county told me in response to a question dealing with this issue, "Let me put it this way. Our unions have shown that they are willing to compromise in order to attract employers." Perhaps this partly explains why even in unionized sectors, the wages of Wilkes-Barre workers lag behind those of comparable workers in the rest of Pennsylvania (U.S. Bureau of the Census, 1980).

Because of the growth of manufacturing, by the end of the 1960s the local economy appeared finally to have rebounded from the loss of the anthracite industry. But there were several underlying structural weaknesses in the Wilkes-Barre economy that did not become apparent until the 1970s, when it became painfully evident that economic recovery had been built on industries in which jobs were proving to be highly vulnerable to elimination because of foreign competition, capital flight, and technological change. For the second time in twenty-five years Wilkes-Barre began to undergo a massive deindustrialization, just as were many other local economies that were heavily dependent on classical forms of heavy manufacturing (Bluestone and Harrison, 1982). Luzerne County experienced a net loss of approximately twelve thousand manufacturing jobs between 1970 and 1980 (U.S. Bureau of the Census, 1980). Many of these jobs were in unionized plants. Officials at the Committee for Economic Growth told me that within the next decade they expect that another five thousand or more jobs will be lost in the garment industry alone. This will come on top of a recent loss of fifteen hundred construction jobs following the completion of a nuclear power plant on the Susquehanna River south of Wilkes-Barre and hundreds, if not thousands, of jobs lost because of anticipated or unexpected plant closings in other sectors of the local economy.

While manufacturing was being devastated during the 1970s and into the 1980s, parts of the local economy experienced rapid growth. Expansion was greatest in the services and retail trade sectors, which together added 10,354 jobs to the county's economy between 1970 and 1980. This gain was almost enough to replace the losses through the decline of manufacturing, but these jobs did not pay nearly as well as those that were eliminated (U.S. Bureau of the Census, 1980).

The shifting nature of the local economy has prompted a mixed response from politicians, businessmen, and workers. Congressman Paul Kanjorski (D.-Luzerne County) has commented: "We're replacing $9.00-an-hour manufacturing jobs with minimum wage jobs at McDonald's. If that keeps up, who's going to buy the hamburgers?" (*Northeast Pennsylvania Business Journal* 1 [April 1986]:4). Other politicians are more optimistic about the new situation. In the same column, the *Northeast Pennsylvania Business Journal* quoted Cindy Bowes from Republican Governor Richard Thornburgh's Press Office, who claimed that: "the transition from manufacturing to a service-based economy has not meant lower wages for workers. . . . Average weekly earnings for workers in the state increased by 25 percent in 1980 and 1984, keeping pace with inflation and with the growth in earnings nationally."

One would be hard-pressed to find union leaders or rank and file who agree with the governor's Press Office; most would agree with Congressman Kanjorski's assessment. It is not difficult to find examples of displaced factory workers or skilled craftsmen who are working for minimum wages either at full-time or part-time jobs in Luzerne County. On two occasions, I have had conversations with parking lot attendants who were in just such a situation. Both had lost skilled jobs and had been unable to find anything else to do except work at a minimum wage job and wait until, as one man put it "something better comes along or until I can get my family to move somewhere where there're decent paying jobs." This man's expressed desire to migrate is in accord with the view of some businessmen about the solution to the problem of displaced workers. A businessman who brought up that issue in a discussion of local economic problems made the following points: "If workers can't find jobs they like or that pay them what they feel they are worth, then they ought to pack up and leave. All of us living here are descended from immigrants who came here to better their situation. . . . Workers have to learn that no one owes them a job or a set income. You only get paid what you're worth. If that's minimum wage, then that's all you'll get."

Businessmen in the area generally agree with the positive assessments of economic change offered by the governor's Press Office. The local business community sees a number of advantages in the current pattern of economic growth in the region. First, the service economy is highly diversified, thereby affording some protection during economic contractions. Second, local businessmen expect that the emerging service economy will dilute union economic and political strength in the county because the levels of unionization in this sector are far lower than in the traditional manufacturing sector. According to the Committee for Economic Growth survey cited earlier, in 1985 only 8 percent of the employees in the sixty-one service firms responding were unionized, whereas 65 percent of the workers in the fifteen heavy industry firms, 71 percent of those in the nineteen light industry businesses, and 68 percent in the eleven construction firms were unionized (Committee for Economic Growth, 1985). In analyzing the future of unions in the county, a businessman commented: "Our unions have been losing members. And matters are likely to get worse. Most of our unions are in sunset industries that are quickly disappearing." Third, local employers recognize that the contraction of the manufacturing sector will result in absolute and relative downward pressures on the local wage rate across most sectors of the county's economy, making it even more profitable for firms to do business.

As Luzerne County's manufacturing crisis intensified, employers began taking steps to achieve a rollback in wages. Many companies began demanding substantial contract concessions as part of the price workers would have to pay to keep their jobs. Concessionary demands took many different forms: lowered rates of pay and reductions in benefits, freezes on wages and benefits, reduced work weeks, changes in work rules, and more. In some cases workers refused to make any concessions, although in others they have been more than willing to accede to owners' requests for givebacks.

Recently, a major local employer reportedly demanded that workers take a 25 percent wage cut or he would move production to Mexico. The employees refused. In another instance, a local manufacturing firm was bought by outside interests. The new owners announced their intention to make the plant a nonunion operation. The unions offered to make concessions, and the new owner accepted them.

At the same time that individual capitalists began demanding concessions from their employees, capital as a whole began to press forward with a broad agenda of political and economic change in the county and the state. Business argued that the region's economy would continue deteriorating unless government tax and expenditure policies were redesigned to create a better investment climate. The specific concessions that were sought were freezes or, preferably, reductions in local property and business taxes and freezes or reductions in government social expenditures and investments. Business also demanded substantial changes in state unemployment compensation and workmen's compensation laws and regulations. When it began seriously pressing these demands in the mid-1970s, local business came into increasing conflict with the county's trade unions and the unions' Democratic allies. This conflict threatened to end the pro-growth coalition, but the coalition managed to hold itself together, despite the strained relations between local capital and labor.

Business, at least in the short run, did not have the political power to gain all of the concessions it wanted from the local state or from the Commonwealth government. The unions, the Democratic party, and the county electorate were too committed to the economic principles of the New Deal willingly to dismantle social programs and roll back public expenditures on the local level. Business did not make major gains on these fronts until after the election of Richard Thornburgh as governor and Ronald W. Reagan as president.

In the midst of this struggle between business on one side

and labor and the Democratic party on the other, Capital Cities purchased the Wilkes-Barre Publishing Company. Local business saw the purchase as a good sign, if for no other reason than that Capital Cities' national connections would help promote the area and provide access to new networks of investors. Furthermore, many local businessmen saw Capital Cities as a potentially powerful ally in their own current struggle with county unions and politicians. Capital Cities had a reputation as a company with an aggressive pro-business philosophy, both with respect to its own internal operations and public policy matters. But local businessmen's hopes that Capital Cities' purchase of the Wilkes-Barre Publishing Company augered well for the future were dashed with the outbreak of the strike in October 1978. The strike showed local businessmen and potential investors across the country that the labor climate might not have changed as much in Wilkes-Barre and Luzerne County as the Chamber of Commerce and other development groups had been claiming it had. The county's unions demonstrated that they still had the militance, solidarity, and power to carry out a successful strike against a major corporation, and the community demonstrated that the popular, mass-based, defensive structures that once had worked so well against the mining companies still could be used to protect local workers who were fighting their employers.

Even though they are long gone from the county, the antagonisms, conflicts, and compromises of the United Mine Workers and the corporate coal operators have exerted a continuing effect on almost all aspects of local life and culture, especially the county's class structure and relations. The mining era taught local workers a number of valuable lessons. First, it showed that workers have little hope for success in their struggles against employers if they are divided. Second, it showed local workers that the best possible means for achieving effective unity was the trade union. Third, workers learned that any given union has a better chance of winning when it can call upon the support and commitment of other unions in the county than when it has to fight on its own. Fourth, workers learned the importance of gaining support for their cause not only from trade unions but from as broad a spectrum of the local population as possible. In addition, they learned the importance of harnessing private, particularistic associations such as ethnic groups, churches, civic groups, taverns, and clubs to labor's cause. Fifth, the mining era taught the regional working class the importance and necessity of political action. Workers learned that if they had to confront a state dominated or directly ruled by a hostile upper class or its agents their cause would be hopeless. Finally, the regional working class learned the value of taking production into its own hands when circumstances required.

On an organizational level, these lessons enabled the county's working classes to maintain the area as a trade union community long after the central organizational force that gave the largest part of the county's workers their unity, the UMWA, had disappeared from the scene. Although none of the unions that survived anthracite's demise or were started during the phase of manufacturing expansion ever had the size or power of the UMWA, the trade union movement as a whole has been able to preserve what the UMWA accomplished and expand its gains. For example, the trade unions have much more formal political power than the UMWA ever had, even at its peak. The unions have been able to maintain their influence and power not only because they have been able to build and maintain solidarity at the point of production but also because they have maintained their connections and their solidarity with virtually all popular institutions in the county. These connections, in turn, have enabled them to maintain mass support among the county's grass roots, which continue to be committed to the practice, program, and objectives of trade unionism as the best available means for defending and improving the conditions of the local working classes.

On an ideological level, the experiences of the mine workers and the lessons that are drawn from them have been incorporated into the interpretive horizon of the local population, especially the working class. Hans-Georg Gadamer defines "horizon" as "the range of vision that includes everything that can be seen from a particular vantage." He continues: "The word has been used in philosophy since Nietzsche and Husserl to characterize the way in which thought is tied to its finite determination" (1982:269). In other words, it is the shared, collective vantage point from which a given group defines, comprehends, and evaluates its life-world.

In Luzerne County the working class's interpretive horizon does not incorporate the experience of the mine workers merely as a series of facts; rather, it invests the mine workers' history with universalistic moral meaning organized around principles of communal responsibility, collective action, and solidarity (Miller and Sharpless, 1985), especially in the face of political and economic adversity. The mine workers, their unions, their strikes, their strategies and tactics, their militance and solidarity, and their hopes and dreams are taken to be universally valid models and guides for action deserving of emulation by all of the county's workers, regardless of industry, status, or historical period.

Because of the moral meaning attached to the mine workers' struggle, each generation is obliged to continue the struggle against economic degradation and exploitation. Failure to do so is tantamount to insulting one's ancestors by rendering nonsensical all of their sacrifices on behalf of labor's cause. This philosophy validates the insult that pickets at the *Times Leader* hurled at local scabs that their fathers or grandfathers would be ashamed of their behavior.

Contemporary workers are expected to continue the struggle the mine workers began not merely because struggle is considered valuable for its own sake but, rather, because struggle is seen to be the only means the working class has to protect itself from those who would take advantage of it. Without the will and capacity to resist, the local working classes believe that they would fall easy prey to any employer wishing to take advantage of them.

The newspaper unions and their community allies applied

all of these lessons in the strike against Capital Cities. As a result, Capital Cities and its local supporters, especially the local business elite, were placed in the unenviable position of battling not only four powerful and militant unions but also confronting the region's moral history.

The *Times Leader* and Capital Cities

2

The Wilkes-Barre Newspaper Market: From Competition to Monopoly to Chain Ownership

Capital Cities' purchase of the Wilkes-Barre Publishing Company ended an era in local journalism. For the first time, ownership of Wilkes-Barre's major daily paper passed out of local hands, repeating a trend in communities across the United States (Bagdikian, 1983).

In the late 1880s there were as many as seven regularly published newspapers in Wilkes-Barre, not counting those that were published in the small cities around Wilkes-Barre or ethnic papers. But daily competition ended in 1939, when the owners of the *Times Leader,* the *Evening News,* and the *Wilkes-Barre Record,* responding to the loss of profits caused by competition, the Depression, and labor problems, merged their papers to form the Wilkes-Barre Publishing Company. Merger brought the owners a Monday-through-Saturday monopoly.

For most of its life, the Wilkes-Barre Publishing Company put out two daily papers, a morning paper called the *Wilkes-Barre Record* and an afternoon paper, the *Times Leader, Evening News.* In 1972, following a major flood that struck Wilkes-Barre, the company switched to an all-day paper published as the *Wilkes-Barre Record, Times Leader, Evening*

News. When Capital Cities bought the company it changed the paper's name to *Times Leader.*

Until the *Citizens' Voice* arrived on the scene, the *Times Leader* was the sole surviving daily paper serving the Wilkes-Barre market. It could trace its history back to 1832, when a paper called the *Anti-Masonic Advocate and Luzerne and Susquehanna Journal* began publication. The *Advocate* was a predecessor of the *Wilkes-Barre Record* and, eventually, the *Times Leader.*

Between 1939 and 1952 the Wilkes-Barre Publishing Company was the leading outlet for advertising in the city's economy. After 1952 it had to compete not only against the *Sunday Independent* but also against television and an increasingly crowded radio market. Although the newer media, along with the *Sunday Independent,* drained advertising revenues from the publishing company, the Monday-through-Saturday monopoly continued to supply the owners with profits and the workers with high wages and fringe benefits.

The situation changed in the late 1960s. Like newspaper publishers elsewhere in the United States, the owners of the Wilkes-Barre Publishing Company found their profits coming under increasing pressure. They faced rapidly increasing costs for utilities and newsprint, their delivery costs were increasing as a result of the rapidly rising price of petroleum products and the dispersal of the region's population, interest rates were soaring, and labor costs were high.

Several other factors added to the Wilkes-Barre Publishing Company's financial problems. For example, as the local economy contracted, the paper's advertising base eroded; a major flood in Wilkes-Barre in 1972 forced the company to invest heavily in repairs to its property and to purchase new equipment; and the owners lost a small fortune when they launched an abortive Sunday edition that was intended to drive the *Sunday Independent* out of business.

The publishers knew that their only hope for improving their profits was to get the unions to moderate their contract demands or, possibly, make contract concessions. In contract negotiations with the Wilkes-Barre Newspaper Guild in 1974, the company asked the union to reduce its wage and salary demands. To convince the guild of the company's perilous financial condition, the owners granted the unions a partial inspection of the company's books. The guild was not convinced that there was a need for a rollback of its demands. Unable to come to terms with the company, the guild struck in late November 1974 and stayed out until early January 1975. The strike could not have come at a worse time because the company lost almost its entire holiday season advertising revenue. The guild returned to work after it persuaded the company to agree to most of its demands. Shortly after the strike was settled, the owners decided to sell the paper. In May 1978, they announced that Capital Cities Communications, Inc., had purchased the Wilkes-Barre Publishing Company.

Capital Cities Communications, Inc.

When Capital Cities purchased the Wilkes-Barre Publishing Company in 1978, it was already among the top fifteen U.S. newspaper chains and the top ten television chains in holdings. Capital Cities was begun in 1954 by a small group of private investors who joined together to buy Hudson Valley Broadcasting in Albany, New York (the information on Capital Cities, except where otherwise noted, is taken from materials submitted as part of the company's Form 10-K for 1981 on file with the Securities and Exchange Commission, file 1-4278). At the time of purchase, Hudson Valley operated WROW-TV (a UHF channel) and a radio station, WROW-AM. In 1957 it bought WTVD-TV in Durham, North Carolina. Also in 1957, Capital Cities offered its first public stock sale.

In 1959 Capital Cities bought a broadcasting group in Providence, Rhode Island. The properties included WPRO-TV, WPRO-AM, and WPRO-FM. In 1961 Capital Cities expanded its New York holdings by acquiring WKBW-TV and WKBW-AM in Buffalo. In the same year it gained a foothold in the New York City metropolitan area when it bought WPAT-AM and WPAT-FM in Paterson, New Jersey. In 1964 the company acquired WSAZ-TV in Huntington, West Virginia.

Capital Cities stock was listed on the New York Exchange for the first time in 1966. During the same year Capital Cities bought radio stations KPOL-AM and KPOL-FM in Los Angeles, which now have the call letters KZLA-AM and KZLA-FM. The company now had holdings on both coasts. The company moved into the Texas market in 1967, when it bought KTRK-TV for cash plus WPRO-TV in Providence, Rhode Island. The company retained ownership of its two Providence radio stations.

Between 1954 and 1968, all of Capital Cities' media holdings were in radio and television. It did not move into the newspaper business until 1969, when it bought its first newspaper, the *Oakland Press,* which served Pontiac, Michigan. Since 1969 the company has expanded its newspaper holdings to become one of the largest chains in the country. In 1978, when it bought the Wilkes-Barre Publishing Company, it owned, in addition to the *Times Leader,* the following papers (dates of purchase are in parentheses): *News-Democrat,* Belleville, Illinois (1972); *Fort Worth Star-Telegram,* Fort Worth, Texas (1974); and *Kansas City Star* and *Kansas City Times,* Kansas City, Missouri (1977). In 1980, Capital Cities purchased the Democrat-Herald Publishing Company, which produces two daily papers and six weeklies in Oregon.

Newspapers are only one part of Capital Cities' publishing operations. In 1968 it bought Fairchild Publications, Inc. At the time of purchase, Fairchild owned eight trade publications, including *Women's Wear Daily* and two other daily business papers (*Editor and Publisher,* 1981). Capital Cities has added through purchase or product development eleven additional publications to its Fairchild Division. By 1981, the Fairchild operation also included a news service and a book publishing company. In addition to the Fairchild operation and its newspapers, Capital Cities runs a Specialized Publications Group, which publishes a variety of newspapers directed to specific professional markets.

With its movement into newspapers and specialized publications, Capital Cities did not lose its interest in broadcast properties. In 1971, the company bought three television stations: WPVI-TV, Philadelphia; WTNH-TV, New Haven; and KFSN-TV, Fresno. In the same year it sold WTEN-TV, Albany (which had been its first television property) and WSAZ-TV, Huntington, West Virginia. The various transactions yielded a net gain for Capital Cities. Its purchases gave the company access to larger markets than it lost through the sale of its Albany and Huntington properties.

When Capital Cities bought Carter Publications, Inc., the owner of the *Fort Worth Star-Telegram* in 1974, it also acquired that company's two radio stations, WBAP-AM and KSCS-FM. Between 1974 and 1981, Capital Cities did not acquire any additional radio or television properties. In 1981 it took over WKHX-FM in Marietta, Georgia, thereby gaining access to the rapidly growing Atlanta market.

Capital Cities has also moved into cable television. By 1981 its property holdings were large enough to justify the establishment of three territorial divisions. In addition to the purchase and development of cable systems, Capital Cities has been trying to develop new systems of electronic journalism. For example, the *News-Democrat* (Belleville, Illinois) was providing four fifteen-minute video news broadcasts over a local cable system. Capital Cities and the Tandy Corporation reached an agreement permitting paid subscribers in the Fort Worth, Texas, area selective access to information from the *Star-Telegram*, using a central computer. Tandy, the owner of Radio Shack, is one of the largest manufacturers of personal computers in the United States. The *Star-Telegram* also was negotiating with local cable systems to provide news services.

Capital Cities had also entered into an agreement with Source Telecomputing Corporation, a subsidiary of the Reader's Digest Association, to provide a daily television version of Capital Cities' publication *Multichannel News*. The company also planned to provide back issues of its *Energy User News* through Nexis, an information system run by Mead Data Central.

Capital Cities runs its own television production company, Capital Cities Television Productions. This unit develops television specials for Capital Cities' stations and for national syndication. In 1981 several of its programs were developed in association with Paulist Productions, a company run by a Roman Catholic religious order. Capital Cities' productions have won a number of awards. In 1981, for example, its series "Family Specials" was given the Ohio State Award. One of Capital Cities' programs received an award in recognition of its contribution to young people's programming by the United States branch of the International Catholic Association for Radio and Television. Two of the local television stations received public service awards: WPVI in Philadelphia for its special "21 Hours—The Pope in Philadelphia" and KTRK in Houston on behalf of its programming about heart disease. Its newspapers, including the *Times Leader*, also have won numerous awards for the quality of their journalism. Its Kansas City operation won a Pulitzer Prize for its coverage of a major hotel disaster in that city.

Capital Cities not only has been recognized for the quality of the work of many of its properties, but the company also participates in funding awards. It is one of the contributors to the Humanitas Prizes, given to selected writers involved in prime time television whose work reflects a commitment to the value and further development of individualism.

The recognition that many of Capital Cities' products have received for their high quality raises the question about how the company's properties fare in the marketplace. In general Capital Cities' television and radio properties have market shares that put them at or near the top of the ratings (Capital Cities Communications, Inc., 1981). Its newspaper operations also do very well because most have a monopoly in their circulation areas. Yet it is not merely because of their monopoly position that the newspapers are so highly profitable. As an observer of the newspaper industry said to me, "Murphy [Capital Cities' president] . . . has a real knack for selecting properties. He is a genius at picking properties with low profit margins and turning their financial situation around in a short time."

Because of Capital Cities' growth and performance since its modest beginning in 1954, its stock has become highly valued by some of America's largest investors. Their judgment about the company and its future seemed justified when Capital Cities purchased the American Broadcasting Company in 1985. This acquisition moved Capital Cities into the front ranks of America's communications conglomerates. To those outside of the media industry and to the casual investor, the news was a shock, but those who paid close attention to media companies were less surprised because Capital Cities was far from being a mouse that was swallowing an elephant.

Capital Cities' Investors

Table 2.1. The Top Seventy-One Stockholders in Capital Cities Communications, Inc.

Principal Stockholders	Shares	Percent
1 Marsh & McLennan Cos., Inc.		
Putnam Management/Funds Combined	841,500	6.28
2 Capital Group, Inc.		
Capital Guardian Trust Co.		
Capital Research and Management Funds		
Combined	793,800	5.93
3 Mackay-Shields Financial Corp.	492,250	3.67
4 Rosenberg Capital Management	449,520	3.35
5 Morgan (J. P.) & Co., Inc.	427,000	3.19
6 Stein Roe & Farnham	330,279	2.46
7 Citicorp	274,240	2.04
8 Kirby Family Group–Allegheny Corp.		
Investors Diversified Ser., Inc.		
IDS Funds Combined	230,000	1.71
9 Bank of New York Co., Inc.	218,479	1.63
10 Murphy, Thomas S. and family	211,265	1.57
11 Starr (C. V.)–American International		
Group		

	American International Insurance Cos. Combined	185,000	1.38
12	State Street Research & Management Co.	181,400	1.35
13	Lasdon, William S.	175,400	1.31
14	General American Investors Co., Inc.	171,900	1.28
15	Ruane Cunniff & Co., Inc.	170,700	1.27
16	TIAA-CREF College Retirement Equities Fund	158,000	1.18
17	New American Fund, Inc.	147,261	1.10
18	Prudential Insurance Co. of America Prudential Insurance Cos./Funds Combined	146,000	1.09
19	Axe (E. W.) & Co., Inc. Axe-Houghton Funds Combined	138,800	1.03
20	Fiduciary Trust Co. of New York Fiduciary Trust/Funds Combined	132,190	.98
21	Chemical New York Corp.	131,100	.97
22	Western Bancorporation	131,100	.97
23	General Electric Co. Elfun Trusts General Electric Pension Trust	130,000	.97
24	Mellon National Corp.	123,400	.92
25	Irving Bank Corp.	117,600	.87
26	New York City Comptroller's Office	114,200	.85
27	Oregon Public Employees Retirement System	114,000	.85
28	Cheswick McRae & Gillespie, Inc.	110,704	.82
29	Seligman (J. & W.) & Co. Seligman/Funds Combined	106,415	.79
30	Fletcher, J. Floyd	105,608	.78
31	Donaldson Lufkin & Jenrette, Inc.	101,692	.75
32	Ford Foundation	100,000	.74
33	State Farm Mutual Automobile Insurance Co.	96,000	.71
34	Dickler, Gerald, and family	95,160	.71
35	Thorndike Doran Paine & Lewis Thorndike-Wellington Funds Combined	92,190	.68
36	Kemper Family Group Kemper Insurance Cos./FDS Combined	88,000	.65
37	First Manhattan Co.	86,500	.64
38	Burke, Daniel B., and Family	86,430	.64
39	BEA Associates, Inc.	81,000	.60
40	INA Corp. INA Insurance Cos./FDS Combined	80,856	.60

41	Atlanta Capitol Corp.	80,850	.60
42	Casey, William J., and family	73,040	.54
43	Columbia Management Co.	70,600	.52
44	Scudder Stevens & Clark Co.	67,800	.50
45	Minnesota Mutual Life Insurance Co.	67,600	.50
46	Dougherty, Joseph P.	63,233	.47
47	Thomas, Lowell J.	61,492	.45
48	Bankers Trust New York Corp.	60,015	.44
49	Fairchild, John E., and family	58,403	.43
50	Wells Fargo & Co.	53,900	.40
51	First Pennsylvania Corp.	51,200	.38
52	First Wisconsin Corp.	50,400	.37
53	RCS Management Co.	50,000	.37
54	Harvard University	47,811	.35
55	International Telephone & Telegraph Corp.		
	Hartford Fire Insurance Cos. Combined	47,600	.35
56	Connecticut State Trust Fund	46,000	.34
57	Connecticut General Insurance Cos./FDS Combined	46,000	.34
58	Heller (Walter E.) International Corp. American National Bank & Trust Co./ Chicago	42,590	.31
59	Rothschild Family Group (France-England) Bank of California NA	41,670	.31
60	Princeton University	37,800	.28
61	U. S. Trust Corp.	36,150	.27
62	Weiss Peck & Greer	35,000	.26
63	Oppenheimer Holdings, Inc.	33,500	.25
64	First Chicago Corp.	33,400	.24
65	SBHU Holdings, Inc.	31,500	.23
66	Sais, John B.	31,050	.23
67	Ranier Bancorporation	30,500	.22
68	Winters National Corp.	30,000	.22
69	Cumberland Associates	30,000	.22
70	Atlanta Capital Management Corp.	29,860	.22
71	McCowan Associates, Inc.	28,700	.21

Source: Abrecht and Locker, 1981:46.

Table 2.1 lists the top seventy-one stockholders in Capital Cities Communications. Compared with other communications companies on *Forbe*'s and *Fortune*'s lists of the five hundred largest American companies, Capital Cities' ownership of Capital Cities' stock is less concentrated than the industry average (Abrecht and Locker, eds., 1981). One reason is that in companies such as the New York Times, Times-Mirror, Washington Post, Knight-Ridder, and Dow Jones the founding families still retain sizable blocks of stock. Capital Cities is different in that there is no founding family in the strict sense of the term. The company is largely a creation of outside investment capital.

Table 2.2 shows how Capital Cities' top twenty owners' investments in other communications companies listed in *Forbes* 500 puts Capital Cities, even before it purchased ABC, in the heart of the "endless chain" of interlocks (Bagdikian, 1983) that exists among America's major media conglomerates. Capital Cities is part and parcel of the information-finance capital complex that has come to dominate the American communications industry over the past twenty-five to fifty years.

Capital Cities' owners with the strongest connections to other media companies are as follows: Capital Group, Inc., which, in addition to its investment in Capital Cities, has substantial holdings in Knight-Ridder, MCA, Time, and Times-Mirror; Morgan (J.P.) and Co., which has top-twenty holdings in Gannett, Metromedia, RCA, Time, Times-Mirror, and the Washington Post Company; TIAA-CREF, the investment fund for university personnel, which holds a top-twenty position in Dow Jones, Gannett, Metromedia, RCA, Time, Times-Mirror, and Warner Communications; and Prudential, a mutual insurance company with holdings in CBS, Knight-Ridder, MCA, Metromedia, and RCA. Capital Group, TIAA-CREF, and Prudential, in addition, all had major holdings in ABC before Capital Cities' purchase of that company.

The corporate owners of Capital Cities and the other conglomerates in the communications sector are interlocked in a

Table 2.2. Capital Cities Top 20 Stockholders' Holdings in Other Forbes 500 Media Conglomerates

| Owners | Media | | | | | | | | |
	ABC	CCC	CBS	DJ	GANNETT	K-N	MCA	MM	NYT
MM	0	1	0	0	0	0	0	0	0
CG	1	2	0	0	0	3	2	0	0
M-S	0	3	0	0	0	0	0	0	0
Rosenberg	0	4	0	0	12	0	0	0	0
Morgan	0	5	0	0	11	0	0	10	0
SRF	0	6	0	8	0	0	0	15	0
Citicorp	0	7	0	9	0	0	9	0	0
Kirby	0	8	0	0	0	0	0	0	0
Bank of NY	0	9	5	0	0	5	0	0	0
Murphy	0	10	0	0	0	0	0	0	0
AIG	0	11	0	0	0	0	0	0	0
SSR	0	12	2	0	0	0	0	2	0
Lasdon	0	13	0	0	0	0	0	0	0
GAI	0	14	0	0	0	0	0	0	0
RCC	0	15	0	0	0	0	0	0	0
TIAA-CREF	13	16	9	3	5	0	0	4	0
NAF	0	17	0	0	0	0	0	0	0
Prudential	12	18	3	0	0	15	8	3	0
Axe	0	19	0	0	0	0	0	0	0
FTNY	0	20	0	12	0	0	0	0	18

variety of ways in addition to their shared stake in the American communications system. Not only do they have shared investments in other parts of the economy, but many of these giant investors own each other's stock. Thus as the linkages among the various companies that constitute Capital Cities' top twenty owners are traced out, the ties become so complex, dense, and overlapping as to make it virtually impossible to describe one owner in isolation from the entire system of ownership.

The *Times-Leader*'s Labor Process and Capital Cities

Capital Cities has been able to achieve its rapid growth,

RCA	TIME	TM	WARNER	WP
0	0	8	1	0
0	3	3	0	0
0	0	0	0	0
2	11	0	5	0
0	4	2	0	3
0	0	12	11	0
0	0	0	0	0
0	0	0	0	0
0	0	0	0	0
0	0	0	0	0
0	0	0	0	0
0	0	0	0	0
0	0	0	0	10
0	0	0	0	0
1	13	5	7	0
0	0	0	0	0
13	0	0	0	0
0	0	0	0	0
0	0	0	0	0

Owners Key:

MM:	March & McLennan
CG:	Capital Group
M-S:	Mackey-Shields
Rosenberg:	Rosenberg Capital Management
Morgan:	Morgan (J.P.) & Co.
Kirby:	Kirby Family Group
Murphy:	Thomas S. Murphy and family
AIG:	American International Group
SSR:	State Street Research & Management
Lasdon:	William S. Lasdon
LCC:	Ruane Cunniff & Co.
NAF:	New American Fund
FTNY:	Fiduciary Trust Co. of New York

Media Key:

ABC:	American Broadcasting Co.
CCC:	Capital Cities Communications
CBS:	Columbia Broadcasting Co.
K-N:	Knight-Ridder
MM:	Metromedia
DJ:	Dow Jones
NYT:	New York Times
RCA:	Radio Corporation of America
TM:	Times-Mirror
WP:	Washington Post

Source: Abrecht and Locker, 1981.

high stock prices, and high rates of profit because of its mix of properties, its market selection, its position within its markets, its management acumen, and its labor policies. Capital Cities' labor policies are geared toward maximizing its workers' productivity. Its success in stimulating productivity is clear in that it has one of the highest profit-to-employee ratios in the communications industry (Forbes, 1986).

Because few of its newspaper properties are totally unionized, Capital Cities has had virtually a free hand in designing and putting into effect high-productivity labor processes. When the company has had to deal with union opposition to proposed changes in labor processes, it never has been hesitant about facing down its unions, as it has done in Fort Worth and Kansas City, or in fighting them to the bitter end, as it did in Pontiac, Michigan. Capital Cities' policy of brooking no opposition to its productivity policies put the company on a direct collision course with the Wilkes-Barre Publishing Company's unions.

When Capital Cities purchased the Wilkes-Barre Publishing Company, it intended to increase the *Times Leader's* rate of return to "somewhere in the neighborhood of 12 percent to 18 percent or higher," according to a manager who was with the company at the time. Even before it purchased the publishing company, Capital Cities' executives knew that such profits would not be attainable under the terms of the existing union contracts.

Having proven its mettle in previous conflicts with newspaper unions, Capital Cities felt confident that if the Wilkes-Barre unions chose to resist any demands it made of them, it could either convince the unions to accept the concessions the company felt were necessary to restore profitability or, failing that, force them to do so, even if a strike resulted. Capital Cities was unwilling to absorb all of the risk of confronting the unions. It forced the old owners to accept part of the costs of a prospective strike by demanding a heavy discount in the purchase price for the company. Capital Cities got the paper for approximately $10.5 million, in addition to assuming all of the publishing company's outstanding debts. At the time of the purchase in 1978, monopoly papers with a circulation the size of Wilkes-Barre's were fetching between $20 and $30 million.

Capital Cities' management team reportedly was appalled by the situation it encountered upon arrival in Wilkes-Barre. According to a former manager: "The Capital Cities' managers couldn't believe the way the paper was run, especially the power the unions had. Shortly after they took over, they brought all of us into a meeting and told us that things were going to change. They told us they expected us to do our job of managing the paper and we shouldn't worry about how the unions responded because they would support us. This was quite a change from the old owners' philosophy. With them you always were afraid to make a decision that might offend the unions. All the unions had to do was threaten a grievance and the owners would reverse your decision."

As Capital Cities' executives tried to get control over the paper's day-to-day operations, they also worked on putting together a package of contract concessions that, if put into effect, would completely change the Wilkes-Barre Publishing Company's labor process.

Formal contract negotiations between the unions and the company began soon after the company took control of the paper. The first locals to begin bargaining with Capital Cities represented the stereotypers and the pressmen, who had been working without a contract with the former owners. During early 1978, according to a member of one of the unions' negotiating committees: "Our international was urging us to sign a contract with the company. They kept telling us that they were hearing rumors that something big was about to happen in Wilkes-Barre and we better sign before it was too late. But we didn't listen. When we finally were ready to sign, the paper already had been sold to Capital Cities."

When bargaining finally began, the International Typographical Union (ITU) and the Newspaper Guild carefully watched developments. Union officials became increasingly angry over the manner in which negotiations proceeded and over company maneuvering away from the bargaining table. Throughout the negotiation period, according to union members, Capital Cities offered a number of workers promotion into management positions if they would drop their union cards. From time to time, the newly promoted managers approached members of the negotiating committee and told them that they, too, could "join our team," if they would drop their cards. At one point in the negotiations, Capital Cities reportedly brought in several of these supervisors and had them stand against the wall facing the union negotiators. This tactic antagonized the unions. A union negotiator described what happened: "They brought all these guys in and stood them along the wall facing us. Then they tried to start negotiating. Well, let me tell you, that session lasted no more than fifteen minutes before we were out of there. . . . They didn't try to pull anything like that again."

It was not merely the tone of the negotiations that angered the unions. They did not like the concessions the company demanded. Knowing what Capital Cities had done in Kansas City and Pontiac, the locals suspected that the company would expect givebacks, but they were not prepared for the breadth of the contract changes Capital Cities was demanding.

As bargaining between the company, the pressmen, and the stereotypers dragged on, Capital Cities exchanged contract proposals with the other unions, the ITU and the Newspaper Guild. This took place in late August 1978. Having seen the fences and having carefully monitored negotiations with the pressmen, the other unions were primed for conflict.

Capital Cities and the four unions had no problems over wages. The company found the unions' wage demands, which asked for a 7 percent increase, well within reason. The major foci of Capital Cities' contract proposals dealt with matters pertaining to union recognition and representation, staffing provisions, forms of compensation, and management control. (From interviews with participants and from published reports in the *Citizens' Voice* and the *Times Leader;* see especially the story headlined "Publishing Company's Position Paper on Contract Talks," November 6, 1978, and the tabloid *Violence in the Valley,* 1978.)

The issue of union representation and recognition pertained mainly to the guild. The company demanded an end to the guild's union-shop clause. It wanted an open-shop provision, arguing that the union and the company should be allowed to compete for the workers' loyalty. In addition, it wanted to increase the number of editorial and managerial positions exempt from guild membership. The old owners had permitted union members to hold almost any management position at the paper without surrendering their union cards. One city businessman familiar with how the paper operated under the former owners saw this as a major reason for the paper's continuing problems: "They had active union members in all types of positions. You would expect many of these people to have divided loyalties. . . . you can't give unions that much power and not expect problems."

The company's staffing demands fell on all four unions. It wanted to eliminate the ITU contract provision requiring that the ITU work force could be reduced only through attrition. Capital Cities saw little chance to improve productivity as long as printers' jobs were guaranteed by the contract. Believing that it might lead to the immediate loss of one hundred or more jobs, the ITU refused to agree to any change in this part of the contract.

After the 1972 Wilkes-Barre flood, the publishing company had installed modern, high-speed electronic composition systems, which included video display terminals in the newsroom and the composing room. At the time, only seven other U.S. papers had comparable systems, and all of these were chain papers. In 1973 the Wilkes-Barre ITU struck to gain protection from layoffs. The new Wilkes-Barre ITU contract gave the union jurisdiction over all jobs working with the new typesetting technology and guaranteed that jobs would be eliminated only when they were vacated by their present incumbents. The Wilkes-Barre contract became a model for other ITU locals across the country.

The company also demanded changes in the staffing provisions in the pressmen's and stereotypers' contracts. Reportedly, it wanted to reduce the number of stereotypers and change the pressmen's room-manning clause. The room-manning clause specified the minimum pressroom crew size and the conditions under which it had to be increased. Capital Cities wanted to raise the requirements for calling in additional personnel. The stereotypers claimed that the company intended eventually to eliminate their classification and assign their remaining functions to other crafts. The stereotypers' job classification had been retained at the *Times Leader* by the old owners despite the fact that the traditional duties of these workers had been eliminated, for the most part, by the switch from a hot-lead to a cold-type production system. The workers who remained in this classification wanted the company to agree to cross-training provisions in the contract to provide them the opportunity to move over to the press room when vacancies developed there as a result of resignations or retirements. Reportedly, neither the old owners nor Capital Cities' negotiators were willing to accede to these demands.

Capital Cities demanded the elimination of all clauses and provisions of Article 4 of the guild contract dealing with staffing. Article 4 required that certain editorial positions had to be maintained on both editions of the paper. It also required that the guild be consulted before any guild job could be eliminated. If the guild did not agree that the job should be eliminated, it had the right to submit the matter to binding arbitration. Article 4 also stipulated that all vacated positions, except the exempt positions, were to be posted by the company. Seniority, experience, education, and past job performance were to be the criteria that had to be used in deciding among candidates bidding for a job. When candidates were equal in the last three categories, seniority was to be the determining factor. Article 4 restricted the company's hiring rights. All vacant positions had to be filled from inside the paper. If there were no internal applicants the company could recruit from outside. The only other way the company could bring in outsiders was by creating new positions, but only two new positions in any guild classification could be created during the life of the contract. Article 4 also limited the company's rights to transfer personnel within and between the two editions. Transfers across job classifications or departments required the approval of the employee and the guild. The company wanted these restrictions removed so that it could rationalize the internal distribution of labor.

Like the ITU, the guild had a contract provision (Article 24, Paragraph 6) guaranteeing that there would be no staff reductions involving its members during the life of the contract. It read as follows: "From October 3, 1976 to September 30, 1978, no Guild member employed as of October 3, 1976 will be discharged for economic reasons and/or as a result of the introduction of new equipment, machines, apparatuses, or processes." The company wanted this removed.

Capital Cities also wanted changes in the two provisions of the guild contract that blocked the company's freedom to hire part-time workers. One prohibited the company from replacing a full-time worker with a part-timer. The other removed the economic incentive for hiring part-time workers by requiring the company to pay them the same fringe benefits as full-time workers in the job classification to which they were assigned. Capital Cities believed that the staffing requirements in the union contracts needlessly raised the wage bill and illegitimately restricted management's rights to adjust the size and composition of the work force as required by market and productivity considerations. It saw no compelling reasons for unions to have a say in such matters.

The theme of management responsibility and rights also can be seen in the compensation changes Capital Cities demanded. The company wanted to introduce a merit system administered and controlled by management. Therefore Capital Cities insisted that the contract be changed so that only the company had the right to determine who received merit pay and how much. The current contract recognized the employer's right to give merit awards but required that all such awards be negotiated by the guild and that the guild be notified of the amount of money each worker received. The company argued that merit awards were private matters between workers and their employer and that the guild had no business negotiating who was to get them and how large they were to be.

The company wanted a merit system for several reasons. First, it wanted to use merit awards to stimulate productivity. Second, it hoped that by introducing a form of compensation that was beyond union control it would be able to stimulate gratitude among the workers and loyalty to the company rather than the union for the raises a worker received. Third, it saw the merit awards as a way of introducing individualized competitive relationships into the labor process, which would help undermine union solidarity. The company also insisted that the contract state that management would be the sole judge of competence. The union was to have no voice in determining the standards for arriving at this determination, nor would it be permitted to participate in designing the evaluation process.

Capital Cities demanded that the guild accede to changes in the overtime provisions in its contract. These provisions imposed a heavy cost on the paper whenever it tried to use workers outside of their normal shift, which the contract defined as seven and a half hours within a nine-hour period. Capital Cities, negotiators maintained that the overtime provisions were an unreasonable and "unprofessional" restraint on the paper's ability to cover the news in a timely, effective manner, especially late-breaking stories and unexpected events. The company also wanted the guild to give up its prohibitions against "free work." The guild contract required that journalists be compensated for all work used by the company, regardless of whether it had been scheduled.

Capital Cities requested several additional concessions from the guild that bore directly on the issue of management control. For example, the company demanded that a management rights clause be inserted into the contract. It also wanted the contract changed to permit the publisher and senior editors to write occasional pieces for the paper. The guild had no objection to the management rights clause, provided agreement could be reached on the wording, but rejected the proposal that senior company officials be allowed to write copy for the paper. It argued that such people had the editorial page on which to express their opinon and that was all they needed.

The company also asked the guild to concede Article 16 in its contract, which required the company to publish an all-day paper during the life of the contract. Capital Cities maintained that this clause infringed on the company's right to determine how its property was to be used.

The guild was asked to accept an ethics clause in the contract. Capital Cities defended this demand by pointing to practices engaged in by journalists that it considered questionable. One of these was a sports publication by several reporters that allegedly directly competed with the *Times Leader* for advertising sales. The company also noted that the clause was needed to prohibit employees from apparent conflicts of interest that jeopardized their credibility as objective journalists.

As an example of ethical practices it considered questionable, the company cited the case of a journalist who ran a public relations firm on the side. One of his major clients was state senator Martin Murray (D.-Wilkes-Barre). Murray was president pro tem of the Pennsylvania Senate. Capital Cities argued that even if this reporter claimed to be unfailingly objective in his coverage of political news, the paper and its readers could never be confident that what he was writing was really objective and unbiased. There would always be nagging suspicions that his work might be colored by his contractual relationships with Murray. Capital Cities also justified its demand by pointing to the case of a courthouse reporter who allegedly ran a private lottery to finance a personal trip to Ireland. The guild dismissed the company's claims that an ethics clause was needed in the contract. It noted that the raffle incident had happened before Capital Cities had purchased the paper and had not seemed to upset the former owners. The guild also asserted that the issue of the sports publication had been taken to arbitration and the arbitrator had ruled that the publication did not compete with the *Times Leader.* The guild deeply resented the way the company presented its request for an ethics clause. The guild felt the company was trying to make it appear that the journalists were engaging in widespread ethical abuses that the union was unwilling and unable to control. The Guild stated that questionable ethical practices were rare and that the union could handle any problems that existed or arose in the future without company interference.

Capital Cities demanded two additional changes in the guild contract's miscellaneous clause (Article 24). First, it wanted reporters to cede control of their bylines. The existing contract gave employees the right to withhold the use of their byline whenever they deemed necessary. The union defended this right by claiming that a byline was the personal property of the journalist and should never be used without the journalist's full consent. Capital Cities argued that the byline was the joint property of the journalist and the company, and therefore the company should have a say on when it was used.

Second, the company asked the guild to eliminate Paragraph 5 of Article 24, which exempted guild members from having to cross picket lines set up by other unions and from handling struck work. Capital Cities wanted to substitute a paragraph that would have allowed guild members only the right to honor their own union's picket lines. The guild knew full well the implications of this change. It was aware that a newspaper strike was doomed to fail if unions were required to cross each other's picket lines, and therefore it refused to agree to contract provisions that would oblige its members to cross lines set up by the craft unions, just as it expected the crafts to reject similar demands made of them. In light of the history of newspaper strike failures across the country because of workers from one union crossing another's picket line, it is small wonder that the guild did not want to accept any changes in the contract that would have required its members to fail to support another newspaper union's labor action.

Capital Cities did not want to change the labor process merely to improve the technical competency of its editorial staff. It also hoped that the changes it was trying to introduce would attract journalists who met its definition of a professional and who, therefore, would be able to produce high-quality work in the appropriate quantity. In Capital Cities' view, building and sustaining a professional work force required a specific labor process.

To Capital Cities this "professional" labor process had to be organized in such a way that it fostered individual competition, for the company believed that competition among professional peers perfected skills and tested competence. Capital Cities wanted to expose its Wilkes-Barre journalists to both internal and external competition. The company firmly believes in the value of market-induced anxiety as a stimulant to improvement in the quantity and quality of a worker's output. Capital Cities' executives felt that the poor quality of work and the low quantity of output among the guild journalists was partly a result of the journalists' immunity from the fear of being replaced by someone better or faster. Because the guild contract insulated reporters and editors from the discipline of the external labor market, they had no reason to care about producing first-rate materials.

The professional labor process, according to Capital Cities, also has to structure rewards so that they are tailored to individual performance levels and not to extraneous factors such as longevity in a job. The professional must not be afraid to have his or her work critically examined and to be rewarded on the basis of the results of such an examination. In the company's view, without individualized rewards tied to performance, journalists will have no reason to produce high-quality work.

Capital Cities believed that even union agreement to reconfiguring the *Times Leader's* labor process would not be enough either to improve the quality of the paper to the standard the company wanted or to raise profit levels. These results would come only by reconstituting the company's editorial work force. Capital Cities wanted to replace the present journalists with men and women who were more technically competent than they believed the workers inherited from the old owners were.

The existing editorial work force was made up almost entirely of men and women who lacked any formal education in journalism other than on-the-job apprenticeship. Capital Cities felt that the apprenticeship system had not given the journalists the skills necessary for producing work that met contemporary quality standards in the field. Capital Cities claimed that the reporters had little understanding of or appreciation for the work methods that led to informative, objective, and unbiased journalistic accounts. Capital Cities' editors pointed to a number of questionable practices that were common at the *Times Leader* before they took over. For example, they claimed that reporters tended to rely excessively on handouts from sources or on the accounts of sources for their stories, rather than moving beyond the surface of a story to generate independent, verifiable or falsifiable accounts, as modern journalistic practice demands (Gouldner, 1976; Schudson, 1978; Gans, 1979). Capital Cities' editors also pointed out that the reporters often were too closely tied to their sources, especially politicians and government officials, to be able to write objective, let alone critical, stories.

It is hard to know whether Capital Cities believed its contract proposals would be accepted by the four unions or whether it offered the proposals hoping that the workers would reject them and strike, thereby allowing the company to replace the old work force with new employees more to its liking, which is precisely what the union negotiators believed was happening. One negotiator recounted his experience as follows:

We'd go in the room, company people on one side of the table, union people on the other. You never knew from one meeting to the next who would still be with you. One guy who left the union later showed up on the company's side of the table. We went through the contract, line by line. When we agreed on something, all of us would shake hands and we'd move to the next point. When we got to the end of a page, everybody would initial it and then we'd start all over again. I had the feeling that every time we'd agree to something the company would raise the ante on the next set of issues. . . . They wanted a strike so that they could hire all new people.

Capital Cities denies that it wanted to force a strike. Nevertheless, the company readily admits that it would not accept contracts that did not provide for the imposition of new labor processes in the newsroom and craft shops. Capital Cities believed that only by changing the basic way in which work was organized at the *Times Leader* could it control costs, increase productivity, improve the quality of the paper, expand its market, and raise profit levels.

Once it got the changes it wanted, Capital Cities had planned to begin marketing the *Times Leader* as a regional newspaper. It felt that the two Scranton papers were of low quality and could easily be defeated in a circulation war. The company also planned to start a Sunday edition. It believed that the *Sunday Independent* was such an inferior paper it could easily be knocked out of the market, even though the *Times Leader*'s former publishers had lost a small fortune on a similar effort shortly after the flood, when the *Sunday Independent* was thought to be especially vulnerable.

Beginning in 1986, rumors began circulating at the *Citizens' Voice* that the *Times Leader* soon would announce that it planned to publish a Sunday edition. These rumors proved true. In June, 1987, Capital Cities revealed that it would begin publishing a Sunday paper in late summer.

The *Citizens' Voice* quickly swung into action. In a "News

Analysis" published June 11, 1987, the *Citizens' Voice* provided a brief recap of the unions' perspective on the strike and ended with a series of questions for its readers.

> "Will Luzerne County and/or Northeastern Pennsylvania end up with one newspaper?
> Will Cap Cities use its millions to force even more newspaper workers into the streets?
> Will Cap Cities continue to use its vitriolic *Times Leader* editorial columns to continually condemn and criticize; to espouse First Ammendment causes when, in fact, the real goal is to eliminate all political, social, and economic opposition?
> Does the community really understand the consequences of what's happening? Do business owners realize the advertising rates they would have without competition? Do readers realize that they would be left with a *Times Leader* even more generic than it is?
> Do those who are being used by the *Times Leader* realize that one day they too could become the abused?
> While the shape of newspapering may be changing in Northeastern Pennsylvania, we at the *Citizens' Voice* pledge to continue our struggle, a struggle that in its own way has served the Wilkes-Barre community by providing the only true daily newspaper."

The *Citizens' Voice* followed this news analysis with an editorial, entitled "Oppose Cap Cities' arrogant agenda," denouncing the *Times Leader* on June 13, 1987. The editorial stated:

> "Capital Cities/ABC has its own agenda for Northeastern Pennsylvania and it goes this way: . . . Use editorial muscle to reshape this area politically into the Cap Cities conservative tone: Lower its own and the area's wage rates."
> The above analysis appeared in Wednesday's edition of the *Citizens' Voice* after the *Times Leader* announced it is going to try to penetrate the area with a Sunday newspaper.
> On Thursday the analysis was proved true. The *Times*

Leader lashed out at Nanticoke Mayor John Haydock because he didn't object to some city employees joining a union. Never mind—if you're the *Times Leader*—that 90 percent of the city's employees are already in the union; that the employees in point have as many as 42 faithful years of service to the city; that these employees don't even have pensions.

The *Times Leader*'s standard is, as stated above, low wages and political control. And the *Times Leader*'s goal is—as the analysis Thursday said—'Use economic muscle to get a monopoly, Make lots of money.'

But the *Times Leader* isn't going to satisfy its agenda. Because we believe the good newspaper people at the *Sunday Independent* are going to (as the daily newspaper people here) show the *Times Leader* what the people of this area are made of. And so are the readers who have—every day of the week for nine years—said 'no' . . . absolutely 'not' . . . to Capital Cities."

While the *Citizens' Voice* went on the attack, the *Sunday Independent*'s editorial columns remained silent. However, it is hard to imagine that its owning family will passively accept such a challenge. In the early 1970s it drove a short-lived Wilkes-Barre Publishing Company Sunday edition from the market. Moreover, a high official at the *Sunday Independent* once told me that if the *Times Leader* ever tried to mount a Sunday paper the *Independent* would try to enter into some type of explicit alliance with the *Citizens' Voice.*

If part of Capital Cities' purpose in Wilkes-Barre was to force a strike, replace its former workers with new employees, and institute a new labor process, it achieved at least some of its goals. There was a strike, and the company has been able to build a new editorial work force made up largely of college-trained writers and editors. Capital Cities also has been able to reduce the number of mechanical craft workers, change work rules in the shops, and raise craft productivity substantially. A former union craft worker who stayed with the company described his work situation as follows:

I work a lot harder now than I used to. But I wouldn't say that they overwork me. They just require that I give a fair day's work for a fair day's wage. . . . Before Capital Cities took over there were a lot of people who didn't have anything to do. They'd punch in and walk around all day. Some of them would leave the building and be gone for a couple of hours. They'd go somewhere and drink coffee or run personal errands. You couldn't blame them—with the new equipment there wasn't enough work to go around. But, still, it wasn't fair to the company. They shouldn't have had to pay people who weren't working.

Capital Cities has raised the quality of the *Times Leader*. Its writing, editing, and graphics have improved dramatically. But at the same time, the improvements in quality, the new personnel, the new work rules, and the increases in productivity have not enabled the company to expand its market into the Scranton area, to develop a Sunday edition, or to increase the level of profits in Wilkes-Barre. Following the strike, the company has had to devote most of the resources it committed to Wilkes-Barre to rebuilding the *Times Leader*'s circulation to its prestrike level.

Capital Cities' decision to alter the *Times Leader*'s labor process and its subsequent conflict with the Wilkes-Barre unions was not an unusual occurrence in the newspaper industry during the late 1970s. Around the same time, strikes took place in Philadelphia; Washington, D.C.; Pontiac, Michigan; New York City; Madison, Wisconsin, and a score of other cities. Most of these strikes ended with unions making substantial concessions. In other cities, unions surrendered and accepted new work rules without a fight. The assaults that publishers were mounting against their workers resulted from a combination of factors and circumstances.

Newspapers across the United States were seeing a marked decay in the "social structures of accumulation" (Gordon, Edwards, and Reich, 1982) put into place after the Depression. Publishers had to contend with rapidly increasing production costs, including wage increases. At the same time, advertising and sales revenues were eroding because of inflation, recession, competition from other media, and, in some cases, declining readership. Although decay was national in scope, it was especially intense in Wilkes-Barre, where the publishing company not only faced industry-specific problems but also had to cope with a local economy that was undergoing its own deindustrialization crisis. It was small wonder that the publishers saw little hope of expanding their circulation and advertising base.

The Wilkes-Barre Publishing Company experienced further limits on its ability to respond to crisis because it had to contend with exceptionally militant and powerful local unions. The local owners knew that they did not have the financial or political muscle to force the unions to make concessions that would help restore their profits. The unions already had rejected any compromise on their contracts. Part of the local newspaper unions' philosophy had always been "no givebacks." They also knew that a unilateral move to impose concessions would be met with a strike that might possibly bankrupt them.

In the face of these circumstances, the owners decided it was best to sell their paper. But they were unable to get the price they had hoped. The publishers blamed the unions' contracts and reputation for militance for the paper's low selling price. Many businessmen in the region agreed with them. One commented: "The publishers were fools when it came to dealing with their unions. They would do almost anything to avoid conflict. They gave the unions everything they asked for. The unions really ran the paper, not the owners. They couldn't even lay anybody off. Because of those contracts, the Hourigans and Smiths lost over half of their capital."

Like the former publishers, Capital Cities believed that higher profits were tied to union concessions. But unlike the former owners, it felt confident that it could either convince the workers to make the concessions it believed were necessary or, failing that, unilaterally impose them. If the unions resisted demands for concessions and struck, Capital Cities felt that the losses would be acceptable because of the long-term gains to be had if the unions were defeated or broken. After all, Capital Cities already had beaten the guild and pressmen in Pontiac, Michigan, and had brought the ITU to heel in Kansas City and Fort Worth.

The company did not plan to cease publication if there was a strike. Because the Wilkes-Barre Publishing Company had the latest printing equipment and presses, the company did not have to depend on large quantities of skilled labor to produce the paper. The craft jobs had been sufficiently "degraded" (Braverman, 1974) that virtually anyone could be taken off the street and trained to do the work in a competent manner within a relatively short time. Production easily could be handled by supervisors, union members who refused to strike, and newly hired employees. As negotiations were proceeding, Capital Cities brought in employees from its other operations to familiarize them with the equipment. The training was conducted when there was no scheduled work. The company made no attempt to hide what it was doing.

The company also knew that it would have few problems finding journalists to replace the guild strikers. With the glut of aspirants for journalism jobs, which was a product of higher proportions of the population acquiring college degrees and a mushrooming of enrollments in journalism schools, publishers have found it easy to replace strikers with new graduates or with workers from other papers.

The guild has no formal means to discipline strikebreakers at a later point in their careers. Because closed shops were outlawed by the Taft-Hartley Act, the guild cannot block strikebreakers from taking jobs at union papers at some later time. As a guild member in Wilkes-Barre put it, "Publishers hire anyone they want. The guild doesn't have any say over who's hired or who isn't. . . . People are hired and they join the union and that's that." At least one, and possibly more, of Capital Cities' nonunion Kansas City journalists who volunteered to go to Wilkes-Barre until the company could hire permanent replacements reportedly later took jobs at guild papers. They had no problem joining the guild. Even if the guild could prevent strikebreakers from getting jobs at union papers, the guild represents workers at fewer than half the papers in the country. The strikebreaker therefore has plenty of opportunities for mobility, should he or she desire to seek work elsewhere. Thus taking a job at a struck paper has few career risks for the scab. Indeed, quite the opposite is the case. It can provide one with an entry into journalism that might otherwise not be available, and it demonstrates to prospective employers that one can be counted on to be a "good employee."

Few of the workers with whom I talked who had signed on with Capital Cities in Wilkes-Barre after the strike began expressed any great fear that they had damaged their careers by being strikebreakers. Most were happy to have had the chance to get a newspaper job and saw the *Times Leader* as a stepping stone to a larger market. When I asked one of these journalists what he would do if he wanted to work for a guild paper, he replied, "I have no problems with the guild. I can take it or leave it. If I had to join the union in order to keep a job I wanted, then I'd join it, even after what's happened here." He went on to say: "The guild has given us a hard time. They've called us names, tried to pick fights, and tried to keep us from doing our jobs. . . . It hasn't been all of them, just a few hotheads. . . . I can understand why these people hate us. They think we took their jobs. We really didn't, you know. They left them. . . . If I were in their shoes, I guess I'd feel the same way, but I don't think I could do the things that some of them have." Others were far less sanguine in their attitude toward the guild, claiming that after what they had witnessed in Wilkes-Barre they would never join the union, even if that meant losing a chance for a better job.

Believing that it had the resources necessary to take a strike and win and being determined to achieve its objectives of restoring management control, lowering labor costs, and increasing productivity, Capital Cities was not inclined to compromise on its major contract demands. It would accept nothing short of a complete redefinition of the labor process, which entailed workers surrendering most of the rights of industrial citizenship that they had won through years of hard collective bargaining, strikes, and struggles on the shop floors, in the newsroom, and in the offices. The workers believed the more important rights they had won were as follows:

1. Protection from market discipline. The craft unions and guild had built an internal labor market that protected the workers from outside competition by more "qualified" or cheaper labor and from displacement because of changes in technology, the organization of production, or even poor market conditions. The workers also were protected from displacement by part-timers. The contracts removed all financial incentives for the company to use part-time instead of full-time labor.

2. Protection from external competition for mobility opportunities. The unions had established an internal mobility ladder that was under their firm control. Union members had to be given the first opportunity to fill any vacated position, except those exempted by contract. These contract provisions also meant that a large number of key supervisors and managers could be union members and, when such was the case, they were subject to some degree of union control.

3. Protection from intensification of the labor process. The *Times Leader*'s contracts provided ample protection from any company attempts to increase output without formal union agreement. The company not only was required to maintain the number of personnel at predefined levels but also to maintain certain functions. Staff could not be reduced without union consent.

4. Control over their "free" time. The contracts prevented the company from capitalizing workers' private time without paying high premiums. The contracts' overtime provisions made certain that whenever employees where given additional assignments requiring work beyond or outside of their normal shift they would be paid a high premium.

5. Protection from the arbitrary and capricious exercise of managerial power in determining competency levels, work assignments, disciplinary actions, raises, promotions, dismissals, and the like. Managers' rights to take such actions were tightly constrained by the contract. Any such actions required union consent.

6. Protection from competition among themselves. Although the workers were able to compete for promotions and raises on a limited basis, the contract kept this competition from becoming too intense and thereby developing a threat to worker solidarity. One guild member made the point that the union was as "important in protecting us from each other and our own greed as in protecting us from an employer."

7. Shop-floor control. Before Capital Cities' purchase, the workers, especially in the crafts, had almost complete control over the shop floor. Each craft worker knew his or her job and exercised a goodly amount of autonomy and self-control in organizing the work, completing it, and determining the quantity and quality of production. The crafts did their work under the supervision of a foreman, but such supervision was nominal. No foreman was likely to do anything that would leave him open to the charge of being a "company man," so, generally, they were careful to avoid infringing on formal and informal union work rules and standards.

As far as I can determine, union members or leaders did not organize these rights into a hierarchy. They insisted on protecting all of them in their negotiations with Capital Cities. Nothing was to be surrendered. All of these rights were inviolable, irreversible, and well worth fighting to defend. They were as fundamental a part of the workers' basic package of human rights as were their political rights of citizenship.

Capital Cities did not look upon such hard-won union gains as rights; it defined them as excessive and archaic privileges that were serious impediments to the company's ability to make a profit. The company has maintained that although these privileges might have been justifiable in the past, current economic conditions do not warrant continuing them. In Capital Cities' view, competent and talented workers did not need a union, which it defined as a superfluous "third party," when all of their minimum rights already were adequately defined and guaranteed by the courts, legislatures, and the National Labor Relations Board. Moreover, Capital Cities argued that its proposed contract changes offered workers in Wilkes-Barre a chance to secure rights impossible to realize under the old contracts, namely, the right to be an individual, to compete, and to be rewarded for personal achievements.

To the unions, Capital Cities' views of an employee's rights and obligations were anathema. To accept them in lieu of the rights built into the union contracts would mean rejecting almost all of the time-honored moral codes and work practices of the craft unions (Montgomery, 1979) and of the particular brand of industrial unionism that the Wilkes-Barre Newspaper Guild had espoused and practiced. In the workers' eyes, Capital Cities was asking them to surrender their human dignity and take degraded work—work that did not meet union standards of respectable employment. And they would have none of it.

To the unionized workers, Capital Cities' talk about the value of individualism, competition, and performance-based rewards was empty rhetoric, a means to disguise the company's desire that its workers produce more without substantially increasing their compensation. In addition, most union members believed that the company's contract proposals, if accepted, would lead to the end of unionism as it had come to be known and practiced at the Wilkes-Barre Publishing Company since the late 1930s, and, if unionism were brought to an end, so, too, would the old forms of work. As a guild member described the situation: "It was clear to us soon after Cap Cities took over that the old owners' values were going to be replaced with a drive to get as much profit as possible. They were going to force a speedup. We weren't going to tolerate that. We're not against profits. An owner deserves to make money, but we weren't going to let ourselves be victims of Cap Cities' greed."

The strikers, however, felt that they were defending not only their own interests but those of all of the county's workers. To have surrendered to Capital Cities would have been to repudiate not only their own traditions as unions but the traditions of all of the county's other unions, past and present. In numerous discussions that I had with them it was clear that union leaders and the rank and file saw their cause as being one not only with their co-unionists in the newspaper industry but also with other trade unionists in the Wilkes-Barre area.

The newspaper unions believed that their contracts expressed everything that the trade union movement in Wilkes-Barre, from the mine workers through the garment workers and other craft and industrial unions, had always stood for: the rights of workers to organize, to bargain collectively, to force owners to take into account workers' needs when setting company goals and the means for achieving them, to ensure a decent wage and adequate benefits, to some degree of autonomy within and control over the labor process, protection from competition from nonorganized workers, protection from unreasonable work standards, protection from arbitrary and capricious management discipline, and to ensure that workers would not be pitted against each other in attempts to better their situation. A clergyman close to the strikers stated that "the newspaper unions saw their cause to be the same as the mine workers. They saw themselves as victims of the worst kind of corporate exploitation imaginable. I don't know how true that is, but that's the way they saw it. . . . This was our Solidarity. They're romantics. . . . The strike was like the old days, the days of the big mine strikes. For a lot of people this was a chance to relive those times."

In the unions' view, then, Capital Cities was asking them to repudiate everything that they and their forebears had accomplished by expecting them to accept degrading working conditions that insulted their human dignity and human rights and undermined their individual self-respect and their overall respectability in the community. One union member expressed this sentiment as follows: "If we accepted the contract, I wouldn't be able to look at myself in the mirror. It would've surrendered everything we fought for in the past. . . . My grandfather and my father would've been ashamed of me."

On the basis of the unions' perceptions and evaluations of the situation, they began devising various strategies that they hoped would force the company to modify its position or, failing that, would allow them to protect themselves should a strike develop. On September 11, 1978, they formed the Wilkes-Barre Council of Newspaper Unions and began developing a coordinated bargaining strategy. No one union would agree to a contract until all did so. It was agreed that no one union would settle its contract on terms the other unions saw as harmful to the collective interests of all the newspaper workers. The company had been led to believe that relations among the local unions had soured over the 1974–75 guild strike. During that strike, several craft workers had attempted to cross the guild picket line but had been turned back. Many of the craft workers, Capital Cities was told, continued to resent the guild walkout during the Christmas holidays, when workers had a chance to make considerable overtime pay handling the paper's heavy advertising.

According to a local Capital Cities official, the company had wanted to carry out independent negotiations with each of the unions. The goal was to reach settlements as quickly as possible with the mechanical trades so that the guild would be isolated and come under increased pressure to sign a concessionary contract or be forced to strike on its own.

From September onward, Capital Cities tried to get the unions to engage in separate bargaining. But they refused, even though Capital Cities received support in its attempt to split the locals from an unexpected quarter—the international offices of the ITU. The ITU sent a negotiator into Wilkes-Barre to try to convince the local to reach a separate agreement with the company. The Wilkes-Barre local literally ran him out of town and informed ITU headquarters that it wanted no further assistance in local negotiations. As a result, when the strike finally came, the international declared it an illegal work stoppage and refused to sanction it. There are several reasons why the ITU was willing to adopt a more conciliatory attitude toward Capital Cities than were the other international unions. First, the ITU was being devastated by technological change. In the late 1970s, its membership had decreased by almost half of what it had been fifteen to twenty years before (Raskin, 1982), primarily because of technological displacement. To cope with this situation, the ITU was taking the position adopted by other unions that in the past had faced the same problem: it wanted to keep its recognition rights in a given shop and negotiate the best possible deals it could for the men and women laid off and for the handful who managed to keep their jobs. Second, the ITU still had not resolved its problems with Capital Cities in Fort Worth and Kansas City, and it did not want to threaten its recognition there by taking an "unreasonable" attitude in Wilkes-Barre. Some members of the Wilkes-Barre local had a somewhat different view. According to them, they were "sold out" by international union officials who had "too close" personal relationships with higher reaches of the company's management.

Despite repeated attempts to break the coordinated negotiation strategy, interunion solidarity held and events moved ineluctably toward a strike. Interunion solidarity had been forged through five major strikes from the late 1930s to the mid-1970s and in countless rounds of contract negotiations, grievance hearings, and arbitration proceedings over the years. Because of their history of mutual support, the leaders of the four unions knew that they could trust and count on each other to maintain the agreement despite pressures from their internationals or their rank and file. Time and again, one or another union had stayed off the job until all of the contracts had been settled or had gone back to work with a contract extension when the others had settled but it still had not. With such a long history of mutual respect, support, and confidence on the local level, it was not surprising that in the face of an enemy as totally threatening to all as Capital Cities was perceived to be, the unions stuck together, even in the face of the opposition of the international ITU.

With union solidarity holding, and neither side showing signs of a willingness to compromise, each party moved ineluctably toward a strike. The situation might have turned out differently for Capital Cities had it been able to break the unions' solidarity or had the company not moved as precipitously against all of the unions. A local Capital Cities official, reflecting on the situation, stated that the company should have come into Wilkes-Barre and shown itself to be a good citizen, signed contracts with the unions, made whatever changes it could in the paper's format and the like, and, then, when the contracts expired, taken an aggressive stand.

But Capital Cities chose to demonstrate that it intended to change the labor process at the paper almost from the moment it assumed control. And the unions responded as everyone expected they would. They went on strike, and they were determined that they would not be defeated, especially when the cost of a defeat would mean their elimination from the paper.

The Strike

3

Capital Cities coupled its demands at the bargaining table with direct pressures on the rank and file. During the summer of 1978, Capital Cities constructed a twelve-foot-high chain-link fence around part of its property in central city Wilkes-Barre, placed surveillance cameras around the outside of the building, and hired a private security force to patrol company buildings (including the shop floors) and grounds.

Capital Cities hired Wackenhut Security, one of the largest private security firms in the country, to handle protective services in Wilkes-Barre. In 1978, Wackenhut was still owned by the man who founded it in 1954, George Wackenhut, a former agent with the Federal Bureau of Investigation. Its board of directors includes Clarence Kelley, a former head of the FBI, several retired military officers with star or flag rank; a former head of the U.S. Secret Service; a former commissioner of customs for the United States, who also was a former official of International Telephone and Telegraph; and several prominent businessmen.

Many of Wackenhut's top executives and managers previously served in the FBI or some other government security force. Wackenhut has held major federal contracts, such as the contract to provide fire protection for the Kennedy Space Center in Florida. It holds contracts with various local government bodies, providing security at stadia, airports, and other public facilities. Wackenhut also has contracts with municipal governments to provide communities with fire fighting and emergency medical services and police support activities (except where otherwise noted, the information on Wackenhut is taken from the company's 1982 annual report).

It also runs overseas security operations. In Latin America it had major contracts and offices in Argentina during the days of the junta and in Peru, Ecuador, the Dominican Republic, Guatemala, and Colombia. In addition, Wackenhut is present in Canada, Bermuda, Italy, Japan, South Korea, and Saudi Arabia. It runs a subsidiary, Wackenhut International Trading Corporation, which peddles security equipment throughout Latin America.

The heart of Wackenhut's operations, however, is its domestic corporate security programs. Wackenhut provides U.S. corporations with a broad range of security services. In addition to uniformed guards, Wackenhut can supply undercover intelligence and investigative operatives, protection from data and information theft, and an employee informer program through which someone can call a Wackenhut number and anonymously charge a person or persons with some illegal act at work. The company also provides private bodyguards for businessmen and their families. Wackenhut runs a training school, the Wackenhut Institute, for its own employees and the security forces of various companies and government bodies.

Among its various security services, Wackenhut markets a strike package. Through Wackenhut Emergency Protection Services, a guard force can be quickly assembled, trained, and dispatched anywhere in the United States under the direction of "labor dispute coordinators." Through Wackenhut Support Services, Inc., a company can purchase additional strike services. Wackenhut Support Services, Inc., provides equipment so that key personnel can stay at the production site during the course of a strike and have as "many homelike comforts as possible for as long as necessary" (Wackenhut, 1982:13).

Capital Cities apparently contracted with both Wackenhut Emergency Protection Services and Wackenhut Support Services, Inc., to provide a full package of strike protection. When Wackenhut arrived in Wilkes-Barre in late September, 1978, it placed guards throughout the publishing company's building. They were at entrances and exits and in rest rooms, eating areas, places where workers congregated on breaks, and the shop floors. It also brought in supplies and equipment that would permit workers to live inside the building in the event a strike took place.

From Capital Cities' perspective, the security system was needed to ensure that the workers would abide by the terms of their contracts because it believed that labor discipline had completely broken down. Furthermore, the new management had been told by the former owners, several of whom continued to work at the paper, that if a strike took place there was sure to be violence, especially if Capital Cities tried to publish while the workers were out.

The workers saw the security provisions as an attempt to intimidate them, curtail the free flow of information inside the building, strip them of time-honored occupational rights and privileges and humiliate them. The unions charged that Capital Cities' security precautions were a part of the company's fundamental assault on the workers' human dignity and an insult to everyone in the region.

To the people who walked or drove past the company's building, located about fifty yards from the city's main shopping district, the atmosphere was that of a mine site preparing for a strike. The mining companies used to barricade and string barbed wire around their property and buildings when a strike loomed. The situation at the publishing company was brought to general public attention in late August 1978, when the weekly *Wyoming Valley Observer* ran a story by Carl T. Davies, along with photographs, which suggested that conditions at the company were comparable to those at a German prisoner of war camp. In a story titled "TLEN . . . [at the time the paper was called the *Times Leader, Evening News*] Staffers

Question 'Security Moves,'" the *Wyoming Valley Observer*
ran a photograph of the building captioned: "STALAG 17?
This 12 foot chain-link fence equipped for the installation of
barbed wire was recently erected along the side and in the rear
parking area of the Wilkes-Barre Publishing Co. on North
Main Street. With negotiations underway between two unions
and the new management, Capital Cities, Inc., employees expressed fears that the fence was erected for security in the
event of a strike. A management spokesman termed the fence
a routine security precaution, while a skeptical reporter said it
reminded him of Stalag 17" (Davies, 1978a:1). The article contained denials from local company officials that the security
precautions were related to strike preparations and a statement from the guild president that he did not accept this explanation. The article went on to note that the contract
negotiations with the pressmen and stereotypers were now at
the arbitration stage and that the negotiation process had had
"a chilling effect on morale." It quoted a source as having
stated that "the contract offered to the pressmen will destroy
the union" and an employee as having said that the negotiations were "stalled over job security, benefits, hours, and jurisdiction" (Davies, 1978a:4). Davies's article also noted one
worker's comments that Capital Cities' Nashville-based law
firm of King and Ballow, which was conducting the negotiations in Wilkes-Barre, had a reputation as a "union neu-
tralizer" (Davies, 1978a:1).

The article quoted extensively from a report issued in May
1978 by John Muir and Company, New York newspaper ana-
lysts:

> The potentially volatile labor situation at the TLEN was high-
> lighted in a May, 1978 market analysis by John Muir and Co.,
> the New York newspaper analysts.
>
> The Muir report cited "a contentious labor environment (the
> paper has had two strikes in the last five years)" as a principal
> disadvantage in owning the TLEN.
>
> "The previous owners of the Wilkes-Barre daily installed a
> modern electronic production system in 1972 after Hurricane

Agnes devastated Wilkes-Barre and flooded and ruined much of the paper's hot-metal production department. However, the paper's owners were not successful in bargaining with labor unions, with the result that the paper has achieved almost none of the labor savings that usually accompany conversion to photocomposition," the report says.

"It is estimated that the paper has about three times more blue-collar employees than it needs to produce the paper," the report continues.

"This obviously represents a marked profit-margin-improvement opportunity for Capital Cities, but gains in this area are not likely to be as easily realized in Wilkes-Barre as in the company's other newspapers.

"Delivery of the Wilkes-Barre paper's bundles is performed by an outside company whose drivers are organized by the Teamsters.

"Thus if management were to take a strike in an effort to win manning concessions, it is likely to be difficult to continue to publish and distribute the newspaper.

"Moreover," the report says, "that part of Pennsylvania has a lengthy union tradition and its residents might not be totally supportive of the newspaper in a strike." (Davies, 1978a:4)

Elsewhere in the same issue, Davies had an article titled "When the Big Fish Swallows the Little Fish: Chain Ownership Portends Change for W-B Daily," in which he reported on interviews with reporters and editors about what they thought would be the likely effect on news coverage of the change from local to chain ownership. The article had a positive tone. It noted that more investigative reporting was one major change readers could expect. Blame for the paper's failure to carry out such reporting in the past was laid at the feet of the former editors and publisher:

The TLEN which shunned in-depth investigative reporting under its previous publisher, John A. Hourigan, Jr., is showing signs that with the new management will come a more professional, aggressive news product.

In the past, the TLEN has avoided the kinds of stories that

win prizes in newspaper contests, such as investigations of corrupt politicians and judges, conflicts of interest involving politicians and zoning decisions, or the awarding of government contracts, and organized crime.

Hourigan, himself, has been chairman of the Luzerne County Planning Commission for many years, although there is no evidence that the newspaper's traditional lack of aggressive reporting on land-use policies and decisions can be attributed to this factor.

One reporter confided that he has received numerous leads of corrupt politicians in the city, but in the past could not pursue them for lack of support by his editors. . . .

For many years organized crime boss Russell Buffalino and his cohorts went about their business in Luzerne County virtually unnoticed by the TLEN.

Recently, however, the newspaper has produced some noteworthy articles on Buffalino as well as Judge Arthur Dellasandro, who is under investigation by the State Judicial Review Board for alleged judicial misconduct. (Davies, 1978b:3).

The article went on to note that the new editor in chief of the paper planned to give reporters more leeway to pursue investigative reports, and it cited Capital Cities' papers' investigative successes in other cities.

But despite this positive appraisal of the company's intended changes for the paper, many readers recalled only the front-page story on the fence and the comparison of the company to a prisoner of war camp. Time and again, people I talked with cited that story as evidence of Capital Cities' "bad intentions toward the unions," as a resident of the region put it.

The security measures added to the antagonism that the union leaders and the rank and file were feeling toward the company. The workers interpreted these measures, especially the placement of security personnel on the shop floor, as a company attempt to tell them that what they cherished as craft rights (see Zimbalist, 1979, and Montgomery, 1979) were nothing more than privileges that could and would be withdrawn if the company felt they were serious obstacles to long-term profit making. This demonstration not only threatened the unions' self-esteem, it also challenged their public status. As word of Capital Cities' actions spread throughout the county's labor circles, they threatened the newspaper workers' status claims in the union movement and in the community. The newspaper unions were shown to be as powerless as the least skilled worker in preventing gross intrusions into and control over their work by management.

The workers thus regarded the use of guards as an attempt not only to control but to humiliate them and to discredit them in the eyes of the community. To the rank and file, the deployment of security forces was a company statement that it did not regard the workers or their unions as capable of maintaining either the spirit or the letter of the labor contract without the use of coercive measures and that they did not deserve the craft "privileges" they traditionally claimed as their right. A worker analyzed the situation as follows:

We had two strikes in the 1970s. There was never any vandalism. We even let some people go through the line to do daily maintenance on the equipment. We were good and loyal workers. When the flood came, we had guys who volunteered to go in and help clean up the building. They did that even though their own homes were a mess. Other guys went up to Scranton to help get the paper out. Does that sound like we were the kind of people who had to be watched all the time? . . .

I'll tell you why they had the guards and fences. It wasn't to protect the building. They were there to show people in the city how afraid they were of us. They wanted people to believe we were dangerous and would attack the building if we had the chance. But that was ridiculous. If we wanted to do something we could have at any time. Some of the people who used to go in early had keys to the whole building. We could've sabotaged the place any time we wanted to. But no one did.

The workers' humiliation was compounded because the front-line personnel of Wackenhut's guard force were almost all black. In a reversal of "normal" social roles in American society, privileged white workers were being supervised, monitored, and scrutinized by a scheduled racial minority. Wackenhut's use of a guard force made up largely of young black men continued a practice with a long history in American capitalism (Cox, 1948; Reich, 1977; Szymanski, 1974; Bonacich, 1980), one with which the Wilkes-Barre region is well familiar. Capitalists have long used minority workers to disorganize unions and break strikes. The Coal and Iron Police often used guards drawn from one ethnic group to police the behavior of another. Thus to the unions and their community backers, Capital Cities' use of black guards harked back to an earlier period in the region's history, when the coal companies deployed their own private security forces, which often were organized along ethnic lines. A city businessman, who sympathized with the strikers, drew a parallel between Capital Cities' use of black guards and the coal companies: "In the mines, they always had guards watching the men. They'd play one group off against another. Irish guards would watch the Poles and Italians, Welsh and German guards would watch the Irish. Capital Cities was doing the same thing, except they used black guards in silly uniforms to do the job."

It is impossible to determine what motivated Wackenhut to send a mostly black guard force into Wilkes-Barre. Some union members and their community supporters suggested that the rank and file and some of the unions' sympathizers considered it an intentional move to provoke the unions. Other explanations, however, might be that the company was grossly insensitive to the region's demographics or that the company hired black males because they were the cheapest labor available. Regardless of the reason, the use of black guards intensified workers' hostility to the company.

Determined not to lose control over the shop floor, the workers resisted and retaliated against the guards almost from the moment they were introduced. Workers and guards traded insults and taunts. Sometimes there were minor physical confrontations. At other times, the workers' resistance was more passive. A former employee told me of an incident in which a large number of men reported back to work just a few minutes before the time they were scheduled to arrive: "The guard had us line up to sign in. Guys would get to the table and say that they didn't have a pen, or they'd fumble around looking for something to write their name with. Other guys would drop their pen and take a while to look for it. It was a mess. A foremen came out to see where his men were. When he saw what was happening he just about went crazy. He stood there yelling at the guard to let his men through. The guard didn't know what to do. So we just stood there until they got their problem worked out."

Not all encounters were amusing. As contract negotiations dragged on and it became increasingly evident to the rank and file that a strike was certain to occur, tensions between the workers and the guards increased dramatically. The tension took its toll on the union men and women and their families. A worker describing those days told me: "It was bad, real bad. I'd go home from work and my stomach would be in knots. I'd get terrible headaches and backaches. The stress was un-believable. There was almost nowhere you could go to get away from the guards. They'd even follow you into the men's room. Everywhere you went you had to sign in and out in a log book that they kept." A striker's wife described her husband's reaction: "He's normally a patient man. He was never short tempered with me or with the children. But during that time, he would come home so worked up that it would take him several hours to unwind. He would yell at the children for the smallest things, and he even started to snap at me. I was really worried about him. I'd never seen him act like that before." Even some management people were upset by the security precautions:

I don't know what they thought they were going to accomplish. The company took an overly aggressive stance. The guards, fences, and cameras really rankled me, and I was not the only manager who felt that way. It wasn't necessary to antagonize the workers in this way. That would have never happened with the Smiths and Hourigans. When they had the paper, it was like a big family. We [referring to labor and management] had our fights, but nothing like that ever happened. The Smiths and Hourigans cared about their employees as people. They would help them out any way they could. I remember one time when heating prices were going through the ceiling, the company gave some people who couldn't pay their bills a little extra money to help them. That's the kind of people they were.

Others had a different view. A former reporter for one of the area's television stations told me that he was informed by an anonymous source at the publishing company that De Witt Smith, one of the paper's former owners, had encouraged Capital Cities to institute strong security measures, arguing that if there was a strike and the company continued publishing, the workers certainly would respond with violent resistance. A worker who was on the picket line claimed that Smith "used to drive one of the buses that carried scabs into the company. People who knew him said he was really getting it off doing that."

The lack of success in the negotiations, the scope of the contract changes the company demanded, the security measures Capital Cities had instituted and the workers' reaction to them, the company's determination to publish in the event of a strike, and the workers' resolve to keep the company from publishing set the stage for an ugly, violent, prolonged confrontation.

Strike Violence

The Newspaper Guild contract expired on September 30, 1978. At the end of the business day on October 6, 1978, the locals struck the paper, claiming that they saw no signs of the company's willingness to bargain on any of the issues that divided them. The company leveled similar charges against the unions. The strike was called despite attempts at informal intervention by various community groups, as well as federal mediators. The sides simply were too far apart for anything to forestall a walkout. The last offer the unions reportedly made was to sign an agreement on wage levels and leave all other terms of the contracts in effect. The company allegedly rejected this offer. As the strikers walked out the door, someone, as the last act as a Capital Cities employee, reportedly wiped out the materials stored in the computer for the next scheduled edition of the paper.

Once on the street, the unions immediately set up picket lines around the company's property in central city Wilkes-Barre. They were joined by volunteers from other unions. The workers' objective was to prevent circulation of the *Times Leader*'s Saturday edition. Shortly before the picket line was set up, the Wilkes-Barre chief of police reportedly had met with the union leaders and told them what the police would and would not tolerate. He reportedly said violence would not be allowed. The union leaders supposedly assured him that they would not initiate any acts of violence against company property or workers. Reportedly, Wackenhut gave similar assurances.

Despite everyone's words to the contrary, the strike immediately took a violent turn. According to a city police officer who claimed to have firsthand knowledge of the events in the first hours after the strike began, "The situation, on the first night, had been in danger of getting out of hand. There was a clear threat to the police department. It was almost overrun that evening. . . . Most of the violence was by the strikers, but they were provoked."

As the situation became more chaotic, Wackenhut officials on the scene called their headquarters for reinforcements. Like the police officer quoted above, they feared that the guards would be overrun. The available guard force was unable to get workers and papers through the picket line and could not protect company property. Whenever Capital Cities tried to bring in workers to keep the paper operating or to ship papers out of the building, the people in the streets sur-

Left, Wackenhut guards arriving for strike duty. *Below,* guards being bused through picket line.

Courtesy, Wilkes-Barre *Citizens' Voice*

Courtesy, Wilkes-Barre *Citizens' Voice*

Above, massed pickets in front of Wilkes-Barre Publishing Company. *Right,* guards spraying fire extinguishers in direction of pickets.

Courtesy, Wilkes-Barre *Times Leader*

Courtesy, Wilkes-Barre *Times Leader*

Above, pickets attempting to prevent company vehicles from leaving premises. *Right,* newspaper delivery truck after a night of violence.

rounded the vehicle to prevent its entry or exit from the company's premises.

Windows were broken, the company's building was defaced, a considerable number of company vehicles were destroyed, and guards were attacked. The reinforcements fared no better. Delegations of strikers and their supporters would surround the buses bringing guards into the city. In some cases, they held them hostage inside the buses, in others they offered to pay the bus fare home for any guard who, having seen what was happening, was willing to resign from the security force. Reportedly several accepted the offer.

Over that first weekend, there were several skirmishes between the guards and the people massed in the streets. The street crowd included strikers, members of other unions, and passersby, who joined the crowd either because they sympathized with the strikers or simply because they wanted to be part of the action. Reportedly, Capital Cities' lawyers conferred with Police Chief John Ruddick during the weekend and he informed them that any attempt by the police to remove the pickets "could start a full-fledged riot." During one incident on that weekend, paint was reportedly thrown on the chief of police when he approached the building shortly after a skirmish between the guards and the people in the street. Rumors circulated that the unions were threatening to hold a labor rally "the likes of which this city had never seen" unless the guards were withdrawn.

Capital Cities was reported to have approached state Representative Bernard O'Brien (D.-Luzerne County), a longtime officer in the stereotypers' union, and asked him for assistance in requesting Governor Milton Shapp to deploy the State Police, which he refused to do (*Citizens' Voice*, October 9, 1978). The State Police, who had observers on the scene, were said to have told the company that it was not their policy to intervene in labor disputes unless the municipal police department could not handle the situation, which did not appear to be the case in Wilkes-Barre. Capital Cities also was said to have contacted the governor and asked him to call up the National Guard. If the request was made, it was not acted on.

The company was not the only one that claimed it was the victim of violence. A Wackenhut guard was arrested by the Wilkes-Barre police and charged with aggravated assault for allegedly having struck a picket with a vehicle. In a subsequent hearing, the district magistrate agreed with one of the guard's three lawyers that the incident did not warrant an aggravated assault charge. The magistrate granted a continuance of the case to give city police time to prepare new charges of simple assault against the guard (*Times Leader,* October 19, 1978).

On Monday, October 9, 1978, when Capital Cities tried to get its delivery trucks on the street, violence resumed. The company was unable to get its trucks out. The guards sprayed the demonstrators with water hoses and fire extinguishers, which, some in the crowd alleged, were filled with paint. No protesters were arrested by city police, but a guard was arrested for having allegedly sprayed James Orcutt, an international official of the guild, with "a liquid." Orcutt eventually withdrew his charges when the guard informed the district magistrate that he was going to leave the area (*Times Leader,* October 25, 1978).

The mayor responded to the crisis in the streets by issuing an emergency order on Tuesday, October 10, 1978, banning sightseers, vehicles, and loiterers from the vicinity of the company's property. On that same day, Capital Cities' attorneys filed for a court injunction to forbid mass picketing around the company's premises.

At the urging of the mayor, the chief of police, and local businessmen, some of whom felt that both the unions and the company "were out of control," Capital Cities decided to suspend operations for four days in the hope that this would give both sides enough time for their "tempers to cool." In the meantime, the Chamber of Commerce reportedly offered to arrange an informal meeting between the unions and the company to try to reach some agreement about curbing the violence. Neither side took up the chamber's offer, and when the company resumed publication, the violence also resumed.

The judge finally issued his injunction on Friday, October 13, but the violence did not stop. Within a few hours after the injunction, a group of people "stormed" the company gates and others cut fences. A guard reportedly was attacked with mace and others hit with stones and bricks. Security was breached, and considerable damage was inflicted on vehicles in the company parking lot.

The unions alleged that that same evening a company executive, Bruce McIntyre, struck two pickets with his vehicle. According to an article published in the *Times Leader* on October 18, 1978:

McIntyre denied he deliberately struck the pickets.

"It was a set up very clearly," he said. "People who allege they were hurt either threw themselves at the car or ran in front of it.

It's pretty hard to run over pickets at a high rate of speed when police are directing the car through the line." . . .

McIntyre said the number of pickets when he arrived were "far in excess of what the court allowed." McIntyre also said the police allowed the pickets to strike the car.

On October 18, the *Times Leader* told of an alleged attack on one of its vans: "Sunday a van carrying employees of the Wilkes-Barre Publishing Company was followed by three cars. One of the cars struck the van, went out of control, and struck a utility pole. The driver of the car . . . was treated for head injuries at General Hospital and released. No one in the van was injured. . . . The driver of the van was arrested by police and charged with leaving the scene of the accident. . . . [The driver's] attorneys contend the following vehicles had been engaged in harassment and caused the accident."

The company became increasingly upset because it felt it was not receiving adequate protection from the Wilkes-Barre police department. Among other things, it accused the chief of being unwilling to enforce the injunction. The chief of police, however, contended that enforcing the injunction was not his responsibility but the sheriff's. According to a source who was in the police department at the time: "John [Ruddick] was happy when the judge issued the injunction. He knew that meant he could wash his hands of the whole mess." The sheriff's office, however, claimed that it did not have sufficient manpower to enforce the court order. It blamed the situation on the county commissioners, who were said to be refusing to appropriate money for deputies' overtime. The commissioners, in turn, claimed that they did not have enough money in the county budget to pay for additional personnel or overtime. But whatever the reasons, everyone involved agreed that the sheriff's deputies could do nothing to stop the violence.

The most serious violent incident took place on October 25, 1978. According to the *Times Leader* of the following day, as many as ten people were injured or assaulted. The paper reported the injured to be Daniel Vladitch, a Wackenhut employee, John Robbins and John Burgess, employees of the Executive Protection Service, David Lindsey, Local 187, ITU, and James Orcutt, a guild representative. The five people allegedly assaulted were John Malloy, the paper's managing editor (a former guild member and longtime company employee), and printers Frank Adams, Ron Clow, William Landmesser, and Harold Fletcher. The paper claimed that as many as fifteen people had attacked its workers. It added: "At 5:45 A.M., a Wackenhut guard informed the city police that more employees would be arriving at 6:00 A.M. and requested two or three policemen be posted at the front door 'for the employees' safety,' the Wackenhut report noted. The dispatcher at police headquarters informed Wackenhut that police could not post anyone at the plant for 'several reasons,' refusing to elaborate. The dispatcher did say that in the event of trouble when the van arrived, the police were to be notified." The article pointed out that the police were called at 6:03 A.M. and arrived at the scene five minutes later.

The most seriously injured person was John Burgess, a police officer in Mount Lebanon, Pennsylvania, a town located in the western part of the state. Burgess was on leave from his regular job while working for Executive Protection Services.

Capital Cities, in its special tabloid *Violence in the Valley*, gave the following account of the violence involving Burgess:

> Burgess, an off-duty policeman from Mount Lebanon, Pa., was employed as a plain-clothes officer by a private security service which had contracted with the Wilkes-Barre Publishing Co.
>
> Unlike the uniformed guards who protected company property, Burgess was armed. He held a valid weapons permit. The plain-clothes officers were retained only after strike violence had made it clear that company employees were in personal danger.
>
> Early on the morning in question [October 25, 1978], Burgess accompanied a group of company workers who were riding to work in a van. They were unloaded on North Main Street to enter the front door of the Wilkes-Barre Publishing Co. building.
>
> As the unloading occurred, one of the uniformed guards was attacked by pickets. Burgess went to the guard's aid and was jumped by a group of pickets, although the original victim escaped.
>
> In the melee, Burgess was so badly beaten that he had to be hospitalized for days. He may have suffered permanent injury.
>
> The unions have published a picture showing James Orcutt, international representative of the Newspaper Guild and leader of the newspaper strike, on top of Burgess during the beating.
>
> The unions' explanation was that Burgess pulled a gun on the pickets and they were merely disarming him.
>
> Both Burgess and other witnesses emphatically deny that version. At the time the picture was taken, Burgess was attempting to prevent the pickets from seizing his gun.

The unions not only disputed Capital Cities' account, as presented above, but raised questions about Burgess's right to carry a firearm. The union alleged that his permit was valid only while he was employed as a police officer, not as a private security guard.

Guards found their situation in Wilkes-Barre precarious even when they were not on company business. There was almost no place in the county where they were safe. When they went to bars or restaurants around the city they exposed themselves to insults, verbal assaults, and beatings. Several guards were attacked and severely beaten by gangs of men in motel parking lots.

Local police kept a careful watch on the guards' behavior. Several were arrested for activities unrelated to the strike. One was arrested for rape (*Citizens' Voice*, October 6, 1982). Whenever such an arrest took place, the strikers' paper gave the story prominent coverage, using the arrest as evidence for its claims that Capital Cities had imported poorly trained, poorly disciplined security personnel of "low character," as a city minister put it, to intimidate and attack local workers.

As the violence on and off the picket line persisted, the company became increasingly disenchanted with local public officials, all of whom were refusing to denounce the unions or the violence, and the city police, whom the company believed were doing nothing to prevent it. According to company officials, city police stood on the sidelines while its property was destroyed and its workers attacked. The company claimed that on several occasions its officials called the police to ask for assistance, which always arrived too late even though the police station was within a block of the company's property. Moreover, according to the company, the police were openly fraternizing with the strikers and, in some cases, "aiding and abetting" their behavior, including helping to "sabotage" the paper's delivery process. In *Violence in the Valley*, the company published a photograph of a picket holding a club preparing to strike a company van that was attempting to move onto company property, while police stood by watching. The company found it incredible that only its people had been arrested for strike violence and no one on the union side had yet to be charged with any offense by the Wilkes-Barre police.

In late October 1978, Capital Cities ran a story about a pending FBI probe of the Wilkes-Barre police department, partly in response to its mishandling of the strike situation. The FBI eventually did send agents into the city to take depositions. They came in response to a complaint filed by

Wackenhut that the Wilkes-Barre police department's behavior constituted a violation of its black guards' civil rights
by failing to provide them with equal protection. The FBI took
no formal action against the Wilkes-Barre police department
or any of the unions.

In the midst of the violence, Wilkes-Barre's police chief resigned his office for reasons unrelated to the strike. In commenting on his handling of the strike, a command officer said,
"John was sympathetic to labor, and he was really worried
about what would happen in the streets if he tried to take a
strong stand with the unions." The new chief was John Swim.
One of his first acts in office was to announce that the department would take a "more professional approach" to the strike.
Swim was careful not to fault the rank-and-file police officers
for lack of action against the strikers and their supporters. Instead, he faulted command officers and elected officials for
not giving officers more explicit directions. Therefore, the
rank-and-file officers had not clearly understood what was expected of them, and it only was natural, under the circumstances, that they would be hesitant to act. On November 3,
1978, the *Times Leader* ran a story on Swim's new policy under the headline "Politics Ruled Policy on Strike, Swim
States." In part the story went as follows:

> Politics influenced the decisions of city officials when they es-
> tablished police policy regarding the strike violence at the
> Wilkes-Barre Publishing Co., says Police Chief John Swim.
> Swim told the *Times Leader* Wednesday that he believes po-
> litical concerns affected "the people who are up for re-elec-
> tion." Swim pointed out that Mayor Lisman and the city's
> councilmen face primary challenges next spring and general
> elections next November.
> Lisman, however, is the elected official with the sole respon-
> sibility for the department and its chief.

The article also noted that Swim had issued a memorandum
to all officers:

The memorandum sets these guidelines for dealing with strike violence:
1. Whenever any police officer witnesses a crime, he is to make an arrest.
2. Whenever any police officer receives information that convinces him a crime has occurred, he will sign a complaint on 'information received.'
3. Whenever any police officer receives information . . . but feels that the information is not sufficient to support charges, he will advise the complainant to proceed by private complaint. (*Times Leader*, November 3, 1978)

The police were not the only part of the local criminal justice system that caused the company problems and about which it expressed disappointment. It also found that the minor judiciary would not proceed with criminal action against any of the strikers or their sympathizers for alleged acts of violence against property or persons (*Times Leader*, November 3, 1978).

With the new law enforcement policy, the announced investigation by the FBI, and the replacement of Wackenhut by a local security firm, mass violence in the immediate vicinity of the company's property in Wilkes-Barre dropped off sharply and attacks on the company and its workers took a different turn. A virtual guerrilla war was carried out against the company. There was almost no street corner in the Wyoming Valley where Capital Cities could leave its newspaper bundles unguarded. Bundles would be unbound and papers blown all over a neighborhood. Indignant residents would call the police, who would call Capital Cities and tell the company to come and clean up the neighborhood or face charges and fines for littering. As late as 1985, newspaper bundles were occasionally sabotaged. They are taken from their normal drop points and hidden so that carriers cannot find them, or they are taken and destroyed. Vehicles left unguarded on company property or almost anywhere in the region were constantly subjected to vandalism.

Capital Cities' workers, especially those who once had belonged to the union but now were crossing picket lines, as well as their families, were subjected to a continual stream of threats, harassment, and vandalism. One worker, a former union printer, told me that he had received a death threat, his children had received calls that threatened him, and he had seen damage to the houses and cars of other company employees. He told of one instance when a bottle filled with oil was thrown through a window of a home, ruining the draperies, carpeting, and some pieces of furniture in the living room. A photojournalist at the *Times Leader* told me that once when he and a reporter had taken a car to cover a story its windows were broken, tires slashed, and antennae ripped off while they were inside a building doing their work. Another Capital Cities craftsman told me that the night after a story appeared about him in the paper, his neighbor's house was damaged. He believed the vandals intended to attack his place but got the houses mixed up in the dark. A television journalist who dated a *Times Leader* reporter claimed that the reporter's tires were slit on several occasions. Another journalist reportedly was involved in at least two scuffles in bars in the city. The fights had started after someone had recognized him and called him a "scab." Capital Cities employees soon realized that while off work it was best either to confine their social activities to a relatively few safe places in the city or hope that no one recognized them as *Times Leader* workers. If they ventured away from these safe places they exposed themselves to threats, verbal abuse, vandalism, and assaults. A local restaurateur told me that during the first year of the strike, employees from both papers would come into his establishment, and if they happened to encounter someone from the other side they would shout epithets at each other. The behavior stopped when he threatened to "throw them out on their ass," as he put it, and not allow them to return. At present, when workers from either paper encounter one another in his restaurant or in other public places, they studiously ignore one another.

In addition to the attacks on property, the threats, and the occasional fist fights, the company's workers and their families experienced heavy social damage. Many found longtime friendships abruptly ending; some were no longer welcome in clubs, fraternal organizations, and even taverns they once frequented. In a few cases, their children were given a hard time in school by their classmates. Like their parents, the children sometimes had to suffer being called "scabs." And, in some cases, the strike caused deep splits in families. For example, a father stayed with the company but his son walked out. The son served on the *Citizens' Voice's* governing board for several years. Reportedly, the two have not spoken to each other for years.

Reporters also sometimes found that their work was sabotaged. Journalists often were ignored or verbally abused by people they were trying to interview or photograph for a story, and they claimed that their work was disrupted by *Citizens' Voice* workers. In addition, their equipment was always at risk. They never knew whether their cars would be in operating order when they finished covering a story or whether they would find broken windows, slashed tires, or other damage.

By 1982 Capital Cities employees began to observe a marked decrease in the levels of vandalism directed against company property and the threats to themselves and their property. Some Capital Cities employees even claim that their professional relationships with their counterparts at the *Citizens' Voice* have become almost normal. Although they do not describe their relationships with the *Citizens' Voice* people as cordial, they consider them far more professional than they had been in the past. One *Times Leader* journalist, who had been hired after the strike began, told me that one night several months after the pickets had been withdrawn, while he was in a restaurant having coffee, he started to chat with a fellow on the next stool, only to discover that the other man worked for the *Citizens' Voice.* As the journalist told it, they sat for several hours discussing the strike, and neither showed any acrimony toward the other. He said that a few months earlier he would have been terrified to learn that he accidentally was talking to a *Citizens' Voice* worker.

The decline in overt antagonistic relationships between the two sets of journalists appears to have been tied to the final withdrawal of pickets from in front of the publishing company. Pickets were removed in the fall of 1982, when the last of the unions were decertified. By the time they left, the unions had only a token presence on the picket line. One or two men walked in front of the building during daylight hours. By early evening they were gone.

Times Leader workers were relieved to see the pickets permanently withdraw from in front of the building because they were a constant irritant to them as well as to the company. A number of the company's employees felt extreme anxiety whenever they had to confront the pickets. During the course of this research, I spent several days, at different times of the year, watching both the pickets' behavior and the various reactions to them. *Times Leader* workers adopted a variety of ways of dealing with the pickets. Their responses were in part related to the individual picketer, for pickets behaved in markedly different ways. Some took up a position on the south side of the building by the driveway and stood there most of the day, only occasionally strolling along the sidewalk. These men saw their job as keeping unionized truck drivers from making pickups from or deliveries to the *Times Leader*. These pickets passed the time chatting with passersby and, on occasion, I saw them exchange acknowledgments with *Times Leader* workers, even if it was only a mutual nod. One former picket, an older craftsman, told me that a young woman who had been hired as an office worker said hello to him every day as she passed through the line. One particularly cold morning, he said, she brought him a cup of coffee.

Other pickets were far more aggressive. They constantly patrolled the front of the building, being sure to pass the front door at regular intervals. From time to time they exchanged taunts and insults with *Times Leader* workers. One day when I was standing in front of the newspaper building, I heard a picket shout at a couple entering the building: "There's a rat scab family going back to its nest!" The man turned and yelled: "Get a job, you lousy bum!" By the time I observed this encounter in 1982, the exchange appeared to have become ritualized. Both the couple, a husband and wife who had stayed with the company, and the picket seemed to expect a confrontation. A woman who had been a confidential employee, and hence not a union member, under the old owners and who had stayed with the company told me the pickets would yell to her, "Your grandfather'd be ashamed of you crossing a picket line." She added that some union people sent her flowers when a death occurred in her family.

Some *Times Leader* workers went out of their way to avoid confrontations. They would time their entries and exits to avoid coming into contact with the pickets; others used a rear door to avoid any possibility of a confrontation. A few *Times Leader* workers, however, not only expected an encounter but seemed to relish it. They made a point of confronting the pickets and exchanging taunts and insults with them.

The aggressive pickets also accosted members of the public who entered the *Times Leader* building. Remarks such as "Why are you going into that scab paper?" were common. It was the aggressive pickets who upset Capital Cities workers the most, as one might expect.

The pickets' presence affected not only the *Times Leader* workers but the general public as well. Many people avoided doing business with the *Times Leader* because they did not want to cross a picket line or be seen doing so. Late one evening, while I was interviewing a Capital Cities photojournalist in a restaurant, I witnessed such a situation. A man approached the photographer and asked if he could obtain a copy of a photograph he had taken of an event the man had attended. The photographer told him that the *Times Leader* sold copies of pictures and explained that he could go to a particular office at the paper and a print would be made for him. The man demurred, explaining that he was a member of a union in the county and did not want to cross the picket line. The photographer gave the man his office phone number and told him to call him and he would see what he could arrange. The photographer told me that "things like this happen all the time."

With the pickets gone, the company employees and the public have relatively free access to the company's building. The company has removed the graffiti from the building, and the fence has been taken down. There no longer are visible reminders of the events of the fall of 1978.

Apportioning Blame: Alternative Definitions of Reality

It is impossible to parcel out responsibility for the violence that took place in Wilkes-Barre. The workers and their community allies blame Capital Cities. They argue that the violence was a direct result of Capital Cities' contract proposals, its use of security measures that could not be considered routine, and its countless other alleged provocations both before and after the strike, chief among which were its decision to publish in the face of a strike and to send the workers letters telling them that they would be replaced if they did not return to work by November 1, 1978.

The company's position was laid out in a sixteen-page tabloid it published and mailed to all postal patrons in the area. The tabloid was titled *Violence in the Valley* and appeared on November 16, 1978. The purpose of the piece was to fix blame on the unions. In reading *Violence in the Valley* one gets the clear impression that Capital Cities saw the violence as a dangerous, mad outburst that threatened the company, its workers, and the entire community.

Violence in the Valley portrayed the strike as the work of outside agitators and local union leaders. It suggested that the strike had little support among the rank and file and that if the average workers knew the true facts they would see the legitimacy of the company's position. The paper was especially critical of James Orcutt, the strike organizer the guild had sent into Wilkes-Barre.

The article that focused on Orcutt detailed his supposed role in strikes at other newspapers. It quoted *Philadelphia* magazine to "show" that Orcutt had been the instigator of the recent strike at the *Philadelphia Inquirer*. *Philadelphia* magazine had described Orcutt as "the hired gun whom the genteel Guild persons of Local 10 had brought in as their chief contract negotiator." It continued that "Orcutt . . . always managed to look like a prop from 'On the Waterfront' . . . [he] was psyching both sides with his costume of scruffy rancher's coat, blue wool pea cap and square wire rimmed which-way-to-the-picket-line-comrade? glasses." According to *Violence in the Valley*, the magazine had said Orcutt "presented himself as a recently rehabilitated revolutionary." Accompanying the article was a photograph of Orcutt in his jacket, wearing his wire-rimmed glasses. Orcutt was portrayed as one of the most violent men on the picket line: "His approach to the Wilkes-Barre strike has plunged from militant to violent. He has sprayed chemicals into the faces of guards, broken plant windows, cut gas lines, punched security guards and rammed his fist through the headlight of a car."

Violence in the Valley argued that not only were the rank-and-file members being manipulated by outsiders and by their leaders, all of whom were said to be putting the interests of the unions ahead of those of their members, but so too were the region's citizens and institutions. This theme is nicely reflected in an article written by Paul Domowitch, a reporter with Capital Cities' *Fort Worth Star-Telegram* and a native of the Wilkes-Barre area. The article, which originally appeared in the *Times Leader* on October 23, 1978, was titled "People Are Falling for It—Hometown Boy's View":

> I came back to this valley last week. In the past it has always been a pleasure. But this time it was on business. I'm here because the people I work for need help in running their newspaper. Unless you've been dead the last couple of weeks, you know that the employees of the *Times Leader* went out on strike two Fridays ago. And according to the newspaper union that makes me a strikebreaker. Or in more blunt language, a scab.
>
> By coming home this time, to do what I'm doing, I think I lost a very dear and a very close friend. Her father is a member of the striking Newspaper Guild, and I'm sure she hates me

right now. I can't blame her, I guess. If the roles were reversed, I'd probably feel the same way.

I feel sorry for people like her father. They are the silent majority who aren't being heard in this strike, the ones who know they've had it pretty good for the past 20 years, maybe too good. And they are willing to make some concessions, to come to terms with management and go back to work. But they aren't being heard.

The trouble with strikes is that management hears only a few voices during bargaining sessions. Those few voices say they speak for everyone. But do they really?

The union has painted a pretty bleak picture of Capital Cities. They have made them out to be a blend of Jack the Ripper and Charles Manson, the unwanted outsider from Madison Avenue who has invaded this valley and taken over by storm. And sad to say, the media and many of the people here have fallen for this martyr act.

I am not an outsider. This is home. It was in 1972 when I stood alongside my father on that sad June morning and watched him cry because a river was about to wash away everything he had worked his whole damn life for. And it is home now.

That is how it is.

But for the past 20 years, there has not been a paper in the United States the size of the *Times Leader* as bad as this one. Considering the population of the Wyoming Valley and the circulation of this newspaper, the previous owners should have been able to get at least $30 million for it when they sold it. But nobody would touch it. Nobody. They finally palmed it off on Capital Cities for a third of that figure, which should tell you something.

I'm not particularly dedicated to Capital Cities. I work for one of their newspapers. Period. I owe them nothing and they owe me nothing.

But they're being wrongly portrayed as the big, bad villain in this whole thing, while the union pretends it's being tied to the railroad tracks. And the people of the Wyoming Valley are falling for it.

Nobody wins in a strike. Not the union and not management. There are going to be scars caused by this whole damn thing that will never disappear, no matter what happens at the bargaining table. (Domowitch, 1978, n.p., excerpted from the *Times Leader*, October 23, 1978)

Several of Domowitch's themes were repeated in a *Violence in the Valley* article written by John Anderson. When the strike began, Anderson had been a member of the guild for six years. He chose to remain with the company rather than go on strike. In explaining why he had stayed at the paper he stated:

> It should be noted that my decision was not based on the pros and cons of unionism.
>
> Instead, I felt the new management of the *Times Leader* was needed in order to bring this newspaper around to what it should be—an aggressive, intelligent, and objective conduit of information to the people of the Wyoming Valley.
>
> As for the issue of human dignity, it is hard for me to understand how such a large number of people were led to believe that working for the *Times Leader* could be such a humiliating experience. (Anderson, n.p., 1978)

The Domowitch and Anderson articles, along with other pieces in *Violence in the Valley*, including selected letters to the editor, expressed Capital Cities' basic position on the strike. The major points were that (1) the union leadership had acted in bad faith with its members when it took them on strike; (2) a large part of the union's rank and file would have preferred to make concessions rather than strike; (3) a major reason why the *Times Leader* was such a bad paper was because of the unions; (4) Capital Cities was a good employer and its workers felt committed enough to the company to volunteer to come to Wilkes-Barre and help management get through its crisis; (5) the community was being manipulated by the unions; and (6) the violence practiced by the strikers was enough in and of itself to discredit their cause.

The workers' paper did not let these points go unchallenged. It noted that Anderson's comments had to be understood in light of his position as De Witt Smith's son-in-law. The *Cit-*

izens' Voice raised the question why, if Anderson was so disappointed in the paper's quality under the former owners, he had never used his family influence with the publishers to try to make changes he thought might be warranted.

To counter the image that Capital Cities was an employer that could generate enough loyalty and commitment that workers would be willing voluntarily to come to Wilkes-Barre and endure the sacrifices doing so entailed, the *Citizens' Voice* ran stories on the situation at the company's Kansas City property. The *Citizens' Voice* reported that some of the Kansas City workers had started a Wilkes-Barre strike support committee, which collected money for the Wilkes-Barre strikers and was organizing opposition to temporary transfers to the *Times Leader.* The *Citizens' Voice* hoped to convince its readers that not everyone who worked for Capital Cities thought the company deserved the support men such as Domowitch were willing to give it. The *Citizens' Voice* reported that after Capital Cities had taken over in Kansas City, it cleaned house in the newsroom, replacing many older journalists with younger ones and raising output standards for all, which was precisely what the strikers were claiming would happen in Wilkes-Barre.

A respondent I interviewed who had worked at Capital Cities' newspapers in Kansas City during the strike claimed that he had heard of the Wilkes-Barre support committee, but he did not know who had started it or how many people belonged to it. He also claimed that although there was no overt pressure on workers to go to Wilkes-Barre, it was "commonly understood" among the staff that those men and women who resisted going could not expect much of a future with the company.

The strikers also attempted to refute Capital Cities' charge that the rank and file in the unions were in favor of a settlement, by continually reminding the readers that only a handful of people had voted against the strike and that 205 men and women had gone on strike, while only 25 chose to remain with the company. The *Citizens' Voice* also stressed that an overwhelming majority of workers had continued to remain on strike, even after Capital Cities had sent them letters telling them that if they did not return to work they would be replaced with permanent employees. That the workers did not respond to Capital Cities' offer was proof enough to the *Citizens' Voice* and its supporters that the rank and file supported the union leadership.

The *Citizens' Voice* seldom mentioned the issue of violence. It carried only stories that reported attacks on strikers and legal proceedings against the guards and company officials. The unions denied most of Capital Cities' charges and allegations with respect to the issue of violence, insisting that, to their knowledge, no striking workers had engaged in any acts of violence except when defending themselves against the guards. The unions also denied that their members had destroyed any property. Some union members allege that the company itself defaced the building to make the unions "look bad."

Finding its offer to take back the strikers without prejudice rejected, Capital Cities went about the business of hiring replacements and decertifying the unions, thus bringing the strike to a legal close. By the time decertification was completed, however, the unions already had established and maintained their own paper as a viable enterprise that clearly dominated the local daily newspaper market. The *Citizens' Voice*, which first hit the streets on October 9, 1978, had a paid circulation in late 1982 of close to forty-seven thousand copies per day, so by that time it did not matter to the unions that they had been decertified at the *Times Leader.*

Capital Cities' local executives admit that bringing Wackenhut Security into Wilkes-Barre was a "public relations disaster." This view is shared by Capital Cities' supporters. None of the businessmen whom I interviewed, for example, saw any deeper significance in Capital Cities' security measures. To them, the company was "well within its legal rights" when it brought in guards to "protect its investment," as one of them explained to me. In his view, the managers' primary obligation was to their stockholders, not to their workers' sensibilities. Moreover, many local businessmen thought the behavior of the strikers and their supporters confirmed the wisdom of having taken security precautions. One prominent city businessman, in talking about the people involved in the attacks on Capital Cities, said that there was no excuse for the violence. In his opinion those responsible for it had behaved "like animals," and if he had anything to say about it they would be "strung up by their heels on the side of the building" to serve as an example to others. Another businessman said that he was "appalled" by the destruction to property and the violence. He went on to say that he was convinced "it was all the work of outsiders. Our [local] people would never do anything like that."

But regardless of whether they attributed the violence and property destruction to local people or "outside union agitators," local businessmen were disturbed over the attacks on property and the response of the local criminal justice system and put most of the blame on the unions. A retired city business executive stated: "Yes, Capital Cities had broken unions in other cities. But it would not have done that in Wilkes-Barre if the unions had been willing to accept their contracts. But these unions would have none of it, even though there were men who had not done any work at the paper for fifteen years."

Needless to say, the local labor unions took a different view. One labor activist, in response to a question I asked about the attacks on the company, said that "it was only property" that was destroyed, and it could be "easily replaced." In his view the loss of the newspaper workers' jobs was far more serious than "mere" damage to property.

If Capital Cities, as the unions charge, had hoped that the security measures would allow it to gain quick control over the labor process, ending many of the informal work practices that kept productivity low, demonstrate to the unions that it was determined to get the concessions it wanted, convey the message that the company did not intend to suspend publication if a strike occurred, and intimidate and politically disorganize the unions so that they would be willing to accept contracts on its terms, the company had to be disappointed with the outcome in Wilkes-Barre.

In Pontiac in 1977, Capital Cities had successfully imposed new work rules, survived a strike by the pressmen and the Newspaper Guild, and forced those unions to walk away from the dispute in defeat. A television newsman who had covered that strike and was also familiar with the situation in Wilkes-Barre claimed that one reason the unions in Pontiac did not mount a stronger resistance was that both pressmen and reporters had other employment possibilities in Pontiac, which was not the case in Wilkes-Barre. Capital Cities had no reason to assume that it could not achieve the same results in Wilkes-Barre. After all, it was using one of the country's best security firms to handle the strike, a firm that not only had extensive experience in dealing with labor disputes but had a personal interlock with Capital Cities. One of Capital Cities' largest individual stockholders and, at the time, a member of its board of directors, was the late William Casey. Casey, who went on to become director of the United States Central Intelligence Agency, had handled Wackenhut's legal business when he had worked at the prestigious law firm of Rogers and Wells (Brownstein and Easton, 1983).

But contrary to Capital Cities' hopes, the guards and other security measures strengthened, rather than weakened, the workers' will to resist. The workers became more convinced that if they granted the company the concessions it demanded they would have to work within a labor process in which overt coercion was the rule, rather than the exception. The workers struck, and Capital Cities was subjected to a continuing series of violent attacks.

The interpersonal violence and the vandalism were polysemic activities, that is, they had multiple meanings for the participants. On one level, attacks on the guards, company workers, and company property can be seen as an expression of pent-up frustration with the company and hostility over

the contract changes it was demanding. And such an interpretation of the reason for the violence, assuming for purposes
of argument that the workers were the perpetrators of the various attacks, has a grain of truth. But there have been other
local workers before and since the *Times Leader* strike who
faced demands for concessions just as extensive and threatening as those put forward by Capital Cities and who have been
every bit as frustrated with and, perhaps, as hostile to their
employers as were the newspaper unions. Yet other strikes
were marked by little or no violence, certainly not to the same
extent as that of the *Times Leader* strike. For the most part,
since the end of the mining era, Wilkes-Barre's working
classes have abided by the rules for conducting a "narrowed,
constrained strike" (Tilly, 1979:135) that grew out of nineteenth-century struggles between employers, workers, and the
state. It has been many years since a local strike has involved
the levels of violence that took place during the newspaper
unions' struggle with the *Times Leader.* Therefore it would be
difficult to account for the newspaper workers' reactions
merely as expressions of discontent, frustration, hostility,
feelings of desperation, and the like.

Similarly, the violence cannot be attributed to the special
character or nature of the local unions involved or their internationals. None of the international unions has a reputation
for especially violent strikes or for being markedly militant.
Indeed, the printing trades are relatively nonmilitant (Wallace
and Kalleburg, 1982). My interviews with participants in past
newspaper strikes and research in historical archives indicate
that past strikes against the Wilkes-Barre Publishing Company were not especially violent.

Some Capital Cities supporters have claimed that the violence was a result of racism—that the workers fought so hard
because most of the guards were black. This theory, however,
does not take into account that many of the people who were
assaulted were white employees of Capital Cities. And white
as well as black guards were assaulted. Burgess, the most seriously injured security officer, was white.

The reason for the violent attack on the company was Capital Cities' decision to adopt a "repertoire of contention" (Tilly, 1979) similar to that once used by the mining companies, which had entered local folklore as an especially odious set of corporate class practices for dealing with workers during labor disputes. Guards, fences, production during a strike, and scab labor all once were staples in this repertoire.

Capital Cities' decision to use means of struggle almost identical to those of the old mining companies opened the way for the newspaper workers to abandon the normal, constrained routines of industrial conflict and return to forms of contention once used by the mine workers—violent attacks on property and scabs. Strike violence long has been part of Wilkes-Barre's trade unions' historical "repertoire of collective action" and "contention" (Tilly, 1979). In the past, especially during the mining era, mass demonstrations and attacks on scabs and company property all had been used by local workers, particularly the miners, in conflicts with their employers.

As during the mining era, the violence in the newspaper strike was not an irrational outburst of collective action. Rather, it had clear purposes: to convince the company that it would be too costly to try to publish during a strike, to disrupt the *Times Leader*'s circulation, to disrupt the company's labor supply by discouraging people from taking jobs by putting their safety in question, and to buy time to get the strike paper on the street. Viewed in this light, violence was a partially successful tactic for the workers. Although it did not force the company to suspend operations for any length of time or totally disrupt the labor supply, it did disrupt the company's distribution system and it gave the workers time to get their paper on the street and into people's homes while the *Times Leader* had suspended publication.

The violence also had an expressive element: it was street theater. As such, it enabled the workers to show their utter and total contempt for the company and its employees; to demonstrate their sense of outrage at the company's assault on their human dignity; to show their power and that of their allies to strike at the company without fear of state reprisals; to delegitimate the company in the community's eyes; and, finally, to show the company its inability to protect its property and personnel and to mobilize local public or private power to protect it. In short, violence served to define Capital Cities as a vulnerable target and the workers as the dominant power with justice on their side.

Capital Cities was as shocked by local government's response as it was by the violence itself. Never before had the company encountered law enforcement agencies that failed to intervene to protect property in a labor dispute. The company was also appalled by the inability of the region's upper class to get the state to act in defense of property. In Capital Cities' view, this failure not only demonstrated the political weakness and ineptitude of the region's upper class, but it also showed the results any corporation could expect when government was staffed by elected and appointed officials who were "too closely tied to the county's unions."

Such a situation, according to Capital Cities, hurt both the publishing company and the entire region. In *Violence in the Valley,* Capital Cities advanced the proposition that the behavior of the striking unions, along with the popular and institutional support they received, would severely damage the prospects of the regional economy for development because sensible investors never would consider sinking capital in northeastern Pennsylvania after having seen the unions and public officials working together to paralyze Capital Cities. The county business elite shared Capital Cities' view. A businessman long associated with county economic development efforts summed up the view of many of his colleagues when he told me there could be "no doubt about it, the publicity hurt this area and it could not have come at a worse time." When I interviewed the former head of the city's Chamber of Commerce, he expressed identical sentiments.

In conclusion, the guards, fences, cameras, and violence were far more than a "public relations disaster." Rather than diminishing the workers' will to resist, Capital Cities' security measures strengthened their militance. Confronting the guards each day, not only in the shops and in the news-room but in the lavatories and rest areas kept the workers' indignation and militance from giving way to apathy or dis-couragement as negotiations dragged on with little sign of progress.

More important, the company's security measures legiti-mated the strikers' use of highly effective historically legiti-mated forms of violent protest without fear of rejection or condemnation by the community's grass roots and without fear of immediate and total state repression. To Capital Cities' chagrin, the company, not the unions, was blamed for the vio-lence.

Perhaps even more than the contract demands, about which few people in the region had much detailed information, Cap-ital Cities' security measures laid the foundation for a grow-ing belief that the company was a moral equivalent of the coal corporations and that the strikers deserved the same public support that the mine workers had received during the days when they struggled for economic and social justice. Once the public began to see the strike in these terms, the violence was seen not as a pathological response of disgruntled workers but as "normatively" appropriate (see Gamson, 1975), the con-temporary moral equivalent of the mine workers' past be-havior. Therefore, when it was attacked, Capital Cities was seen to be "getting what it deserved," as more than one person told me.

Such beliefs helped seal Capital Cities' fate in Luzerne County. Domowitch was right when he said the community saw Capital Cities as a "blend of Jack the Ripper and Charles Manson . . . who has invaded this valley and taken it over by storm," as the clergymen cited earlier put it. Capital Cities was seen as corporate evil incarnate, a practitioner of "the worst form of corporate exploitation imaginable." And having reached this interpretation of the company, the community responded as it had to the mining companies: it joined in the workers' struggle against the "unwanted outsider from Madison Avenue" (Domowitch, n.p., 1978).

The *Citizens' Voice*

4

Strike newspapers are relatively common. Unions often use them to provide strike benefits and to maintain workers' morale during a walkout. The Wilkes-Barre unions had one in 1954, when they struck the publishing company for six months. Therefore it was not surprising that they would start another in 1978.

A few days before the strike started, papers were filed in the Luzerne County Courthouse incorporating a strike newspaper called the *Citizens' Voice*. The owner of record was listed as the Wilkes-Barre Council of Newspaper Unions, Inc. There are no records on file showing when this organization was formed, its makeup, owners, or its officers. It appears to be a dummy corporation set up by the four local unions to protect themselves from economic and legal liabilities that might ensue from the strike.

The evident legal ambiguity was reflected in the workers' understandings of who owned the paper. As late as 1982, many of the rank and file thought they were the owners of record. It was not until sometime in 1983 that the paper's governing body explained to the strikers that the paper was not owned directly by the workers. Reportedly, this announcement created quite a stir, and a normal, relatively calm meeting turned into a stormy session. Some of the workers demanded to know who owned the paper. From all reports, that was never made clear. The governing board merely insisted that it was owned by the Council of Newspaper Unions.

Because the workers have no equity in the paper, the *Citizens' Voice* is not an employee-owned enterprise in the conventional sense of the term—one of two forms of direct employee ownership: either a producer cooperative or an enterprise incorporated as an employee stock ownership plan (ESOP). In coops workers own equal shares in the enterprise; theoretically, they have an equal voice in policy making and formulation because the enterprise operates according to the principle of one person, one vote; the horizontal division of labor is fluid; there is an attempt to minimize the vertical division of labor and to have egalitarian compensation systems. According to Joyce Rothschild and J. Allen Whitt (1986), coops' goals often differ sharply from those of other economic enterprises. They go far beyond merely securing profits. Producer coooperatives frequently are established and maintained so as to provide the employee-owners with an opportunity for realizing values such as creativity and self-expression in and through work, freedom and autonomy in the workplace, a chance to supersede the wage system, full participation in governance of the enterprise, and the like (see also Rothschild-Whitt, 1979).

ESOPs differ markedly from producer coops in structure, operation, and goals. Whereas the producer cooperative is owned entirely by the workers, in the ESOP workers may own varying shares of the enterprise. They may be minority or majority partners, or they may own the entire business. Unlike the coop, the ESOP has varying wage and benefit levels, and individual employees own varying amounts of stock, with the amount tied to level of compensation. Votes generally are weighted in proportion to the employee's equity.

Typically, the ESOP, unlike the producer cooperative, is not designed to facilitate workers' full participation in the management of the enterprise. The numerous case studies summarized by Rothschild and Whitt (1986) show that often there is no greater worker participation in ESOPs than in conventional firms, especially when the ESOP comes about because of a buyout or the conversion of an already existing enterprise.

The organizational structures and labor processes of ESOPs also tend to resemble those of conventionally owned enterprises. ESOPs' horizontal and vertical divisions of labor are highly formalized and rationalized, and personnel assignments are made according to skills and education; compensation levels are tied to job classifications, seniority, and performance; and the enterprise is oriented toward profit maximization. Partly because of their emphasis on profit maximization, ESOPs generally are less interested than coops in conducting social experiments to create alternative worlds of work.

The *Citizens' Voice* is neither a conventionally owned nor a worker-owned enterprise because none of the strikers has equity in the paper. As a result, the workers at the paper are neither employees nor employee-owners. Nonetheless, because the paper is self-managed by workers, if not self-owned in the legal sense, it can be compared with ESOPs and coops for the purpose of determining how the paper is organized, how it functions, and what the workers might have accomplished by setting up the paper, other than merely having protected a certain number of jobs.

The Organizational Structure of the *Citizens' Voice*

As it became increasingly evident that no agreement would be reached between Capital Cities and the four unions, the unions began to make preparations for starting a strike paper. The Wilkes-Barre unions were no strangers to such acitivity. In 1954 they had published an economically successful strike paper for six months. When that strike was settled, they closed their paper and returned to work. During the 1954 strike, the publishing company had ceased operations.

Sometime during the late summer of 1978, the unions decided to make contingency plans for a strike. Included in
these plans was a strike paper. By the time the strike came on
October 6, 1978, the unions had secured large interest-free
loans from the Newspaper Guild and from the recently
merged international union representing pressmen and stereotypers. They also received strike benefits from these
unions. The international ITU, however, declared the Wilkes-
Barre strike a wildcat action and provided no financial support
for the paper. Not only did it not lend money, but it also refused to send strike benefits to Wilkes-Barre. To add insult to
injury, the international ITU also refused to sanction its members who stayed behind to work for Capital Cities. At one
point, it even sent a representative to Wilkes-Barre to present
a commemorative anniversary pin to one of the men who had
chosen to return to work for the company after having been
on strike for a brief period.

The unions also secured access to printing equipment,
presses, and production facilities at nominal costs by renting
the facilities of the *Wyoming Valley Observer*, which supposedly was sympathetic to the unions' cause and also needed
the money. As one striker put it: "They were nearly bankrupt.
We helped bail them out for a couple of months." The unions
also secured regular access to scarce newsprint, reportedly
supplied by a "sympathetic" local and unionized printing
business.

By defining the *Citizens' Voice* as a strike paper the unions
gained a number of continuing financial advantages, the
cumulative effects of which made the paper more competitive
with the now mainly nonunion *Times Leader*. Among these
financial gains are, first, freedom from the obligation of paying union-scale wages and supplying union fringe benefits
such as contributions to union pension plans and health benefits. Second, because a strike paper is a nonprofit corporation
it does not have to pay corporate income tax. Third, it has
claimed that since it is a strike paper and technically its workers are receiving strike benefits it does not have to pay various

Above, first newsroom of the *Citizens' Voice. Below,* first composing room of the *Citizens' Voice.*

taxes. These claims were disputed by federal and state authorities; the dispute with the federal government is still unresolved, but the paper reached a compromise settlement with Pennsylvania. Fourth, the *Citizens' Voice* has not had to honor union work rules or job classifications, giving it the freedom to reassign personnel, to restructure jobs, and to redefine job standards as needed. At first glance it might seem to be a paradox that the rank and file were willing to impose on themselves greater cuts than those Capital Cities wanted to introduce. Closer examination, however, shows that the workers' behavior is not so paradoxical. They were willing to take these cuts primarily to keep their jobs. The strikers, with good reason, believed that if Capital Cities had its way many of the workers would have ended up unemployed and those who managed to retain their jobs would have to meet higher output and performance standards.

In designing the structure of their paper, the unions agreed to a system of governance that gave each union an equal voice in the paper's management. A governing body, the Unity Council, composed of two members from each of the four locals, was formed. Neither the creation of the Unity Council nor the formal definition of its powers emerged from the rank and file. The council was created and its powers were defined by the local union leaders, in consultation with and with the support of their advisers from the internationals, except the ITU.

Council members are elected for one-year terms. Council elections have not been competitive. In the years since 1978, only three different members of the Newspaper Guild have served. The one turnover took place because a council member left the paper to take another job. The guild's president has served on the council since the start of the strike. The stereotypers have had no turnover, and, like the guild, their top officer has been on the board since 1978. The pressmen have had three representatives over the years. They had to elect a new member when one of the men left the paper. The ITU has had six different members. One of the original two left the strike to take a job somewhere else. The others served for given periods and then decided to step out of office. Like the guild and the stereotypers, the ITU has elected its top official at the paper to the Unity Council. Members of the Unity Council are not full-time managers in the same sense an executive board would be in a conventionally owned firm. All of the members have full-time positions within the paper, and they are expected to perform their normal jobs while also serving on the council.

The Unity Council formulates policy, manages finances, engages in long-range planning, assigns personnel, and oversees the general operation of the paper. The council operates on a principle of the public unanimity and collective responsibility. Members, regardless of their private reservations about any decisions, are expected to support the decisions publicly and take full personal responsibility for them. There is no formal mechanism of review or appeal of council decisions. Theoretically, the council is responsible only to itself.

Despite the absence of formal, institutionalized means for the workers to block or reverse council decisions, the rank and file have a number of formal and informal participation opportunities (Pateman, 1970) that they can and do use to make their individual and collective voices heard in the running of the *Citizens' Voice.* Through elections to the council the workers have the power to punish members for "bad" or unpopular decisions. And through the electoral process in the unions and in the paper it is theoretically possible that the workers could abolish the council and establish some other form of governing board. The strikers also have a number of formal and informal means for participating in the *Citizens' Voice*'s policy process, defined as the means through which various policy-planning networks bring policies to the attention of decision centers (Domhoff, 1983:116).

Two of the more important formal participation opportunities are the monthly council meetings and the periodic mass meetings. According to several informants, the monthly meetings normally draw somewhere between fifty and sixty strikers, roughly 25 to 30 percent of the total *Citizens' Voice* work force. The council's monthly meetings are divided into two parts, an open forum and an executive session. During the open part of the meeting, workers are free to ask council members to explain their decisions, to account for their behavior, and to provide information on any facet of the strike. The rank and file also are free to debate council members or each other on any topic pertaining to the strike. Most of the council's policy and personnel decisions, as well as its internal debate, take place in executive sessions rather than in open meetings. Some strikers object to the use of executive sessions. One told me that he felt such sessions gave the council too much power, but others see nothing wrong with the executive sessions. As another put it, "If the council had to debate every decision in an open meeting, they'd never be able to get anything done."

It is impossible to gauge the influence of the rank and file on council decision making through various formal and informal participation opportunities because the council apparently makes most of its key policy decisions in executive session or in informal, private discussions. The council uses executive sessions for a number of reasons. First, secrecy prevents premature disclosure of policies. Second, by using executive sessions the council is able to maintain a public face of total unity and unanimity. The council does not want outsiders, especially Capital Cities, or the rank and file to know the extent of its internal differences. Interunion solidarity would be seriously threatened if council members were free to repudiate publicly decisions that went against their members' special interests but were thought to serve the general good. Third, the council does not want divisive issues to be known. Fourth, private decision making provides council members with some freedom from their individual constituencies, thereby allowing them to take actions that are designed to serve the common good of the paper, rather than special interests within it. This freedom is critical in the case of decisions that require unequal sacrifices by one union or individual. In general, the council does try to balance sacrifices and burdens. It knows that whenever it violates principles of equality of sacrifice, controversy surely will follow. For example, one Christmas the New York pressmen's union took up a collection for the Wilkes-Barre strikers. A delegation came to Wilkes-Barre to distribute the proceeds of the welfare fund and held a Christmas party for the strikers' children. The council decided to support a request made by some of the younger strikers who had dependent children that they get a larger share of the money from the collection than the older men, who, it was claimed, had fewer financial responsibilities. Some of the older men grumbled about the decision, and a few complained vociferously. But the council distributed the money according to its interpretation of "need." Fifth, individual council members and the council as a whole use secrecy to augment authority. It is able to control the paper's agenda by determining, in large part, what issues will be stressed and when a matter will be brought forward for public debate. The council can use its control over the timing of bringing up issues to develop a consensus for its policy before potential opposition has the opportunity to emerge and become organized. As an example, the council began receiving complaints that jobs were being filled on the paper without being posted. Before this could become a major issue, it required that all jobs be posted and that all workers be given the opportunity to apply for them.

The council uses mass meetings to announce new policies and any new developments in the strike that it feels warrant special attention. The mass meetings are scheduled at times when almost all of the work force can attend. Generally most of the workers come to them. In the early days of the strike, spouses also were invited, but this no longer is common. As in the monthly meetings, the rank and file are given a chance to express their opinions, vent their frustrations, and engage in open debate and discussion with each other and with the council members.

Although the meetings offer members of the rank and file

an opportunity to hear the council and to voice their personal and collective opinions, the council also tries to use the meetings for its own ends. The meetings are a principal avenue for the council to manufacture or demonstrate consensus for its actions, policies, and programs.

Workers also have the opportunity to influence council decisions by serving on the ad hoc advisory committees that the council sets up for various reasons. When plans were being drawn up to purchase new equipment and move to new facilities, committees were established to help the council decide what composition system and printing presses were most feasible and what equipment would be installed in the newsroom. These committees, according to informants who served on them, were given wide latitude in researching the paper's needs and making final recommendations to the council.

The rank and file also can exercise influence through the international unions, working with regional representatives to effect council policies. This tends to occur when a given union feels that a policy violates principles of equal treatment and equal sacrifices for all of the unions. Some of the strikers, however, have complained that the internationals are unwilling to do anything that will weaken the Unity Council and that international representatives ignore their complaints.

Finally, the workers can influence council policy by threatening to strike and set up a picket line. Reportedly, they did so only once, in a dispute between pressmen and the council over work rules and work assignments. When the pressmen began to feel that the council was unresponsive to their needs, reportedly they threatened (half-seriously, some claim) to set up an informational picket line at the *Citizens' Voice.* Hearing about the threat, the council quickly descended on the pressroom, and there was a stormy meeting between the two sides. Fortunately for both parties, they eventually were able to reconcile their differences and avoid a public display of their disagreement.

More than any other incident, the threat of setting up a picket line showed that at least some members of the rank and file were willing to resort to extreme measures if and when they determined that the council had violated their fundamental interests or rights. If the council previously had felt that it had almost unlimited power to exercise its will over the workers, it was forced to modify or, at the very least, reassess this view following this incident. But the pressmen did show that if they choose to do so, workers could force the council to take account of their views and needs, even when the council thought these were not in the paper's best interests.

Although one can find examples of the council's willingness to accommodate opposition to its policies and decisions, it would be a mistake to conclude that the council will easily abandon unpopular policies, especially those it believes are best for the paper. On several occasions, the council has made decisions it knows will be unpopular with all or part of the rank and file. A good example is its decision about distributing the money it received from the ITU, when that union finally agreed to begin making strike payments to Wilkes-Barre sometime late in 1982 or early in 1983.

Many of the strikers expected a substantial raise in their weekly benefits because of the ITU payments. Some were surprised and angry when they found out that the council had decided to raise their weekly compensation to $295, even though it had enough money to raise them to $315. The council explained that $10 per week would be set aside in an escrow account to help the strikers pay their taxes at the end of the year and the other $10 would be used to help pay for new delivery trucks.

Because the *Citizens' Voice* operates as a strike paper, all workers receive the same pay, whatever their job title or functions. This system worked to the benefit of some of the lower-paid workers, but most of the reporters and skilled craft workers took significant pay cuts. Even at $295 per week, they still earned less than they would have had they stayed with the *Times Leader*, provided, of course, that they were not dismissed by the company.

Although not a few workers publicly complained about the

way the money was allocated, the council had its way. In part it was able to contain the opposition by pointing out that there was no other source of funds to purchase trucks and by convincing the workers that it would be politically unwise to have their strike benefits exceed $300 per week, when many of their community supporters received far lower weekly wages.

The Unity Council also has been able to make and effect unpopular decisions about personnel assignments and classification, despite the discontent generated. For example, at one point the craft workers who were assigned to Newspaper Guild jobs proposed that they be allowed to convert their union cards into guild memberships, retaining their seniority rights and other privileges. Reportedly, the guild balked at this suggestion and the Unity Council supported its objections. The council also has supported the newsroom's requests for hiring additional personnel, even though there continues to be a surplus of craft workers.

Overall, although the council has had its way in defining policies at the *Citizens' Voice,* more often than not, it has faced opposition and cannot ignore the needs and wishes of the rank and file. To keep conflict at a minimum, the council has learned that it must be solicitous of workers' opinions and must provide opportunities for formal and informal input at all points in the policy process.

The concept that best describes the role of the council in the paper's internal life is that of oligarchical domination, which G. William Domhoff (1983:150) defines as "the ability of a class or group to set the terms under which other classes or groups within a social system must operate." Domination, as Domhoff rightly observes, does not rule out the possibility of dissent or the possibility that the dominant group may occasionally be defeated in the policy process. It does mean, however, that the conflict and dissent that occur are structured so that the system of unequal power relations is left unchallenged and unchanged. And this is precisely the case at the *Citizens' Voice.* Dissent has never become so great that an organized movement has been directed at dismantling the

Unity Council and replacing it with some other system of governance. Debate and conflict have gone only far enough to challenge specific policies and raise questions about the wisdom, judgment, and competence of individual council members. The council, as a structure of governance, has remained sacrosanct.

The Unity Council has been able to generate mass loyalty and support from the rank and file for a number of reasons. First, it has been highly successful in managing the strike. Among other things, the council has been able to maintain internal peace and solidarity among the unions and the individual members; under its leadership, the *Citizens' Voice* has the largest circulation in the local newspaper market; the council has been adept at securing whatever resources the paper has needed from the internationals and from the local community; it has neutralized the papers' enemies in the community; it has raised compensation levels; and it has effectively transformed the *Citizens' Voice* from a temporary publication that was using outmoded equipment into a permanent paper with modern facilities and the latest production equipment.

Second, the council has been able to generate mass loyalty and commitment by keeping alive a sense of crisis and threat, keeping the workers from being either overconfident about their chances of beating Capital Cities or unduly pessimistic because the *Times Leader* continues to publish, despite the losses it has sustained.

Third, by providing the workers with a variety of opportunities for exercising influence, by maintaining open channels of communication with the rank and file, and by being careful to explain to the strikers why it cannot meet all their needs all the time, the council has been able to maintain its internal support. So concerned was the council with the need for communication that early in the strike it mailed a regular newsletter to the strikers' homes and invited spouses to the mass meetings. Reportedly, the spouses were given the right to speak and to ask questions from the floor.

Fourth, the council, as previously noted, has been extremely adept at issue management. Because of its considerable formal and informal powers, the council can (and does) determine what issues will and will not be made public, how issues will be defined, and when they will appear. This power gives the council the capacity to structure the levels of consent and dissent on a broad range of topics, making sure that dissent seldom becomes strong enough to threaten the strike.

Fifth, the council has been able to maintain support because of its ability to reward its allies and punish its opponents. The council has a broad range of privileges that it can dispense to or withhold from workers, especially the craft workers. The council has complete control over who will stay in a craft position and who will be reassigned. In addition, the council determines the jobs to which these workers will be reassigned. Craft workers who run afoul of the council risk being given insignificant, if not distasteful, job assignments. And it does not appear to be hesitant about using its control over privileges and punishments to reward supporters, to discipline dissidents, and to create its own cadres of loyalists. One man who returned to the *Times Leader* after having been on strike said the primary reason why he crossed over was that the council refused to give him Sundays off from his picket-line duties. That privilege, he claimed, was given to an ardent council supporter. The council, with the support of the internationals, has suspended the seniority principle. A worker who objected to his assignment, in part because someone with less seniority was given preference for a better job, claimed that he was told by both the council and his international representative that "this is a strike and seniority rules don't apply." But despite these examples, it should not be thought that the council uses its power to control job assignments and to discipline workers arbitrarily. A striker who once had a supervisory role at the paper told me he sometimes had difficulty in getting the council to take action against workers who were shirking their duties. The council reportedly told him that it would be bad for morale to take too hard a line against the rank and file.

In sum, although the Unity Council does not have the broad managerial powers and rights in governing the *Citizens' Voice* that upper management has in a conventionally owned firm or even in a large number of ESOPs, it does have a greater capacity to dominate the policy process and the day-to-day operation of the paper than would seem to be the case in most producer cooperatives (Rothschild and Whitt, 1986). Yet the council does not completely control the rank and file. They can and do exercise some influence over the policy process and the operation of the paper through a variety of participation opportunities, which give them a much greater chance of having their voices heard and their wills realized than was the case at the old *Times Leader* and certainly more than they would have had they continued to work for Capital Cities.

The workers have the means to influence the Unity Council and can occasionally "force it to take account of their interests, needs, and demands to produce decisions that it may not have wanted to make. For this reason, the council, like other trade union organizations (Offe, 1985), must continually deal with the problem of maintaining worker solidarity and discipline. To generate and maintain solidarity, workers must think of and evaluate the benefits of membership in the organization in collective, rather than individual, utilitarian terms (Offe, 1985). The problem of solidarity is especially acute at the *Citizens' Voice* because it is composed not only of individual workers, each of whom has personal needs, interests, and aspirations, but also of four distinct locals, each having its own organizational history, its own set of needs and interests, and its own internal problems in achieving unity. Although relations among the newspaper unions have been fairly good at the local level, there have been some strains. In addition, there have been problems among the various unions at the national level, especially between the pressmen and the ITU, and the Newspaper Guild and the ITU. At the time of the strike, the pressmen and stereotypers had recently merged at the national level, and the ITU and guild were conducting negotiations for a merger, which did not come about. Relations between the international Newspaper Guild and the ITU and between the pressmen and the ITU were strained because of the ITU's apparent unwillingness to provide unequivocal support for strike actions these unions had called, a case in point reportedly being the action both unions had taken against Capital Cities in Pontiac in 1977.

In addition to the problem of solidarity, trade union organizations must be able to ensure that the rank and file will possess and maintain a continuing "willingness to act" (Offe, 1985:185) on behalf of their collectively defined interests. In the case of the *Citizens' Voice,* such a willingness has entailed the willingness not only to strike but to stay with the paper and not return to the *Times Leader* and to continue to make personal and organizational sacrifices for the good of the whole. Included among these sacrifices is a willingness to abide by the decisions of the Unity Council and not to take precipitous actions on behalf of individual and union-specific interests.

According to Claus Offe (1985), bureaucratic, oligarchical control cannot generate either a collective orientation or a willingness to act in labor organizations. To overcome the internal heterogeneity of interests characteristic of any labor organization so that its members think collectively and are willing to act collectively, "dialogical patterns" (Offe, 1985: 193) of collective action must be available within the organization so that the rank and file at least occasionally have an opportunity to participate in debate, and these patterns must be reconciled with the "instrumental-monological" (Offe, 1985:193) patterns of collective action in which debates about policy, objectives, and the like occur only at the leadership level.

The *Citizens' Voice* thus far has been able to achieve the reconciliation between the two patterns of collective action that Offe has discussed. As a result; it has developed the collective identification and willingness to act that are essential for organizational survival and success. Not only were the unions able to get 205 workers to walk out in 1978, but in

1986, approximately 140 of the original strikers were still working at the paper. Of those no longer with the paper, the vast majority took other jobs or retired. Fewer than a dozen returned to the *Times Leader.*

The Labor Process

The *Citizens' Voice* has incorporated the "production re-gime" described by Michael Burawoy (1979) from the pre–Capital Cities Wilkes-Barre Publishing Company. There is no sign that this was done with any critical reflection on the strikers' part at the time the paper was being established. They simply assumed that they had no choice but to put into effect the labor process they had known at the *Times Leader* before Capital Cities bought it. There also does not appear to have been any major internal debate since the strike began about alternative production regimes.

It has never been proposed, for example, that managerial functions and structures put into place by the previous owners be abolished or collectivized, or that management, at any layer in the organizational structure, be rotated, selected by democratic processes, or be subject to more democratic controls. Just as managers are appointed by owners or by managers at other papers, at the *Citizens' Voice* managers are selected by and directly accountable to the Unity Council.

Managers and supervisors at the *Citizens' Voice* exercise many of the same functions as their counterparts in other enterprises. They are charged with organizing and overseeing the labor of others so as to ensure that labor discipline is maintained, production quotas are met, and output meets acceptable quality standards. All of this, however, is done within a production regime that continues to honor a *system of craft production.* There has been no pressure from the rank and file or from the Unity Council to dissolve the horizontal division of labor and replace it with a job-rotation sheme similar to those found in cooperatives (Rothschild and Whitt, 1986).

On the shop floors, traditional craft practices govern the organization and pace of work. In the craft rooms, the workers set up their own production teams, determine shift assignments, job assignments, job content, days off, vacation schedules, and the like. For the most part these decisions are made using standard union procedures and rules and are then forwarded to the council for routine review and approval. The council usually accepts the crafts' recommendations without objection.

Although craft workers have maintained their traditional forms of work and their traditional prerogatives at the *Citizens' Voice*, there is no telling how long they will continue to be able to do so. The biggest threat to their autonomy and self-control and to their traditional patterns of organizing their work is the technological modernization program that the *Citizens' Voice* put into effect in 1984. In 1983 the paper purchased and began renovating an abandoned warehouse in Wilkes-Barre, where it planned to consolidate its operations. For most of its existence, the *Citizens' Voice* had its newsroom in Wilkes-Barre and its craft rooms at Plymouth, a West Side suburb some five miles south of Wilkes-Barre.

The paper bought a Goss Urbanite press and a Compugraphic One System, complete with video display terminals in both the newsroom and the composing room. When it relied on older equipment, the *Citizens' Voice* maintained craft positions for a large number of pressmen and printers, and for two workers who still carried the designation of stereotyper, even though with the advent of cold-type production they no longer practiced most of the skills traditionally associated with the stereotyping craft. The remaining workers in the stereotyper classification were shifted to other jobs; one, for example, supervised a shift of pickets, and one has been moved to a job as an advertising salesman. Even though some former stereotypers are now in jobs under the control of the guild, they continue to hold union cards in the stereotypers' local and continue to be represented at the strike paper by that local's delegates to the Unity Council.

To maintain jobs in the composing room, the printers shared work, a practice they last used during the Depression, when Wilkes-Barre Publishing Company printers reportedly reduced their hours voluntarily so as to maintain employment levels. But even with work sharing at the *Citizens' Voice,* not all craft persons could be absorbed. Some had to be reassigned to other positions at the paper.

With the introduction of new equipment, the problem of occupying redundant craft workers became more intense, and more of them were moved into other jobs. A further complication is that more than a dozen people were hired into guild positions since the strike began, initially, according to reports, without opportunity for displaced craft workers to bid on the positions. Technically, these newly hired workers have more seniority in the guild than do craft workers moving into guild positions after the new workers' dates of appointment. Some printers have resented the hirings because they have reduced the options for employment in "better" guild jobs.

Courtesy, Wilkes-Barre *Citizens' Voice*

Computerized composing room in new building of the *Citizens' Voice.*

Technological change at the *Citizens' Voice* has also led to job "degradation" (Braverman, 1974) in the positions that have been retained. Because of the new production technologies, many jobs were transformed from skilled into semiskilled or lesser positions. The new equipment could also reverse the traditional relationships between the crafts and the newsroom. Before the advent of this modern printing technology, the shops dictated the volume, pace, and form of work in newspapers. Contemporary technologies allow the newsroom rather than the craft rooms to drive the paper. In conventionally owned newspapers, the only constraint that the newsroom and those who command it face on exercising their customary control is union contracts that were negotiated at a time when the crafts had a tight monopoly over the supply of skilled labor that was essential for production. Now that craft work has been simplified so that virtually anyone can be trained to do it in a short time, the political will and economic strength of the owners determine whether they will try to reverse traditional patterns. The same can be said of the Unity Council. Like owners, it is capable of subordinating the crafts and allowing the newsroom to take complete control over the production process. Should this be done, the crafts will no longer have the capacity to set work standards and define the quantity of output for each job, let alone for the rooms in their entirety. And craft workers will be in approximately the same position with respect to the loss of traditional craft privilege and control at the *Citizens' Voice* as are their counterparts at the *Times Leader.*

Like the craft workers, the *Citizens' Voice*'s editorial employees have had to face major changes in their patterns and styles of work. Because of competitive pressures from the *Times Leader,* the *Citizens' Voice*'s reporters and editors have had to make adjustments in the ways they collect information, the stories they produce, and the features and articles that are put into the paper.

Reporters no longer can rely only or mainly on handouts for stories. They know that if there is more information available than the sources give them, the *Times Leader* reporters will press to discover it. As a result, *Citizens' Voice* reporters are becoming more aggressive in their reporting practices, if for no other reason than to avoid being scooped by the *Times Leader.*

Competition from the *Times Leader* also has forced the *Citizens' Voice* journalists to pay more attention to the quality and the nature of their writing. The *Citizens' Voice* reporters have had to write far more analytical copy than they did in the past. Many have had difficulty adjusting to these new demands because their training, education, and previous job experience did not prepare them for producing such copy.

The hardest adjustment for the *Citizens' Voice*'s reporters and editors is to produce independent accounts such as are the hallmark of contemporary professional journalism (Gouldner, 1976; Schudson, 1978; Gans, 1979). Under the former owners, journalists were rewarded for work styles that took the news at face value. News was what newsmakers said it was. Capital Cities had a different orientation. Like other news companies, it demanded that its reporters and editors offer an independent, if not alternative, point of view to that proffered by the subjects of news coverage. *Citizens' Voice*'s reporters and editors initially had a hard time producing such copy. Their difficulties did not stem only from deficiencies in technical skill. They also involved politics. The *Citizens' Voice*'s survival depends on staying in the good graces of local newsmakers, especially politicians. If the *Citizens' Voice* began practicing even a mildly critical or skeptical political journalism, its relationships with established centers of power could be threatened.

The *Citizens' Voice* has been forced to add new sections on food and entertainment in response to the *Times Leader*'s introduction of such features. Few, if any, of the *Citizens' Voice* reporters or editors had previous experience in producing special sections or soft-news features. Because of competition from the *Times Leader*, the *Citizens' Voice* also has had to add a photojournalist and daily columns and features by local reporters. Ironically, the *Citizens' Voice* has had to resort to using part-time workers to produce some of its copy, which the guild's contract had virtually prohibited the *Times Leader* from doing. Some of these part-timers write under pseudonyms out of fear that if their employers were to discover their identity, they would be disciplined or lose their jobs.

The *Citizens' Voice*'s early efforts at matching the *Times Leader*'s offerings often were little more than crude approximations of their competitor's material. When the *Times Leader* decided to hire full-time photojournalists, it found a staff by hiring recent graduates of a leading university. The *Citizens' Voice*, on the other hand, converted one of its workers who was an amateur photographer into a full-time photojournalist. Over the years, however, as the *Citizens' Voice* has gained more experience with new features and forms of presentation, its quality has shown a marked improvement and it is now a respectable competitor with the *Times Leader*. *Times Leader* workers grudgingly acknowledge the improvements that have taken place in the *Citizens' Voice* and realize that they face additional pressures to outdo the strike paper.

In sum, the strikers have had to cope with major changes in the nature of their work. First, they faced the difficulty of producing a newspaper under strike conditions using old equipment with which they were not completely familiar. Because of the limitations of the equipment, the *Citizens' Voice* began publication as a tabloid. Many of the workers with whom I talked seemed embarrassed by this format. They wanted me to understand that they would have published as a broadsheet if that had been possible. There also were serious imbalances in the *Citizens' Voice*'s work force; there were too many printers and stereotypers and not enough trained editorial workers to produce a paper that matched the *Times Leader*'s quality standards. Finally, both the craft workers and the editorial employees have had to adjust their jobs to meet the competitive pressures of the *Times Leader*. The craft workers have had to learn new techniques of design, layout, and color graphics, and editors and journalists have had to produce new sections and learn new styles of journalism. As a result, the *Citizens' Voice*'s labor process has been continually evolving, which has added to the pressures and uncertainties facing the workers throughout the course of the strike.

In analyzing the *Citizens' Voice*'s system of governance and labor process, as well as its vertical and horizontal divisions of labor, one may conclude that the Unity Council and the strikers have not used the establishment of the paper as an opportunity to conduct a broad, wholesale experiment in workplace democracy. It should not be surprising that the strikers have been content with creating and maintaining a production regime (Burawoy, 1979) closely approximating traditional craft norms and models in view of the circumstances surrounding the paper's founding, the continuing uncertainty of its environment, the nature of the work force, and the nature of the groups on which it relies for external support.

The paper was started in a crisis situation, and initially the union leadership and the rank and file wanted only that the paper provide an effective, temporary defense of their interests. Had they tried to develop a more democratic paper or one with a less clearly defined production system, it might not have been as effective in dealing with the uncertain, crisis-ridden environment as the *Citizens' Voice* thus far has proven to be. Paul Bernstein (1976), for example, has noted that centralized systems of decision making appear to be more effective at handling a crisis environment than are decentralized, democratized decision systems. If the strike leaders had been completely dependent on the rank and file for approval of their day-to-day decisions, they might have been paralyzed in trying to reach decisions quickly.

Continuing competitive pressures from the *Times Leader* also obstructed an inclination to experiment. The strikers are convinced that as long as Capital Cities continues to operate in the local market they should avoid taking risks. Therefore, any change that even remotely could threaten the economic well-being of the *Citizens' Voice* is pushed to the side in favor of the tried and true.

The data presented by Rothschild and Whitt (1986) indicate

that high levels of workplace democracy may be a luxury that only coops or ESOPs functioning in noncompetitive or highly restricted markets can afford. If this is the case, it is understandable why the *Citizens' Voice* has shown little inclination to experiment with its internal structures and its labor process in the face of immense competitive pressures.

In addition to crisis and competition, the nature of the *Citizens' Voice's* work force helps explain why there has been little effort to create greater workplace democracy. As is true of other U.S. workers, the strikers' past experience would not have led them to believe that they either were able to or ought to have *complete* control over all facets of an enterprise.

The thrust of working-class socialization and the paucity of participation opportunities afforded to working-class populations (Pateman, 1970), in the family (Aronowitz, 1973), the schools (Bowles and Gintis, 1976; Apple, 1979), the community (Gaventa, 1980), or the larger society (Ricci, 1971; Wolfe, 1977) have left most of the U.S. working class bereft of the desire or the confidence in their ability to control an economic enterprise. The working class seldom thinks of the enterprise as something that ought to be democratically organized and managed. Therefore, it is small wonder that the *Citizens' Voice* workers have shown little interest in taking direct control over the entire paper but have been satisfied with partial participation opportunities and conventional, hierarchical and vertical divisions of labor, as long as they were assured that traditional craft rights and privileges of autonomy, control, and the like in the labor process would be maintained.

Because they were satisfied with traditional craft rights and privileges, the rank and file saw no need to dissolve the vertical division of labor and debureaucratize the enterprise. They accepted bureaucratic domination based on office, function, or expertise as normal, natural, and inevitable. It was almost as though they could not conceive that production could take place without hierarchy.

Just as the rank and file believe the vertical division of labor is a necessary part of production, so, too, they believe the horizontal division of labor should be a permanent feature of their enterprise. The workers' insistence on maintaining the horizontal division of labor is a function of their trade union consciousness and has led them to demand that traditional craft rights, privileges, and boundaries be maintained at almost all costs, short of the loss of the strike. This attitude has perpetuated traditional modes of work organization and reduced the chances of installing a more flexible horizontal division of labor. Because of their trade union consciousness and craft identifications, the rank and file have not shown any interest in abolishing craft classifications and craft or occupational control over jobs. Nor have they demanded that workers be allowed to move from one assignment to another either as their needs and interests change or as production requirements might demand.

Similarly, the technical and managerial cadres at the paper have not wished to see their power and authority dissolved through the redesign of the vertical division of labor. Their position has been strengthened by the installation of new production technologies, which, among other things, have transferred power and control away from the crafts toward those who manage the machines.

Experimentation also has been blocked by the way the paper's goals have evolved. When the paper started, many of the rank and file saw it as a temporary defensive measure. It was not until late 1978, when Capital Cities sent the workers letters telling them that it intended to replace them unless they immediately returned to work, that it became evident that the paper would be permanent. There is no sign that the rank and file expected the strike to end as it has. All my interviewees insisted that though they felt that the strike would be long, they expected eventually to return to work. If the strike leaders had from the beginning planned a permanent walkout, as Capital Cities has claimed, they did not so inform the rank and file. As one striker told me: "When this strike started, all of us figured that we'd be out for a long time. But none of us thought that it would be forever. But here we are, still out."

With their economic future completely tied to the financial

success of the *Citizens' Voice*, it was natural that the rank and file and the union leadership would direct the enterprise toward a goal of maximizing profits, or more appropriately, revenues, since the *Citizens' Voice* continues to operate as a nonprofit strike paper. Accepting that goal, the paper's workers came to be dominated by the same laws of accumulation that control any other conventional, capitalist enterprises. To generate a revenue surplus, they had to accept wage and benefit levels, work rules, and, potentially, forms of organization many of which were lower and more onerous than those Capital Cities would have imposed on them. The workers felt such sacrifices were justified as the price that had to be paid to defend their unions and their principles and to maintain their jobs.

In addition, several other factors have obstructed the development of innovative changes in the organizational structures and the labor process at the *Citizens' Voice*. For example, the international unions, especially the Newspaper Guild, which seems to have played the most critical role in shaping the internal structure of the *Citizens' Voice*, wanted management structures and production processes that assured orderly and regular output, believing this was the only way the strike would succeed and their substantial financial commitments to the paper would not be squandered. The internationals were not disappointed. Within four years of the start of the strike, the *Citizens' Voice* had repaid all the loans it had received from the internationals to that point. The national office of the guild continues to provide heavy financial subsidies to Wilkes-Barre.

The internationals also were hesitant about encouraging an experiment in worker ownership or self-management that might bring into question the roles of the unions within the enterprise. Because of the ambiguous role of unions in worker-owned enterprises, unions have been reluctant to become involved in establishing such businesses. Therefore, had the local unions tried to establish a highly democratic production system, it is unlikely that the internationals would have been

willing to sink nearly as much capital and organizational resources into the *Citizens' Voice* as they eventually did.

Had the local unions wanted to establish an organizational
structure that was more internally flexible and more fully
democratic and had the internationals supported these attempts, the larger community environment would have im-
peded their efforts. Even with the paper's strong centralized
system and traditional organizational structure, many outsiders, including some of its strongest supporters, initially
were skeptical that the four unions would be able to work
together and that they would be able to guarantee labor discipline and productivity. Early in the strike, a prominent figure
in the city who supported the *Citizens' Voice* expressed his
doubts about the strikers' ability to hold together: "They're a
contentious bunch, you know. When they worked for the publishing company, they were hard to manage. Whoever ends up
running things at the *CV* is going to have his hands full keeping the unions together and the people working." Fortunately
for the *Citizens' Voice*, this assessment proved incorrect. One
could only imagine what the reaction would have been had
the paper launched a bold experiment in worker self-management and flexibly organized production. Surely doubts about
the paper's chances for success would have been stronger than
they already were, making it more difficult for some parts of
the local community to accept the risks associated with backing the *Citizens' Voice* against the *Times Leader*. For example,
had the *Citizens' Voice* not followed conventional practices, it
would have faced even more serious problems than it did
when approaching private creditors for loans. One striker told
me that when the Unity Council first approached a city bank
about a loan, it was told that the board of directors would have
to review the application. The loan eventually was approved.
The paper met its repayment schedules and was granted
further loans. By concentrating power in a central committee
and preserving conventional hierarchical and horizontal divisions of labor, the union leaders demonstrated to outsiders
that the strike would not be allowed to degenerate into anar-

chy, that there was one center of power that was responsible for governing the strike and ensuring that the paper would meet its financial and political obligations, and that the paper was being managed according to sound business principles.

In sum, the *Citizens' Voice* created a production regime differing in few critical respects from those of conventionally owned and managed newspapers whose labor process is based on traditional modes of craft production. To fend off external threats from Capital Cities and later to maximize profit, the *Citizens' Voice* built a management system that permitted only partial and limited forms of rank-and-file participation, created a division of labor organized around hierarchies of specialization and expertise, and invested in technology designed to reduce the number of skilled workers and to increase the output of those who retained their jobs.

Apparently not conscious of alternative possibilities, the rank and file did not resist the imposition of the old divisions of labor or the new production technologies. Indeed, most workers seem to be enthusiastic about the technological changes, despite the personal consequences involved. They consider their future more secure with the *Citizens' Voice* having an increased capacity to secure greater and greater revenues. Being content with preserving minimum levels of control over their day-to-day tasks, the *Citizens' Voice* workers, like many of those who labor in ESOPs (Mulder, 1971; Mire, 1975; Bernstein, 1976; Russell, Hochner, and Perry, 1979; Rothschild-Whitt, 1979), have missed a chance to gain even greater freedom within the labor process than was secured by contemporary forms of craft work.

Because there is so little interest in and support for fundamental change in the organization of power and production at the *Citizens' Voice,* it was only logical that in 1983, when the Unity Council began to explore ways to pass ownership to the rank and file, it found the ESOP a more attractive model than the producer cooperative. Transforming into an ESOP would change little at the *Citizens' Voice.* Work could go on much as always, and the paper could continue unimpeded in its course of profit maximization.

Movement toward creating an ESOP has been slow, however, because the Unity Council has had to resolve a host of ancillary issues related to the decision to transfer ownership to the rank and file. Among the more important of these are the amount of money to be paid to the unions for the paper, the distribution of stock and voting rights, the composition of the board of directors, the relationship of the board to the rank and file, the role of the unions in representing the workers in an enterprise they own, whether the wage and benefit structure will be pegged to union scales, whether union work rules and seniority provisions will be recognized and implemented, the position of workers hired since the strike began, and the fate of the surplus craft workers whose jobs have been eliminated by technology. In addition, the transformation has been blocked by the continuing litigation initiated by Capital Cities and the dispute between the *Citizens' Voice* and federal tax authorities over the paper's tax status. Until these issues are resolved and the Unity Council can generate rank-and-file consensus for its proposals, the paper will not be converted to another form of ownership but will continue to operate as a strike paper.

5

The *Citizens' Voice* and the Community:
Mobilizing Support and Neutralizing the Opposition

The newspaper unions, like any other actors attempting to put together a protest movement (see Schwartz, 1976), knew that if they tried to fight Capital Cities using only their own resources they would quickly be overwhelmed. From the earliest planning stages, the locals recognized that although inter- and intraunion militance and solidarity were necessary for a successful action, they were not sufficient conditions for enabling them to fight Capital Cities. The unions were well aware that the conduct of a successful strike required the support of key actors, groups, institutional elites, and the community grass roots. Such support had been vital to every victory the newspaper unions had won in Wilkes-Barre. In 1937 public support led to the Newspaper Guild's recognition at the *Times Leader* following a bitter strike, and in 1939 public support contributed to the guild's victory in a strike against the newly formed Wilkes-Barre Publishing Company. In 1954 public support enabled the four unions to carry out a six-month strike, during which time the workers survived in part on the proceeds of a successful strike paper.

To secure community support, the newspaper unions used a mixture of strategies, tactics, and incentives. They applied a broad range of material incentives to secure support and neutralize opposition within the community. When they had no control over appropriate material incentives or their application, the strikers made effective use of symbolic, collective incentives. Combining material and symbolic incentives, the strikers built a multiclass support system that tied together a broad range of actors, groups, and institutions. Without its highly committed support system the *Citizens' Voice* would have neither prospered nor been able to inflict heavy financial losses on Capital Cities. Some of the elements of this support system were directly incorporated into the paper, others were used as "nonaffiliated supporters," to use a term from Michael Schwartz (1976: 169), and still others became allies in a broad coalition whose aim was to displace the *Times Leader* from its preeminent market position.

The *Citizens' Voice* and Its Affinity Groups

When the strike began, there were three groups on which the *Citizens' Voice* relied heavily—trade unions, politicians, and newspaper carriers. Each of these groups had an interest or preexisting structural solidarities with the newspaper unions that *predisposed* it toward alignment with the *Citizens' Voice.* The strikers recognized, however, that even though the politicians and carriers might have natural sympathy for the *Citizens' Voice,* they would support the paper only if the unions could offset the countervailing pressures that the *Times Leader* and its local allies would apply to them. Of the three, only the county's trade unions could be expected to provide more or less automatic support for the *Citizens' Voice.*

In part, the support from other unions was a direct result of the special circumstances in which trade unionism developed in Luzerne County. The county's trade union movement has had a long history of mutual support, cooperation, and solidarity. But it was not only historical factors that made the county's trade unions willing to provide assistance to the newspaper workers. The county's unions believed that a victory by Capital Cities would be a disaster for all of the region's working people because it would set a dangerous precedent that other employers might be tempted to follow. The unions believed that a victory for the newspaper workers would send a clear message to the county's employers that trade unionism was alive, well, and capable of mounting an effective program of resistance against any employer demanding "unreasonable" concessions from workers.

Local unions also supported the *Citizens' Voice* in the hope that the strike might result in the creation of a permanent prounion paper. The *Times Leader* and the *Sunday Independent* both were conservative, Republican-oriented papers that supported the county business elite's political and economic agendas. The unions, with good reason, feared that their political program would suffer major reversals unless they could get their message to the general public.

Early on, local and state trade unions supplied the striking newspaper workers with a broad range of services. In the first days of the strike, union volunteers poured into strike headquarters and offered to help with any tasks that needed to be done. Some stuffed envelopes and helped with chores around the office, others manned phone banks soliciting subscriptions to the *Citizens' Voice*, and pressmen and printers from around the city helped produce the paper. Several of the volunteers became involved in activities at the picket lines in front of the publishing company's building. A volunteer described his impressions of those first days as follows: "I went over there to see if I could be of any help. It was amazing. There were people there from almost every union in the city. People were tripping over themselves. Everybody wanted to lend a hand any way they could. . . . It made me feel good to be part of all that."

One local union official told me that her retirees were the most ardent supporters of the paper. When the strike started, a large number of the younger members could not understand why their union was devoting so much time to discussing it when they had their own problems. But gradually, this view disappeared and the younger people came to share the older workers' belief that they were obligated to see the *Citizens' Voice*'s cause as their own.

The trade unions also provided the *Citizens' Voice* with *indirect* financial support. Union leaders asked members to make donations to the *Citizens' Voice,* encouraged them to take subscriptions to the strikers' paper and cancel their subscriptions to the *Times Leader,* and took out advertisements in the paper. During the first two weeks of the strike, before payments from subscribers and commercial advertisers began to come in, union ads were the *Citizens' Voice*'s financial lifeblood, providing a much needed cash flow. Local unions continue to advertise in the *Citizens' Voice,* especially in its annual anniversary issue. Trade unions also helped the *Citizens' Voice* by imposing a news blackout on the *Times Leader. Times Leader* reporters found that local labor leaders would not send them news releases, would refuse to be interviewed, and would not allow them to attend any union meetings.

Unions also made important political contributions to the *Citizens' Voice.* Through the county's trade unions, the strikers were able to mobilize a large number of politicians and harness parts of the system of local government to their cause. A number of politicians and elected officials were products of the trade union movement and continued to maintain close ties with it. At the time the strike began, for example, one member of the county's delegation to the Pennsylvania General Assembly had belonged to the UMWA, another had been a president of a stereotypers' local (although he had not worked at the Wilkes-Barre Publishing Company), and several had links to the county's teachers' unions. In addition, other union men and women held lesser offices in local and county government. These politicians supported the strike with little prompting from their unions. They acted as a matter of principle. Other politicians, however, clearly would have preferred to remain neutral in the strike or to delay committing themselves to supporting either side until they could judge the political costs of such a decision.

The county trade unions made clear to local political elites that unions regarded support for the strike as a litmus test of an official's commitment to labor's cause. Unions demanded prompt and unambiguous declarations of support from politicians; hesitation or proclamations of neutrality were unacceptable. Politicians were expected to refrain from taking any steps, official or unofficial, that would hurt the *Citizens' Voice* or help the *Times Leader.* Anyone unwilling to profess support and match it with action was taken to be repudiating not only the striking newspaper unions but also the county's entire labor movement.

The unions could make such political demands and expect politicians to comply because labor was the key group in the Democratic party coalition in the county. Without labor's financial and organizational support, the Democrats never would have been able to displace the powerful Republican machine that had once controlled public office in Wilkes-Barre and Luzerne County. No Luzerne County politician, whether Democrat or Republican, can expect a successful career in the face of determined trade union opposition. All politicians in the county must reach an accommodation with the trade unions, even if they do no more than offer public support for New Deal programs and their subsequent embellishments. From time to time, however, politicians are expected to go beyond a minimum commitment to labor's cause, and the *Times Leader* strike was one such case.

Although the unions demanded that all politicians comply with their request for support, they did not insist that everyone respond in the same way. The unions knew that they could not expect the handful of Republicans who represented suburban and rural voters to sign their own electoral death warrants by becoming too closely identified with the *Citizens' Voice.* In such cases, the trade unions were content with private assurances of support, provided they were backed up with discreet but appropriate action. On the other hand, Democrats were expected to demonstrate their support for the *Cit-*

izens' Voice and all of organized labor with more visible and dramatic gestures.

One way politicians and appointed officials helped the *Citizens' Voice* was by participating in a news boycott of the *Times Leader.* Many refused to meet privately with *Times Leader* reporters, granted them no exclusive stories, sent news releases to the *Times Leader* only after giving the *Citizens' Voice* the chance to break a story, gave the *Times Leader* no background information, held press conferences to which the *Times Leader* was not invited, and placed no political advertisements or announcements in the *Times Leader.* Many elected and appointed officials provided the paper with only such information as the law required. Even then, in some cases, the *Times Leader* got the information it wanted only by threatening to sue or by actually suing an official or agency.

For the first two to three years of the strike, the boycott virtually destroyed the *Times Leader's* political news network in the county. Having few sources with whom they could talk, either on or off the record, the *Times Leader's* political reporters had to work long and hard to produce copy, and even then they often could get little more than basic facts that already had appeared in the *Citizens' Voice.*

The politicians' boycott gave the *Citizens' Voice* a considerable competitive advantage because anyone who wanted to keep abreast of local political developments had to read the *Citizens' Voice* or wait until the *Sunday Independent* ran the story. At present, the boycott seems to have been partially lifted, and more politicians appear to be willing to talk with *Times Leader* reporters in public forums. Some, however, still refuse to deal with the *Times Leader.* Until he retired from office in the early 1980s, state Senator Martin Murray (D.-Wilkes-Barre), president pro tem of the Pennsylvania Senate, would have nothing to do with the *Times Leader.* While running in a heated primary in 1984, the incumbent Democratic congressman from Luzerne County refused to participate in a debate that the *Times Leader* had helped organize on the grounds that he wanted no contact with Capital Cities. Another elected state official told me that he had as little to do with the *Times Leader* and its reporters as possible and that he never sent them news releases or gave them exclusive interviews.

Although such ostentatious displays of hostility to the *Times Leader* seem to be less frequent now than in the early years of the strike, the paper continues to suffer because its political reporters have been unable to build large stables of well-placed confidential sources. Many of these sources will deal only with *Citizens' Voice* or *Sunday Independent* reporters. Such sources are the sine qua non of all political reporting. This support has helped the *Citizens' Voice* maintain its competitive advantage as the daily paper to be read for local political news.

The county's political elite did more than merely lend personal support to the strikers. Equally important, this group allied the county Democratic party with the *Citizens' Voice's* cause, thereby providing the paper with influential advocates and organizers in the vast majority of the county's precincts and wards.

Furthermore, the politicians prevented local and state government from intervening in the strike on the company's behalf. Government neutrality took a form that benefited the workers rather than the company. The Wilkes-Barre police and the county sheriff's office stood idly by while strikers, their supporters, and company guards fought each other on and off for days on end. Law enforcement agencies throughout the county followed the early example of the Wilkes-Barre police. Municipal police departments were less than vigilant in protecting company property, especially undelivered newspapers, and workers. Additionally, many police departments in the small cities and towns surrounding Wilkes-Barre participated in the news boycott of the *Times Leader.* The police gave Capital Cities' reporters only the barest outlines of stories, while providing *Citizens' Voice* reporters with substantially more background information.

Several municipal councils and even one of the county's school boards supported the *Citizens' Voice* by passing resolutions condemning Capital Cities' behavior in Wilkes-Barre. The *Citizens' Voice* made much of these resolutions, using them as further evidence of the justice of its cause and the legitimacy of its claims against Capital Cities and its call for public support. No one mentioned that relatives and other people with close personal or organizational connections to the strikers sat on these bodies. In a move that Capital Cities found particularly appalling, the Wilkes-Barre city council went on record asking the company to clean up its building, which bore the marks of the strike violence and subsequent acts of vandalism.

In sum, because of the role the trade unions play in the county's politically dominant Democratic party the trade unions' power to discipline politicians they consider errant, and the personal histories of many of the region's leading political figures and public officials, the *Citizens' Voice* was able to win and hold the support of the local political system and its key elites. The politicians, especially those in the Democratic party, along with the trade unions, became part of the *Citizens' Voice*'s local coalition.

Most politicians and officials did not have to learn the hard way that it was better to be identified as a *Citizens' Voice* supporter than as an ally of the *Times Leader.* One exception was Congressman James Nelligan, who defeated Rafael Musto for Daniel J. Flood's seat in 1980. Musto had been appointed to fill the remainder of Flood's term. Flood had resigned after he had been tried on alleged corruption charges in federal court. That trial ended with a hung jury. Flood's support in the area was so strong that he was reelected to Congress in 1978 despite his problems with the federal government. The *Citizens' Voice* backed Flood until the bitter end, when he finally resigned from office.

Nelligan's problems with the *Citizens' Voice* began shortly after he took office. The *Citizens' Voice* distrusted his conservative, Reaganite political ideology, but this was not the

key factor in turning the paper against him. The *Citizens'
Voice* had reached accommodations with other conservative
Republicans. Relations between the *Citizens' Voice* and the
congressman turned nasty after Nelligan agreed to act as the
official starter of a charity race sponsored by the *Times
Leader.* Accusing him of having sided with the *Times Leader,*
the *Citizens' Voice* relentlessly attacked Nelligan. Nelligan
was skewered for everything from taking junkets to supporting Reagan's economic agenda. Although some of the crit-
icisms were sound, others were silly. But that did not seem to
matter to the *Citizens' Voice* or its readers. While the *Citizens' Voice* continued to attack Nelligan, even after his key
aides had met with the paper's editorial board in a vain attempt to reconcile the congressman and the paper, the *Times
Leader* supported him. But it did not help the congressman's
cause. The *Citizens' Voice*'s attacks helped to erode Nelligan's
base of support and ultimately contributed to his defeat in a
bid for a second term. Nelligan's debacle showed local politicians that the *Times Leader* was just as incapable of protecting
its allies as it was of punishing its enemies. The *Citizens'
Voice,* on the other hand, could do both. This power alignment
further reduced the chances that any sensible politician
would ally with Capital Cities in Wilkes-Barre.

But even though the Nelligan matter showed the political
weakness of the *Times Leader* in protecting elected officials
who supported it, local politicians knew that the paper was
not a toothless lion. The *Times Leader* has been as vituper-
ative in denouncing the *Citizens' Voice*'s allies as the *Citizens' Voice* has been in attacking politicians who support the
Times Leader. Carefully monitoring both the public and private behavior of its political enemies, it has served as a local
muckraker. Given Luzerne County's long history of alleged
political corruption, marked by the resignation of Congressman Flood, the trial and conviction of a former Democratic party county chairman on voting fraud charges, trials
and convictions of school directors, investigations of judges,
charges against a board member of the county's public com-

munity college, a number of investigations of public officials for mishandling disaster relief funds after the Hurricane Agnes flood in 1972, and a host of other incidents, not to mention the fact that the county is the base of operations for an alleged Mafia family that reportedly has intimate connections with some local politicians, the *Times Leader* should be able to mine this news vein for years without repeating itself. But linking them to corruption is about the only way the *Times Leader* has been able to damage its local political opponents. Otherwise, politicians have found that they can gain or hold votes by wearing *Times Leader* attacks as badges of their political courage and their solidarity with the strikers and the local community.

Along with assuming the role of a muckraker, Capital Cities has tried to make a virtue of its political isolation by casting the *Times Leader* as a voice of progressive reform. The *Times Leader* has supported the county's "good" government reformers and their calls for structural changes in local government systems, tax and spending reductions, more equitable property tax assessments, the elimination of "one-party, machine politics," higher levels of professionalism among government workers, and the like.

If the *Times Leader* had hoped to make political capital by advocating such a position, it must be sorely disappointed because such an agenda appeals to few people in the region. Although the local electorate from time to time will "throw the rascals out," few of the county's voters appear to be willing to support structural changes that could weaken the Democrat and Republican machines. For example, for a brief period Wilkes-Barre experimented with a city manager form of government, but that was soon abandoned and the city adopted a mayor-council system. County voters also have continued to reject government political and service consolidation that, if combined with civil service reform, could weaken the job patronage system that serves as one of the bases of machine power. Because of the general lack of voter enthusiasm for broad structural changes in local political processes, identifying with the "reforming minority" has not won Capital Cities the support or gratitude of the community's grass roots. On the contrary, it has isolated the company even further from the community's political mainstream and has complicated, if not weakened, the *Times Leader*'s competitive position.

The third major affinity group that supplied the *Citizens' Voice* with critical support early in the strike was the carrier work force. In Luzerne County most carriers were adolescents ranging between thirteen and eighteen years of age (Keil, 1984). According to sources at the *Citizens' Voice,* approximately eight hundred of the roughly one thousand carriers supported the strike. This was a major blow to Capital Cities. Had the strikers not been able to secure the carriers' support they would not have been able to get their paper on the street as quickly as they did or rapidly assemble a distribution system reaching into almost every neighborhood in the metropolitan area.

The strikers began mobilizing the *Times Leader*'s carriers the moment the strike began. During the first weekend, circulation supervisors called the carriers' households to ask their parents if they would permit their children to deliver the unions' strike paper. Apparently, the supervisors, unless asked, did not mention that the *Times Leader* would continue publishing during the strike.

If the parents were unavailable, the circulation supervisors spoke directly to the carriers. Parents and carriers were told that the strikers would give the children a small pay increase for each paper they delivered. Carriers who agreed to deliver the *Citizens' Voice* were told that they could pick up their newspaper bundles at their usual collection points.

The carriers had various motivations for going with the strikers. Some did so for no other reason than at the time they made the commitment they thought the *Times Leader* would suspend publication for the duration of the strike. Others agreed to deliver the *Citizens' Voice* because their parents told them to. Still others agreed because of the increased pay. Some surveyed their customers and, finding that most people wanted the *Citizens' Voice,* decided that it made economic sense to switch to that paper. And, finally, some chose to deliver the *Citizens' Voice* because they or their parents believed in the strikers' cause (Keil, 1984).

When Capital Cities learned that the unions had taken control of the company's carrier force, the company began calling carriers' homes to get them to return to work for the *Times Leader.* Carriers were informed that since they were not part of any recognized collective bargaining unit the company would consider that they had abandoned their jobs and if they did not return promptly they would be replaced with other youngsters. Futhermore, they allegedly were told that if they refused to return there would be no guarantee that they would get their paper routes back if and when the strike was settled. The company sweetened its demands by offering the carriers pay increases.

The vast majority of the carriers stuck with their decisions to deliver the *Citizens' Voice,* despite the uncertainties many faced about their customers' reactions once it became known that the *Times Leader* would publish during the strike and what would happen to them if and when the strike was settled. The *Citizens' Voice* was unable to give them any assurance that it could get them rehired in the event the unions returned to work with a settlement.

Once the carriers made the commitment to stay with the *Citizens' Voice,* they became an active social force on behalf of the strikers' efforts to secure grass-roots support for the *Citizens' Voice* in the county's neighborhoods. Carriers generally had their paper routes in their own or nearby neighborhoods and often had extensive personal ties with their customers. The households they served often contained their friends, friends of their parents, the parents of their friends, and their kin. Even in the absence of such intimate bonds, carriers and customers had personal relations, if for no other reason than that the company required carriers to make their own bill collections.

The multiple and often overlapping social connections and

relationships between carriers and customers meant that when the carriers decided to deliver the *Citizens' Voice* rather than the *Times Leader* they could exercise powerful personal claims on subscribers to make the switch with them. This factor was especially important in bringing over to the *Citizens' Voice*'s side households that were indifferent about who won the strike. Many such households took the *Citizens' Voice* merely because their carriers asked them to do so. One carrier told me she had gone to each of her customers and told them that she intended to deliver the *Citizens' Voice* and asked them if they would be interested in taking that paper. Some of her customers refused, but the vast majority agreed to take the strikers' paper. Some did so, she felt, because of the way they felt about her rather than because of any clear-cut commitment about the strike.

The loss of the vast majority of its carriers threw Capital Cities' distribution network into disarray. Capital Cities has never been able to recover completely from this blow. It has not been able to regain access to the traditional labor pool of stable working-class and middle-class families on which the company relied for carriers before the strike. It has difficulty recruiting and keeping the youngsters it does hire. One former *Times Leader* carrier told me that though he never had any problems with the company, he quit because it "wasn't worth his time." He was covering a route that was about twice as large geographically as that of a friend who was delivering the *Citizens' Voice* and had far fewer households to serve. As a result, the company had a chronic carrier shortage. Because of its inability to find a steady and reliable pool of carriers, the *Times Leader*'s household distribution system has been in shambles for most of the time since the strike began. In the meantime, the *Citizens' Voice* has more applicants for routes than it has positions. According to more than one source at the *Times Leader*, the defection of the carriers "during the company's time of need" was one of the most lethal blows the paper took early in the strike.

Capital Cities has offered a number of incentives to local

youngsters to try to get them to sign up as carriers. The company has announced competitions for college scholarships, prizes, bonuses, and the like. For years nothing seemed to work. At one point during the strike, Capitals Cities' circulation office tried to recruit carriers with the help of officials of one of the county's school districts. The teachers' union objected to the school administrators' cooperation with the company, and the *Citizens' Voice* used the incident to charge that Capital Cities once again was trying to bribe the region's adolescents into working for it.

That Capital Cities lost most of the carrier work force should not be altogether surprising. Many of these adolescents were from union households or families and they were familiar with the demands of the region's labor culture. Like their predecessors during the mining era, they and their parents believed that their age did not excuse them from contributing to the success of a strike, even if they might suffer a loss of income or even a job. Nor should it be surprising that adolescents continue to avoid working for Capital Cities. Although the current crop of carriers can take comfort from the knowledge that the *Citizens' Voice* is firmly entrenched in the local newspaper market, the attitudes of many carriers and parents continue to reflect the same judgments that carriers and parents made in 1978: it is better to take one's chances with the *Citizens' Voice* than to become involved with a company that they believe has totally violated and repudiated local cultural sensibilities about how an employer should behave with respect to its workers.

Just as the *Times Leader* had problems with the carriers, it also had difficulties with other parts of its distribution system. Many newsstand operators refused to carry the paper, and some merchants would not put *Times Leader* vending machines inside their businesses or on their property. In the first few months after the strike began, it was almost impossible to find anyone who was selling the *Times Leader* in central city Wilkes-Barre, in the outlying neighborhoods, or in many of the inner suburbs. A city businessman, recalling the time when he could not purchase a copy of the *Times Leader* anywhere in the central business district, stated his belief that the paper's absence constituted a "serious violation of my constitutional right to read what I wanted. Those unions had no right to keep me from buying the *Times Leader.*"

Capital Cities has had more success in rebuilding this part of its distribution system than it has in reconstructing its carrier work force. At present most newsstands are selling the *Times Leader,* and the paper has made its way back into vending machines in restaurants, taverns, and other business places. As late as 1986, however, some businesses still refused to sell it. In April 1986 I walked into a newsstand in an office building in Wilkes-Barre that had not sold the *Times Leader* in the past. I asked the owner for a copy. I was politely told that I could buy it in the vending machine in the lobby. When I informed the owner that the machine was empty, she held up a copy of the *Citizens' Voice* and said, "Why don't you buy this?" I told her that I had already read it and there was something in the *Times Leader* that I needed to see. At that point she said, "Well, you'll have to buy it somewhere else. I don't sell it." I asked her why. She responded that the *Citizens' Voice* was "the union paper and that's all I want to carry."

The three groups discussed thus far—trade unions, politicians, and carriers—became the nuclei of the *Citizens' Voice*'s support network. All had preexisting working relationships with the newspaper unions, which facilitated their organizations into the strikers' support system. Once these groups were incorporated into the strikers' support system, in part because each group saw some of its interests to be isomorphic with the *Citizens' Voice*'s, each became an active agent that helped the strikers organize further support among the community's grass roots. By securing the active involvement of these three groups, the strikers were able to reach deeply and widely into the structures of community life and present their appeal to individuals and groups which they might not otherwise have been able to reach. In the process they were able to create a widespread popular movement to work on their behalf. The term "popular movement" indicates that there was no well-developed formal organization that directed the protest against Capital Cities. Rather, much of the response in the neighborhoods and towns in and about Wilkes-Barre and its suburbs apparently was spontaneous and uncoordinated by any formally organized group or social network.

Mobilizing the Community's Grass Roots

The newspaper unions recognized that even with the support of their affinity groups they could not win the strike without broad-based support from the community. To secure such support, they had to generate a conscience constituency that embraced most of the county's population. To this end, the strikers coupled their own organizing work and that of their allies with a carefully orchestrated ideological campaign. The ideological campaign had a double purpose. It sought to discredit Capital Cities and the *Times Leader,* while simultaneously providing individuals and groups with collective, symbolic incentives for supporting the *Citizens' Voice.*

The strikers used a moral discourse to attack Capital Cities. The company was portrayed not merely as a bad employer but as a radically evil presence in local life that threatened the entire community. This representation drew on the classical meanings of evil identified by Paul Ricoeur (1969). Capital Cities was depicted as an external, alien force that polluted the local community and threatened to overwhelm local institutions and culture. The *Citizens' Voice* and its supporters presented the company as a defiler and a seducer that was leading otherwise decent people astray. As a result, its presence brought chaos and disorder into local life.

The key negative moral label the strikers affixed to the *Times Leader* was that it was a "scab paper." Most commonly the word "scab" is applied to individuals who, putting self-interest ahead of the collective well-being, are seen to threaten the social, political, moral, and economic integrity and solidarity of working-class community life. To be a scab is to break ranks with all *decent* people, especially one's former colleagues or, in the case of replacement workers, those whose jobs are taken.

In sociological terms, a person labeled a scab takes on a new, dishonorable, "master status" (Becker, 1963). As Edwin M. Schur (1971: 24) observes, such negative labeling permits others to "isolate, treat, correct, or punish" the devalued person. Such was the case in Wilkes-Barre. Capital Cities' employees felt the full fury of the community's reaction to them as scabs. By cooperating with Capital Cities, they transformed themselves from respectable people into legitimate targets of hostility and aggression. They lost friends; they received anonymous, threatening phone calls; the homes and automobiles of some were vandalized; they were shunned by former coworkers or friends; in some cases neighbors reduced their contacts with them or ceased having any relations with them; and for some their relations with their families were compromised.

Individuals often are designated as scabs, but less frequently is an entire company and its products so labeled. But because the larger part of the community accepted the validity of designating Capital City as a scab, the unions were able to break through the boundaries that normally confine industrial disputes in the United States to specific institutional spheres (Dahrendorf, 1959; Aronowitz, 1983), and the strike was transformed into an issue of communitywide moral significance. All people who considered themselves part of the local community were placed under an obligation to avoid any contact with Capital Cities or the *Times Leader.* Capital Cities became an object that was to be isolated, avoided, and punished, just as were the individuals who worked for it.

Even the slightest contact with the *Times Leader* or its employees was likely to expose one to community censure. People have told me a variety of stories about how they got themselves into trouble with relatives, friends, family, and neighbors for having read or subscribed to the *Times Leader* or for having social relationships with the paper's employees. For example, a local woman who had dated a Capital Cities reporter told me that at first she was afraid to tell her parents where the man worked, and, later, after she did tell them they would not tell anyone else in the family or any of their neighbors and friends. I also was told that people made negative public comments to neighbors who subscribed to the *Times Leader*. Other people told me they would hide copies of the *Times Leader* when friends or family visited so as to avoid the possibility of an argument about the strike. A retired executive, in talking about how the strike had divided the community, reported that on more than one occasion he had seen bitter arguments break out between friends or colleagues over the strike. He said: "You could be sitting in a meeting or be at a social gathering and someone would ask 'Did you see the article on such-and-such in the *Times Leader*?' Then all hell would break out because someone would be sure to respond that they didn't read that 'scab paper.'" One person even told me he was accosted on a bus by a stranger who told him he ought to be "ashamed of himself" for reading the *Times Leader*.

Although the primary reason the company was made an object of moral opprobrium was its labor policy, which the community took to be an assault on all local workers and all that the county's trade unions had accomplished in the past, that was not the only reason why Capital Cities was viewed as a threat to local life.

Local society also came to see the *Times Leader* as a threat because of the news policy it reputedly wanted to put into effect. The newspaper unions claimed that the company planned to turn the *Times Leader* away from its long-standing practice of providing heavy coverage of local social news and events, substituting a variety of prepackaged hard and soft features. Prepackaged features generally cost less to produce than do other news stories. They often arrive at a paper already written, edited, and proofread, thus substantially reducing the local labor costs involved in producing news copy. The unions charged that because of the shift to prepackaged materials, less space would be available for covering stories about local events; they claimed that Capital Cities wanted to change the paper's content for the same reason it wanted to change the workers' contracts: to raise its profits. Although prepackaged features can be given a "local slant" by assigning a reporter to write a few lines of additional copy, cost-conscious editors may be tempted to view such assignments as unnecessary luxuries. To the general community, the reputed decision to shift the *Times Leader* away from its traditional reporting of news commonly published in what Morris Janowitz (1967) has called a "community press," that is, a press that focuses on local institutions, organizations, and personalities, was further evidence of the company's disrespect and disregard for local tastes and culture. It was thought that the company was willing to reduce the community to invisibility on the pages of the *Times Leader* for the sake of profits. This impression about how the company looked on the local community was reinforced when Thomas Murphy, Capital Cities' chief executive officer, was quoted as having said that the company intended to "inflict" its newspaper on the community whether it wanted it or not. The *Citizens' Voice* made much of Murphy's alleged comment and Capital Cities' supposed new plans for the paper. For example, in a story run under the headline, "Thanks to You, the Voice Is Growing," in the *Citizens' Voice*'s fourth anniversary edition, October 6, 1982, it made the following points:

> When Capital Cities took control of the *Times Leader* its plan for the paper called for cutting costs, increasing revenues and sending increased profits to headquarters in New York.
> To us, its employees, this meant pressure on those aged 50 or more to quit or retire. And pressure on younger workers to accept low wages and benefits or move on. There was no respect for past service or the desire to stay within the community.
> To the readers, the Capital Cities plan meant less local news, less news overall in the paper. Items such as bowling scores, club news and school news were to be eliminated.

To the advertiser, the plan would have meant bills doubling and even tripling. And diminished service.

Instead the establishment and success of the *Citizens' Voice* has preserved the careers of veteran newspeople in their 50s and 60s and a stable work outlook for younger employees.

It preserved the opportunity for area people to see the important events of daily life—club activities, engagements, bowling scores, school accomplishments—receive the publicity they deserve.

It preserved the ability of the local businesses—from department stores to mid-sized shops to individual operations—to afford newspaper advertising.

Today, more than four years since Capital Cities came to town with this plan, they are not always as obvious as they were in 1978. The wolf has donned sheep's clothing. They no longer brag they "will inflict a newspaper on that town."

But their plan must remain the same, only more so. When they arrived in 1978, they had a $10 million investment to recoup. Today, they admit to being more than $30 million in the red. How much would they cut local news and increase advertising rates to make this up if they could?

And even if they claim to give you "more," the *Citizens' Voice* contains far more local news and the same amount of national and world news. Does their slogan mean that they give your [*sic*] "more" than they would really like to?

For these reasons, Capital Cities still is trying to smash its striking employees and the *Citizens' Voice*. Its commercials, its management, its salespeople and its reporters continue to try and pound their way, smile their way, deal their way, even buy their way through the barrier that prevents them from having this area for themselves.

For these reasons, this area's working people and families and business people do the right thing when they continue to resist the advances of the *Times Leader* and Capital Cities to stand on principle and firmly say "no."

Having accepted the strikers' definition of Capital Cities as an unwanted, outside intruder that, in the name of higher profits, had a master plan for the area that threatened the interests of everyone from the casual reader to the local businessmen to its own workers, young and old, and that depicted the company as having little respect for the area and its people, the larger part of the county's population participated in a boycott of the paper. People often refused to give *Times Leader* reporters interviews; they did not send social information to the paper; they refused to be photographed for the *Times Leader*; and the like. The boycott was not limited to news. The majority of newspaper readers stopped buying the *Times Leader* and began subscribing to the *Citizens' Voice*. As tens of thousands of subscriptions were canceled within the first two to three weeks of the strike, the *Times Leader* found itself virtually shut out of a large part of its former market, especially in Wilkes-Barre and in the towns and small cities that made up the heart of the county's urbanized core, the part of the county referred to as the Wyoming Valley. The Wyoming Valley and the towns to the north and south of it along the Susquehanna River were the former mining areas. If one were to overlay a map of the *Citizens' Voice*'s major areas of support on these areas, they would coincide almost exactly.

When subscription cancellations began pouring in to the company, Capital Cities at first refused to acknowledge them. It tried to deliver as many papers as it could without charge. The company was prepared to accept the financial losses incurred by giving the paper away so that it could maintain its advertising rates. People receiving the free paper called the company and demanded that they be removed from the delivery lists. Some who received the paper even called their local police departments to complain that the company was littering their porches. Several police departments reportedly called the company to complain about the way the paper was being delivered.

When it became evident that its strategy was failing, Capital Cities began mailing the paper to all postal patrons. Again, many households refused delivery. Some went to their post offices and filled out cards stating that they did not want to receive the paper. A letter carrier informed me that on his route only 13 out of approximately 460 households took the paper when Capital Cities was mailing it out. He believed that the reactions of people on his route were not atypical. Other letter carriers had similar experiences. He claimed further that Capital Cities was shipping "thousands of pounds" of newspapers to a city waste recycler every day during that time. Reportedly, the company still is doing so, but at a substantially reduced rate.

To restore its circulation, Capital Cities has offered free trial subscriptions for various time periods and has cut the newsstand price of the paper at different times to ten cents a copy. In commenting on this strategy, a *Citizens' Voice* employee remarked that he felt that the price reductions hurt Capital Cities' subscription business because subscribers were not receiving similar discounts. The precise effect of these various incentives is next to impossible to gauge. Capital Cities does not release circulation figures for the *Times Leader.* In 1982, however, I was told by a local Capital Cities source that the paper's circulation was "around thirty-two-thousand" papers a day. In early 1986, however, the paper was claiming that it had finally surpassed the *Citizens' Voice's* paid circulation.

The *Citizens' Voice* dismisses Capital Cities' circulation claims, charging that they represent an unaudited estimate and are counts of the press run, not the paid circulation. If Capital Cities' claimed circulation figures are correct, it is anybody's guess how it has rebuilt its circulation, given that there has not been any appreciable drop in the *Citizens' Voice's* circulation and little growth in the county's population. It would seem that the only ways Capital Cities could have improved its circulation would be if there were a sharp increase in the number of two-paper households and/or vending-machine sales, or if circulation had expanded into the rural and semirural hinterland, taking circulation away from small-town papers and the two Scranton papers. A circulation increase does not seem likely because of the sustained animosity toward the paper in the community and because, according to a local company source, earlier Capital Cities market studies reportedly found that about thirty thousand households claimed they would never subscribe to the *Times Leader,* even if it were the only paper in the city. Therefore, if Capital Cities has succeeded in repairing its circulation levels in the area, it most likely has done so by developing new markets and gaining new subscribers in the outlying rural and semirural areas of northeastern Pennsylvania, where Wilkes-Barre papers had few subscribers before the strike and by rebuilding its sales at newsstands and vending machines.

Thus even if the company indeed has been able to draw even with the *Citizens' Voice,* it has not been at the expense of the strikers' paper's circulation. Support for the strikers in the community has held firm over the past eight years. The unions' moral campaign has accomplished at least part of its objectives: Capital Cities was constituted in the public's mind as a moral pariah whose presence a large part of the community deemed unacceptable. So morally worthless was the company taken to be that any persons who had even the slightest contact with it, its paper, or its workers or who expressed mildly favorable opinions about the company were deemed guilty of having committed the moral equivalent of crossing the picket line. They were not considered guilty merely of "collaboration" but of the far more serious infraction of "collaborationism." Ad Teulings (1982) defines the former as cooperation out of necessity and the latter as cooperation out of conviction or belief in the rightness of an enemy's cause. In Wilkes-Barre any act that could be construed as helping Capital Cities was looked upon as a form of the more serious moral offense of "collaborationism."

At the same time that the *Citizens' Voice* was stigmatizing Capital Cities, it worked to link itself and its cause with the moral history of the county's workers. The *Citizens' Voice* identified its cause with that of the United Mine Workers and all the other local unions that had built up and maintained the region's trade union culture. To make clear to its readers that the newspaper unions stood within the moral halo of the UMW, its antecedents, and its successors, the *Citizens' Voice* ran a series of articles, beginning in April 1979, detailing past and present labor struggles in the county and the extent of suffering and misery that the local population had endured at the hands of absentee-owned mining companies. The series was called "Coal Crackers . . . OUR ROOTS!" These articles carry the strong message that the struggle against corporate power did not end in the county with the demise of anthracite, that there were parallels between the struggle of the newspaper workers and that of the miners, and that it was only through trade unionism that all workers, regardless of time or industry, could defend their interests and achieve self-respect and dignity. For example, in Part II of the series, entitled "Coal Mining—Hell on Earth," there was a sidebar with the headline "Owing One's Soul: The Company Store." It read as follows:

> The miner's misery didn't end at the finish of each working day.
>
> Every aspect of his life—political, religious, and social—was dictated by the company.
>
> But perhaps one of the most effective and notorious indignities the miner and his family had to endure was the company store.
>
> Many coal operators maintained their own store and compelled employees to trade there. It was at this store that a man's wages determined the extent of his credit. Bookkeeping departments of the coal companies submitted a daily report of the earnings of each employee, and no person's bill could exceed his earnings.
>
> But the real rip off came because payroll deductions for store bills meant a reduction in real wages—because of higher prices as well as less pay.
>
> One independent merchant in the late 1880s noted that company store prices ranged as high as 160 percent above his.
>
> The end result of low wages and numerous payroll deductions was little or no pay.
>
> One of the most humiliating things a miner could suffer was being issued a "bob-tail" check from the company at payday. The check was simply a statement that the total deductions equaled wages.
>
> One miner during that period told a story of a man who

worked for five years and never drew a dollar in wages. All the
money he earned went to the company store to pay for his
"indebtedness."

The story added at the end of the five year period the man
was finally issued a $5 check and on that occasion it brought
tears to the old miner's eyes. (*Citizens' Voice*, April 10, 1979)

The main story dealt with the early efforts to organize
miners' unions in the mid-1860s, and it detailed other examples of miners' suffering at the hands of corporate capital. The
story concluded with a discussion of the Molly Maguires, an
Irish mine workers' terrorist society that flourished in the
southern anthracite fields in the middle decades of the nineteenth century. In part, the story stated:

It was the act of desperate men. The highly secret Mollies were
charged with destruction of mine property and outright murder
of foremen and mine superintendents.

It was the stuff that made for lurid newspaper sensa-
tionalism. It also prompted the bitterly anti-labor head of the
Philadelphia and Reading Railroad to call in Allan Pinkerton
and his detective agency. Pinkerton detective James McParlan
developed evidence against the Mollies that led to the wholesale conviction of 24 of the leaders; 10 of them eventually
hanged.

During the years 1876 and 1877, trials of Molly Maguires
were numerous throughout the region. But the hands pulling
the hangman's rope were not clean. Subsequent disclosures in-
dicated that mine operators and Pinkertons deliberately insti-
gated violence in order to discredit legitimate union activities.

"The facts show that there was as much terror waged against
the Mollies than those [*sic*] illiterate Irishmen ever aroused,"
commented historian Aleine Austin. (*Citizens' Voice*, April 10,
1979)

Anyone familiar with the charges the newspaper unions were
making against Capital Cities could not help but draw the
parallel between the mine workers and the newspaper strikers
that the *Citizens' Voice* intended.

The theme of corporate exploitation and the suffering and struggle of workers was repeated in Part III of the series, which dealt mainly with the events leading up to the 1902 coal strike and the strike itself. The article "John Mitchell: Hope for the Miners," in discussing the interim between the end of the 1900 strike and the beginning of the 1902 strike, described relations between the company and the workers as follows: "But it was a hollow peace. The owners hired 'coalies' to guard the properties and began stockpiling in anticipation of the next showdown" (*Citizens' Voice*, April 11, 1979). The story went on to note that the strike was marked by violence and that the National Guard was sent into the region. It closed with an account of how the strike was settled:

> But when the strikers' morale was at its lowest, something un-expected happened. William F. Clark, a Wilkes-Barre photographer, had written to George F. Baer, president of the Reading, asking him to settle the strike. Baer responded:
>> "I beg of you not to be discouraged. The rights and interests of the laboring man will be protected and cared for—not by the labor agitators but by the Christian men of property to whom God has given control of the property rights of the country, and upon the successful management of which so much depends."
>
> Baer's letter, made public, led the *New York Times* to note: "A good many people think they superintend the earth, but not many have the egregious vanity to describe themselves as its managing directors."
>
> From that point on, public sympathy was almost all on the side of the strikers. The federal government intervened and President Theodore Roosevelt appointed a commission. Both the coal companies and the UMW agreed to abide by the decision of the commission which, after lengthy hearings, recommended wage increase [*sic*] and other improved working conditions for the miners.
>
> By the 1902 strike, coal was a basic in American life, but outside the coal fields, few knew what it took to deliver the fuel. Publicity of the strike changed that.
>
> The open hearings of the Roosevelt Commission also gave

the public a glimpse at many of the coalfield owners. Famed lawyer Clarence Darrow represented the United Mine Workers at the federal commission hearings. Among statements made were from Baer [*sic*]: "If a man comes to me and offers to work for me and I am willing to pay him $2 a day and he is content to take it, that is a bargain as good and as sacred in the eyes of the law as any bargain could be. . . ."

And from Darrow: "Mr. Baer and his friends imagine no doubt that they are fighting for a grand principle when they for what they say is the God-given right of every man to work for any wages he sees fit. . . . But that is not the God-given right these gentlemen are interested in. They are interested in the God-given right to hire the cheapest man they can find. (*Citizens' Voice*, April 11, 1979)

One could not find a more eloquent statement of one of the strikers' major charges against Capital Cities, recalling that one of the guild's points in defending the strike was that the company wanted to fire experienced workers and replace them with younger and cheaper laborers.

A sidebar to this story titled "A Grim Cargo" read:

The wagon wheels rolled slowly down the coal patch street, grinding anthracite into dust.

It was a grim cargo hauled by the two tired mules. A father and son had died that day in a rockfall . . . the man and boy were going home for the last time.

Such incidents happened more than once. A Nanticoke miner tells the story of the coal company officials who took the bodies home, deposited them on the porch and told the grief-stricken widow and mother, "Here are your men!"

In a Pittston cemetery, a tombstone tells the story of the father who carried his 14-year-old son's broken body home after a mine accident. The lad died on the kitchen table.

Up and down Wyoming Valley, the death of the mines visited hundreds of families, and thousands more lived with the pain of injuries. Pain, physical and spiritual, was the daily lot of the coal miners. (*Citizens' Voice*, April 11, 1979)

Part IV of the series, "Depression: The Long Hard Days," as the title indicates, focused on the Depression and its effects on the mining industry. The article detailed the way the Depression exacerbated the already bad conditions in the coal fields; the violence inflicted on miners by the companies; the weakened condition of the UMW, which led to organizational splits and, for a time, dual unionism; bootlegging; and the 1932 strike. It also discussed the beginnings of the textile industry and chronic mass male unemployment in the region.

The article glossed over a number of other salient events during the Depression. For example, it failed to mention the open rebellions that the rank and file carried out against the UMW leaders, whom many accused of having collaborated with the companies. District 1, the anthracite district, was in turmoil. Bombings, shootings, and small-scale riots occurred throughout the region, especially in Luzerne County. In March 1932 dissident miners called a wildcat strike that was supported by forty-four locals (Miller and Sharpless, 1985). The strike lasted from March 12 to March 31, when, facing opposition from the union's national leadership, mine operators, and the state, the leaders called a halt to the action.

In 1933 dissident miners formed the United Anthracite Miners of Pennsylvania with the man who had led the 1932 strike as its president. The break-away union became involved in several strikes in Luzerne County, which were marked with violence as the men fought strikebreakers and the police. According to Donald L. Miller and Richard E. Sharpless, "Brawls broke out between strikers, police, and miners attempting to work. Pitched battles occurred at collieries throughout the Wyoming Valley. The violence soon spilled over to the mining towns. Beatings, shootings, bombings, and burnings became commonplace" (1985:306–7). The head of the new union agreed not to conduct any more strikes when he was persuaded that the federal government would investigate the miners' grievances. When no action came, he called another strike in January 1934. Most of the Luzerne County's mines were closed, and as many as fourteen thousand men stayed off the job. This strike also was marked by violence. It was suspended in February 1934, when the union was assured that the National Labor Relations Board would listen to its grievances. The board, however, was unsympathetic to the dissidents' cause. It made several rulings against the union, and the strike was renewed in February 1935. Again there was violence. The car of a local judge who jailed the union leaders for failing to obey an injunction was bombed, and county authorities declared a state of martial law. According to Miller and Sharpless,

The UAMP threw all of its remaining resources into the strike. Women and children in line with the region's strong tradition of family and community solidarity, played active roles in this, the union's last desperate effort. Schoolchildren organized support activities; in Nanticoke several hundred high school students struck in sympathy with teachers who had relatives working for Glen Alden [one of the major companies targeted in the strike]. The UAMP women's auxiliary was everywhere, soliciting help from local unemployed councils and recruiting speakers who could talk to mine workers in Slavic languages. Twelve of the ninety defendants charged with contempt of court for violating the strike injunction were women. In Hanover and Nanticoke, women were arrested by state police for stoning miners attempting to work. In Wilkes-Barre ten women attacked and beat three strikebreakers. One hapless miner was stripped of his clothes and was sent home naked to the women's taunts of "scab." The intensity of feeling often resulted in deplorable acts. Stacia Treski of Nanticoke tells of "a young man . . . [who] had to work because he had two children and his wife was expecting another. He went to work—crossing the pickets—and was killed in an accident in the mines." Before the burial the dead miner's funeral procession was stoned and his open grave was filled with tin cans. "The people were so mad that he went to work they wanted to dig him out," Treski recalls. "They had to get the police to keep him in his grave." (1985:308–9)

The strike eventually was broken by the combined power of the UMW, which participated in blacklisting the dissidents, the companies, and the State Police, who were especially brutal in suppressing the strikers. One resident of the region whom I interviewed about the *Citizens' Voice* strike brought up the 1934 strike in the course of our conversation. He recalled that his father, a miner, was beaten by State Police officers, who were mounted on horses, while he was standing in his own back yard. He went on to tell me that a few years later his father and a few of his friends, while drinking in a tavern, saw one of the state policemen who had beaten him, and they grabbed him and "beat the hell out of him."

Miller and Sharpless also point out that during the 1930s there was a communist presence in the region, led by an ethnic Croat party activist. The communists helped set up highly effective unemployed councils to put pressure on the local political structure to respond to the desperate economic straits in which many families found themselves. By mid-1931, the councils had a membership in excess of twenty thousand in the coal fields. The councils were "authentic popular organizations that developed to meet real and urgent needs" and were not merely party front groups (Miller and Sharpless, 1985:319).

Because of the *Citizens' Voice*'s obvious desire to extol the virtues of established trade unions, it is understandable why the paper did not deal with the UAMP in any great detail. The region's strong anticommunism and the need to neutralize the opposition of the local business elite to the paper also explain why the *Citizens' Voice* did not mention the councils and the role of the communists in helping organize them, even though that information was readily available.

The remainder of the series, which ran for several more days, dealt with the decline of the anthracite industry and its replacement by the garment and textile industries, the region's chronic unemployment as a result of mine shutdowns, and the attempt to rebuild the local economy. Part VI of the series, "Knox Breakthrough Ends an Era," made the following points:

The diversification, the efforts to reshape the land, the programs to improve the region's image—all are part of a continuing evolution that can never deny the past.

Directly or indirectly, every person in the anthracite region has been touched by the good and bad of mining.

The cruelties, the indignation, the suffering [sic]. All contributed to the toughness needed to maintain an existence, and in later years to overcome recession and depression.

The resiliency of coal country people is a reflection of the toughness, stubbornness and faith of the coal miners. They forged lives in the most difficult of times. Their sons and daughters face their hard times with a faith born of coal cracker heritage. (*Citizens' Voice*, April 14, 1979)

A sidebar story on the same date, titled "Sirens Scream, Miners Moan" read:

The shrill of the colliery whistle and the scream of ambulance sirens sent chills down every spine.

In a coal town it meant disaster. Something was wrong in the mine.

May 31, 1950. The whistle blasts and the sirens scream. It's 7 A.M.

A cage carrying eight miners to the bottom of the 800-foot Baltimore shaft of the Huber Coal Company, Ashley, plunged to the mine floor from the 220-foot mark.

All eight men aboard the cage suffered broken legs and other injuries.

The men were hauled from the mine via the Red Ash cage.

Unbelievable but true, the men lay moaning on stretchers in a hospital corridor until 1:30 P.M. They got no pain killers and no treatment until mine officials arrived.

Even at the halfway mark of the 20th Century, coal mining meant suffering in Wyoming Valley. (*Citizens' Voice*, April 14, 1979)

Although the "Coal Crackers . . . OUR ROOTS!" series ostensibly was a historical presentation (albeit nicely sanitized and reworked so as not to offend established trade unions or even the local upper class, failing to mention the latter's role in building the mining industry and suppressing local workers) of how the region and its people had fared at the hands of the coal barons and of the way they were delivered up from what one of the articles called "economic feudalism" by the united action of the workers in their unions, it could just as easily have been read as an indictment of Capital Cities and the *Times Leader* and as praise for the newspaper unions in their struggle against the company. All the charges of which Capital Cities stood accused were shown to have had precedents in the behavior of the mining companies. Like the coal companies, Capital Cities had been denounced by the unions and their supporters for its alleged corporate arrogance, its total indifference and disregard for its workers' "human dignity," its interest in securing the cheapest possible work force regardless of the costs to the men and women who lost their jobs, its use of a private security force, and its having provoked violence. In the same vein, the newspaper unions' self-justifications for their strike and its results could be seen to have had a precedent in the region's labor history. In the past, when workers had become sufficiently desperate, they had used violence, had taken over the means of production by operating bootleg mines, and had found that the only way to protect themselves from the depredations of the companies was to build strong unions. It was not hard for even the casual reader to understand the underlying message that the newspaper unions were the moral equivalent of the United Mine Workers, just as Capital Cities was the moral equivalent of the coal companies.

It must be remembered that this series ran six months after the strike began, so it cannot be argued that it was meant to generate a motivation for the larger part of the community to act. The community had already decided whose cause was just: the first day it published, the *Citizens' Voice* had sold more than forty thousand copies, and within the first month it had reached sales of roughly forty-seven thousand copies per day. Rather, the series' function was more to provide the paper's supporters with an explicit ex post facto justification for their action so as to sustain their commitment for the long haul and to try to expand the paper's base of support to include other social classes and strata, especially people in white-collar jobs, small businessmen and women, professionals, and others whose personal or family origins were in the county's working classes. For that reason, the point that all people in the region had a share in the legacy of the mining industry was emphasized.

The county's working classes, especially those in trade unions, needed no a priori and *explicitly formulated* justification to act in behalf of the *Citizens' Voice*. They had seen or heard what was happening at the paper and already had made the decision to support the newspaper unions by the time the strike began.

The local working classes could respond as rapidly as they did not only because they were motivated to support the newspaper unions but also because the community knew how to engage in mass collective action in defense of workers' interests. Such responses had long been part of the local working classes' repertoire of contention, and the community's social organization was conducive to such action. In Chapter 1 I showed how important collective action was to mine workers struggling to defend their interests. The miners were able to mobilize ethnic groups and, in many cases, whole communities to act on their behalf. Miller and Sharpless demonstrate that collective action on behalf of workers continued well into the twentieth century, and they correctly see it as part of a larger tradition of communal solidarity, collective responsibility, and mutual self-help. The collective orientation was broad enough in the twentieth century to include most of the major ethnic groups; large parts of the working classes, not just miners; and some members of the middle strata (see especially Miller and Sharpless, 1985:312–13). The only real worry that the newspaper unions had was whether the community still had the structural capacity to act. When the strike began, however, they were pleasantly surprised, to put it mildly, to find that it did.

Fortunately for the strikers, not only did the old moral traditions of collective responsibility, collective obligation, and mutual self-help continue to survive, but so did the institutional structures that had been forged during the mining era. The strong families; the neighborhoods and towns; the centers of informal sociability such as the tavern; the parishes and churches; the fraternal, civic, and mutual benefit organizations; the ethnic groups; and the social networks that linked these various subsystems, institutions, organizations, and groups together had retained enough vitality to enable collective action to take place. For example, the strikers received assistance from their nuclear and extended families. Children and spouses went to work, and kin either gave them part-time jobs or helped them find other ways to supplement their meager strike benefits ($40 per week when they first walked out), sometimes with gifts of money, food, and clothing. Such family support is not confined to the newspaper unions; it has long been part of the region's working-class culture, as Miller and Sharpless (1985) observe. During layoffs or strikes, working-class families often mobilize in this way.

Entire neighborhoods took the side of the *Citizens' Voice,* often without prompting and usually without action by any formal neighborhood organization. Neighbors supported the strikers in indirect ways. They participated in the news boycott of Capital Cities by refusing to send personal announcements to the *Times Leader;* refused to allow their children to be carriers; lobbied politicians to voice public support of the newspaper unions; subscribed to the *Citizens' Voice;* urged local merchants to advertise in the strikers' paper; helped apply pressure to businesses refusing to advertise in the *Citizens' Voice;* sometimes put up signs in their yards and on their cars saying "Cap Cities Go Home" or similar words; and exerted considerable moral pressure on people they knew who sub-scribed to the *Times Leader.*

Like local neighborhoods, many religious organizations sprang to the strikers' defense. Protestant and Catholic clergy (Luzerne County is more than 50 percent Catholic according to figures cited by Carroll, Johnson, and Marty, 1979) partici-pated in a major rally that the county's trade unions held on behalf of the newspaper unions; preached sermons advocating support for the strikers (one clergyman allegedly told his con-gregation that it was "sinful" for anyone to work for the *Times Leader*); participated in the news boycott by refusing to send announcements about parish events to the *Times Leader;* and more than one clergyman wrote articles for the *Citizens' Voice.* Reportedly, a clergyman who headed up a youth organization in the county unceremoniously turned down a gift that Capital Cities had offered his group because of his personal feelings about the strike. At the same time, church organizations invited *Citizens' Voice* reporters to cover their activities, and some invited the strikers to come speak about their conflict with the company.

Just as the strikers were able to mobilize a significant number of religious organizations to their cause, they also succeeded in securing the support of a large number of volun-tary and civic organizations, including numerous ethnic fra-ternal organizations. Many of these associations, like the churches, invited the strikers to send speakers, sent the *Cit-izens' Voice* news items and photographs, and studiously and self-consciously avoided any overt contact with the *Times Leader.*

The actions of neighborhoods, churches, and civic and vol-untary associations helped strengthen the *Citizens' Voice*'s moral claims for support from other segments of the county's population, especially the middle classes. The *Citizens' Voice* was able to use this outpouring of support to secure critically needed advertising accounts from a large number of the county's small businesses, especially those whose customers were mainly working class. But not all of the small business

Billboard appeals to civic patriotism.

advertisers sided with the strikers for material reasons. A fairly large number of those that early in the strike placed ads in the *Citizens' Voice* did so because their owners had roots in the county's working classes or shared the strikers' definition of the situation. A vehemently pro-*Citizens' Voice* small businessman described his reaction to the company: "Capital Cities is no good. They tried to give their people the shaft. Even though I'm not union, I'd never treat my people that way. I've got more self-respect than to do something like that." Of course, not all small businessmen shared this man's sentiments. Probably more sided with the company, although I have no quantitative data on the distribution of small business support for either paper and cannot draw any definitive conclusions.

Small businessmen were not the only parts of the local middle classes who supported the *Citizens' Voice*. The strikers also garnered the support of managers, professionals, and other white-collar workers whose occupations place them in

what Erik Olin Wright calls "contradictory class locations."
According to Wright:

> Contradictory class locations between the bourgeoisie and the
> proletariat can be defined as those positions which:
> (a) occupy a contradictory location within the social rela-
> tions of production, i.e., positions which involve a non-coinci-
> dence of relations of control over money capital, physical
> capital and labor power; or,
> (b) are linked directly to contradictory locations through
> families or class trajectories; or,
> (c) occupy a contradictory location within the political and
> ideological apparatuses, i.e., execute but do not create state
> policy, or disseminate but do not control the production of
> bourgeois ideology.

Generally, those people in contradictory class locations who
were more likely to support the *Times Leader* held positions
more closely approximating those of the classical bourgeoisie,
which Wright defines as

> those positions which:
> (a) occupy the bourgeois position within the social relations of
> production, i.e., positions of control over money capital, phys-
> ical capital and labor power; or,
> (b) are linked directly to the bourgeoisie through families or
> class trajectories; or
> (c) occupy bourgeois positions within the political and ide-
> ological apparatuses, i.e., positions which involve the control
> over the creation of state policy and the production of ide-
> ology" (1978:97).

Those whose occupations more closely approximated the
classical working-class position, that is, lacked control over
any form of capital, had family or class trajectories that linked
them directly to the working class, and were excluded from
"either the creation or execution of state policy and ideology"
(Wright: 1978:97), supported the *Citizens' Voice*. Of course,
this was the general pattern. As already seen, there were ex-

ceptions. For example, many people occupying the "bourgeois" position in the political apparatus, contrary to what one might expect, supported the *Citizens' Voice* rather than the *Times Leader.*

Although, as in the case of small businesses, I have no systematic data to indicate how many people from contradictory class locations or how many who occupied the bourgeois position in either the public or private sectors may have supported the *Times Leader,* or, equally important, why they might have done so, my general impression is that non-working-class support for the strikers came from men and women who had family or personal roots in the local working classes and hence identified with the county's trade union culture, served a working-class clientele, lived in largely working-class neighborhoods, and participated in various voluntary organizations and informal social networks that were largely working class or had a mixed class composition. If one or more of these factors was present, the non-working-class resident of the county was likely to have supported the *Citizens' Voice.* Such was the case with the county's teachers. The teachers' unions in the county were among the *Citizens' Voice*'s strongest supporters. Many of the local teachers had the same social origins as the strikers. They came from working-class or lower-middle-class families, had attended college in the county or had gone to school at a former state teachers' college, and had strong attachments to local social structures and local culture.

The exceptions to the general patterns of support did not always benefit the *Citizens' Voice.* Sometimes they worked in favor of the *Times Leader.* Parts of the county's working classes supported Capital Cities, at least in the sense that they did not cancel their subscriptions to the *Times Leader* and did not subscribe to the *Citizens' Voice.* The majority of such workers live in the rural and semirural townships outside of the old urbanized core. Workers in these areas responded differently than did their counterparts in other parts of the county for a variety of reasons. Some were skilled craft workers who once had lived in the urban core but, as part of their aspirations for mobility, had moved out to the suburbs and participated in different social networks and organizations than those to which they once had belonged. Others supported the *Times Leader* for political reasons, objecting to the *Citizens' Voice*'s identification with the Democrats. According to a striker who lived in one of these areas, one of the main reasons why his neighbors refused to subscribe to the *Citizens' Voice* was that they saw it as a "Democrat paper," and they were Republicans. A third factor explaining the lack of working-class support in these areas is historical. Few of these towns had been mining communities. As a result, few of their workers or their workers' ancestors had participated in creating or sustaining the great tradition of working-class solidarity, communal support, and collective responsibility built up by the mine workers and their successors. Indeed, a generation or two ago, many workers in these communities had been active opponents of the miners, especially immigrant mine workers. These towns and townships, along with a few in the urbanized area, reportedly had been centers of Ku Klux Klan strength in the 1920s and earlier had been centers of power for the Know Nothings. Workers living in the fringe areas have their own social networks and organizations that are only loosely connected, if at all, to those of workers in the urban core. They therefore stand outside of the formal and informal social control systems that helped shape and maintain support for the *Citizens' Voice.* Although workers living in the county's fringe areas have not been as responsive to the *Citizens' Voice*'s cause as have the rest of the working class, their loss has been more than outweighed, quantitatively and qualitatively, by the continuing support the strikers secured from a significant number of small businesses, as evidenced by the paper's early advertisements, and from parts of the middle classes.

In sum, through a judicious and selective application of material and symbolic incentives, especially collective moral incentives, the strikers were able to build and maintain overwhelming community support for their cause. It is not surprising that a moral appeal could prove to be an effective instrument for mobilizing and maintaining community commitment. A growing body of literature on social movements (see Wilson, 1973; Tillock and Morrison, 1979; Gamson and Fireman, 1979; Moe, 1980; Jenkins, 1983) shows that support networks can be constructed even in the relative absence of the material incentives Mancur Olson (1968) believes are essential to the success of social movements. Had the newspaper unions not presented their case as a moral one, they would not have been able to connect themselves to the ongoing community traditions of collective responsibility, mutual self-help, and solidarity. Therefore it is unlikely that they would have been successful in transforming the larger part of the community into an active and supportive agent working on their behalf because they had few material incentives to offer the general public to secure its commitment to their cause. For example, during the first months of the strike the *Citizens' Voice*, lacking access to wire service copy and syndicated features, could not provide its readers with adequate coverage of national and international news, sports coverage, or their favorite comic strips. The only news it covered well was on the local front.

But its supporters did not mind that the *Citizens' Voice* was relatively primitive in its early days or that its content was largely irrelevant to them. If content was all that mattered, people would have read the *Times Leader* or switched to another newspaper, such as the *Philadelphia Inquirer* or the *New York Times*, both of which were sold in the county. But people were interested in more than content. They bought the *Citizens' Voice*, in part, to make a personal statement about the strike and their relation to local history, culture, and society. To buy the *Citizens' Voice* was to affiliate with local traditions and society, to acknowledge that one stood on the side of the community and all that it held sacred. To buy the *Times Leader* was a sign that one rejected hallowed local traditions, values, beliefs, and social practices. The *Citizens' Voice*, then, was not merely a newspaper; it was an expression of and a symbol for the community. It was taken to embody the unity of local popular material and cultural interests that had been forged through the continuing struggle of the county's trade union movement against "outside" corporations that had little regard for the dignity of their workers and the intrinsic value of local life. As stated earlier, the strike was Luzerne County's "Solidarity." To resist it was to identify with alien forces, which people thought intended to overwhelm local society and culture and remake them in their image.

Neutralizing the Opposition

As the conflict between the newspaper unions and Capital Cities spilled over the "normal" institutionalized boundaries (Dahrendorf, 1959; Aronowitz, 1973) and became a strike, the county's business elite rallied to the *Times Leader*'s defense. The business elite's response represented a clear threat to the *Citizens' Voice*, for not only did this elite put pressure on local politicians to "enforce the laws" and end the street violence, but, more important, many of its members refused to place ads in the strikers' paper. The strike leaders knew that unless they were willing to enter into direct conflict with the local business elite they would not be able to survive. Without access to advertising dollars from that sector, the *Citizens' Voice* could not compete with the *Times Leader*, no matter what its circulation advantage.

Though displaced from direct control of the state at the time the strike took place, the business elite, a lineal descendant of the old patrician bourgeoisie that had ruled Luzerne County for most of its history, still was a formidable foe. It was composed of a number of families who could trace their upper-class ancestry back to the years shortly after the revolutionary war, descendants of families that had made their fortunes during the mining era, and successful ethnic entrepreneurs, whose family fortunes were of more recent vintage.

The business elite represented a broad range of local economic interests. It included manufacturers, wholesale and retail merchants, bankers, utility owners, lawyers, a smattering of other professionals, contractors, realtors, and other businessmen.

On an economic level, the business elite's unity was achieved and expressed in and through the city's three largest banks: Wyoming National, United Penn, and First Eastern. Over the years these banks had bought up or merged with weaker city and suburban banks to become the centers of county financial activity and power. Each bank organizes specific subsets of the county's largest and most socially prominent capitalists into a coherent fraction of local finance capital within the overall business elite. In turn, the various fractions achieve a more global economic unity through the multiple interlocks among the banks' stockholders and boards of directors. At the time of the strike, several of the wealthier families were represented on more than one bank board either by family members or top managers of their firms (Moody's, 1982).

In addition, the banks are partially organized into a more comprehensive unity through their directors' joint investments and board seats in other local companies. Especially important in this regard is Pennsylvania Enterprises, Inc., the local gas and water company (Moody's, 1982).

Pennsylvania Enterprises is a highly diversified company whose subsidiaries include the Pennsylvania Gas and Water Company, Pennsylvania Energy Resources, Inc., Penn Gas Company, Shavertown-Kingston Township Water Company, Hillcrest Water Company, Homesite Water Company, Pennsylvania Energy Resources, and Theta Land Corporation. The last two are service subsidiaries. They sell supplies, "manage" forests, sell forest products, develop real estate, and Theta holds coal and gas leases (Moody's, 1982:4550).

Pennsylvania Enterprises' investments and board of directors at the time the strike took place linked individuals, families, and businesses from all over northeastern Pennsylvania who were involved primarily in banking and real estate development. Its board includes not only representatives of Wilkes-Barre's financial capitalists but also those in Scranton and other cities in the region (Moody's, 1982). Although Pennsylvania Enterprises is an important institutional means for organizing the interests of urban capitalists from the two major cities in the region—Wilkes-Barre and Scranton—it is not the only means for doing so. The Economic Development Council of Northeastern Pennsylvania and the board of Northeastern National, a Scranton bank that operates in both counties, play similar roles.

Because of the economic assets the members of the business elite possess individually and collectively, they are able to exercise domination over other parts of their class and over county economic life in general. Their domination is exercised through the banks and a host of ancillary organizations directly or indirectly under their control. Among the more important of these are the Greater Wilkes-Barre Chamber of Commerce, the Wilkes-Barre Industrial Fund, and the Committee for Economic Growth, all of which organize as much local capital as possible under the hegemonic domination of the county business elite.

The business elite is economically as well as socially and culturally integrated, even though it no longer is the largely white, Anglo-Saxon, Protestant (WASP) patrician establishment it had been until shortly after the turn of the century. The social expansion of the county's business elite was slow in coming. The WASP groups tried to protect their social exclusivity as long as possible. Until late in the nineteenth century, they restricted membership in the four major elite institutions—the Westmoreland Club, the Wyoming Valley Country Club, the Wyoming Historical and Genealogical Society, and Lodge 61, F&AM—to their "own kind."

The Westmoreland Club was the first of these organizations to open itself to upwardly mobile achievers, including even Irish Catholics, in the 1880s and 1890s. In the well-appointed rooms of the Westmoreland Club, the arriviste could eat, drink, play cards, and discuss business on an almost equal basis with the patricians. When the latter tired of dealing with the newly wealthy, they could always escape to one of the other clubs that still was closed to those who lacked proper pedigrees.

Gradually, however, even those barriers began falling in the twentieth century, and wealth, rather than only background, became increasingly important in determining social membership in the local upper class. Whether this opening of upper-class institutions represented a more egalitarian spirit, a rational attempt to co-opt the newly rich, or some other factor is an open question. Nevertheless, more and more ethnics, including eastern and southern Europeans, Italians, and Jews, began acquiring memberships in the formerly exclusively WASP clubs. The Westmoreland Club reportedly "even had a Jewish president," as one member, who wanted to demonstrate the toleration of the upper class, said. As barriers to membership in these clubs fell, more formerly marginal families could make claims for public recognition and acceptance as respectable members of the local bourgeoisie.

In addition to the club system, the social unity of the local upper class is reinforced through common residence. Most members of the county business elite live in a handful of neighborhoods in the Back Mountain, a semirural suburban area located just west of the Wyoming Valley, separated from the valley by mountains. Living in these neighborhoods, the upper class seldom comes into informal, spontaneous social contact with the rest of the county's population, especially the urban core's working classes. They can drive in and out of Wilkes-Barre on an expressway that rises above the working-class neighborhoods, and should they care to glance to the left or right from their car windows they can easily look down on the people and houses in the Wyoming Valley.

The local upper class also has its own private elementary and secondary schools. For well over a century, Wyoming Seminary, a secondary preparatory school, has been a major training ground for the local upper class. Ten of the county's congressmen and countless businessmen and professionals received their early educations there. Attendance at Wyoming Seminary was the local equivalent of attendance at Phillips, Hotchkiss, Deerfield, and the like for the national upper class. It was a means for initiating a youngster to the behaviors, values, and practices of upper-class life and for early incorporation into upper-class social networks.

The newspaper unions were not surprised that the business elite and most of the county's upper class sprang to the defense of the *Times Leader*, if for no other reason than that the paper's former owners, several of whom were given jobs with Capital Cities, were part of the city's stratum of finance capitalists. But there were additional reasons why the business elite and the upper class supported the *Times Leader*. The business elite was involved in a struggle with local unions over wages, benefits, and work rules and with the local state over public expenditures and business taxes. The strike presented an opportunity to deliver a major setback not only to the newspaper unions but to the county's trade union movement in general and its allies in the Democratic party, making it easier to get concessions from the elite's own workers and from the local state. The business elite was convinced that if the newspaper unions won the strike their own workers' resolve, as well as that of public officials, to continue resisting concessionary demands would strengthen. In addition, the elite feared that control of the county's major newspaper by the trade unions and (by extension) the Democrats would be a serious setback to its efforts to redevelop the local economy. The business elite was "simply appalled," according to one member, by the "wanton" destruction of property during the strike, the "unwillingness" of the police to enforce the law "impartially," and the "cowardice" of local politicians in the face of union power. More than one city businessman thought it was "high time" someone taught the unions a "lesson" that there were "limits" to their power. As a result of such interests, beliefs, and sentiments, many members of the business elite refused to place advertisements in the *Citizens' Voice*, instead maintaining their accounts with the *Times Leader.* The one problem with this strategy was that it failed to take into account a critical variable—consumer response.

In mid-October 1978, the *Citizens' Voice* began applying pressure to businesses that refused to buy advertising space from it. The newspaper unions set up "informational" picket lines in front of a supermarket that was part of a locally owned chain and a car dealership. The *Citizens' Voice* covered the informational picket lines as if they involved a straight news story, explaining in detail that the pickets were trying to educate the public about these businesses' "unfair" advertising practices, defined as taking advertising space in the *Times Leader* but not in the *Citizens' Voice.* At the same time, the *Citizens' Voice* ran editorials and signed and unsigned letters to the editor vilifying the *Times Leader* and Capital Cities so as to whip up public indignation against the company and, by extension, its supporters.

The supermarket chain, finding that a large proportion of its customers would not cross the picket line, soon announced that it was changing its advertising policy. Henceforth, it intended to place ads in both the *Citizens' Voice* and the *Times Leader.* The newspaper unions were less successful with the car dealership. It would not accede to the *Citizens' Voice's* pressure. It was able to resist the *Citizens' Voice's* demands in part because of the nature of its product line. It sold expensive domestic and imported cars and had less worry about losing customers than if it sold cheaper imports and and domestic autos.

The *Citizens' Voice's* settlement with the supermarket chain became the model for agreements with a number of other local businesses. The picket lines, however, added to the hostility of some businessmen toward the strike. They believed that unions had "no right to dictate" their advertising policies. Even some of the strikers were not altogether pleased at having taken coercive action, which they feared would antagonize local businessmen.

Most local business resistance to advertising in the *Cit-*

izens' Voice crumbled after the strikers forced the city's largest locally owned department store, Fowler, Dick, and Walker, to agree to terms similar to those reached with the supermarket chain. Initially, the store's owners refused to purchase any advertising space in the *Citizens' Voice*, but after a brief suspension of its advertisements in the *Times Leader* it resumed its business with Capital Cities.

Reportedly, the day after the advertisement appeared "all hell broke loose," as one employee described the situation. The store began receiving hundreds of telephone calls complaining about its "unfair" advertising policy, and scores of people "stormed" the credit department to close out their accounts. Some customers were said to have walked in and torn up their credit cards; others mailed them back, explaining that they would not do business with the department store until it adopted a "fair advertising policy," as more than one customer put it.

Soon afterward, Fowler, Dick, and Walker agreed to purchase advertising space in the *Citizens' Voice* and the consumer pressure ended, even though the company was purchasing more space from the *Times Leader* than from the *Citizens' Voice* and continues to do so. One striker explained that even though the department store had more lines of advertising in the *Times Leader*, the *Citizens' Voice* did not mind because the department store supposedly was getting a heavy discount from Capital Cities but was paying full price for the *Citizens' Voice* space. According to the strikers, the only reason Capital Cities is getting any local advertising business is that the company is "practically giving its advertising space away," a charge the company denies.

Local businesses were not the only firms that experienced pressures. A city businessman told me that paint was thrown on the house of the local manager of a national retail chain after his company had placed an advertisement in the *Times Leader* and before it began advertising in the *Citizens' Voice*. A Capital Cities supporter in the city's business community claims that the *Citizens' Voice* received most of its early advertising business through intimidation. He said that a friend of his was told by an anonymous caller that his store windows would be broken unless he advertised in the strikers' paper. The unions deny that they ever used or threatened violence to get advertising business.

Although the support of consumers was critical to the *Citizens' Voice*, sometimes it could backfire. I was told that once a member of one of the city's trade unions went into a business and denounced the owner for advertising in a "scab paper." The owner, who also advertised in the *Citizens' Voice*, quickly called the paper to find out why he was being harassed because he had treated both papers equally "all along." The *Citizens' Voice* apologized to the businessman, as did the president of the union to which the complaining individual belonged.

Soon after Fowler, Dick, and Walker's capitulation, most major local businesses fell into line and signed advertising contracts with the *Citizens' Voice*. Today, only a handful of local companies and advertising agencies do not have advertising contracts with the *Citizens' Voice*. Among the largest of these is a regional department store chain that places ads with the *Citizens' Voice* during the Christmas holiday season but otherwise gives the strikers no business. But this case is rare; most businesses in the county now seem resigned to advertising in the *Citizens' Voice*. When I asked one businessman who initially had refused to put ads in the workers' paper why he had changed his mind, his response was simple: "I found out that it would bring in customers." And this now appears to be the dominant attitude in the business community. They may not like the *Citizens' Voice*, the values it represents, or its politics, but it does have a large circulation, and if businessmen want to reach its readers with their advertisements, they know that they have to accommodate themselves to the paper's presence.

Although responses of consumers helped the *Citizens' Voice* secure advertising contracts that it might not otherwise have gotten, consumer behavior did not help the strikers stop the flow of advertising dollars to the *Times Leader.* The *Times Leader* has continued to have advertising contracts with all the major businesses in the city. This continued support has helped the *Times Leader* control its losses, which undoubtedly would have been far greater had the *Citizens' Voice* been able to get enough support from consumers to force local businesses to stop advertising with Capital Cities.

Although the *Citizens' Voice* has been successful in forcing local businesses to support it with advertising, it has been far less successful in securing a reasonable share of national advertising. The *Citizens' Voice* receives far fewer national ads than it deserves based on its circulation figures. Conversely, because the *Times Leader* is part of a national chain, it receives far more national advertising than its alleged circulation figures suggest it should.

Its heavy national advertising business has helped Capital Cities to reduce its losses in Wilkes-Barre. These national ads are high-profit items. Advertisers pay top dollar for the space, and they send camera-ready copy. In addition, many of the ads include coupons for products, which are run in packages every Tuesday and have had a dramatic impact on the paper's sales for that day.

Advertising resistance was not the only expression of business support for Capital Cities. The owner of WLKY, a Wilkes-Barre radio station, editorialized on several occasions about the strike violence and the vandalism to company property. WBRE-TV, the city's only television station, hired the wife of a top local Capital Cities official for an on-the-air position. She was brought in to train for a co-anchor position on the 6:00 and 11:00 news program. Her hiring generated considerable controversy both inside and outside of the station. Other broadcast personnel resented being denied a chance to apply for the position, especially since the person hired had no previous broadcast experience. Many of the technical personnel and some of the off-camera editorial people were angered by the decision because they were *Citizens' Voice* sympathizers. After a period of training, it was decided that rather than giving her the co-anchor position, she would be given another on-the-air assignment as a general features reporter. In that position she has developed a considerable local reputation for the quality of her work. One of the reasons why it was eventually decided to find someone else for the co-anchor job was because of what some insiders at the station insist was systematic "sabotage" of her work by the technical people.

Hostility inside the station was matched by an adverse community reaction. A news executive employed at WBRE when the hiring occurred said that "getting involved" with Capital Cities had "definitely hurt our book at the time," meaning that it had hurt the station's ratings. He said the station had received numerous complaints from viewers and from several advertisers, who told the owner that if they began to experience problems because they were advertising on WBRE, they would have to switch their ads to one of the Scranton stations. Community reaction was directed not only at the station but at the woman hired. Some people refused to be interviewed by her. For example, a female union official turned down a request for an interview for a special series the reporter was doing. In other cases, people made rude remarks to her when she and her cameraman were filming at various locations around the city. Nevertheless, the owner stuck to his decision, and the woman stayed with the job and developed into one of the area's better special features broadcast journalists, despite the innumerable handicaps she had to face because of her husband's job.

The local business community further demonstrated its support for Capital Cities when it reportedly gave one of the company's officials a position on a Chamber of Commerce board. This angered local union officials, who accused the chamber of having taken sides in the strike. As a result, the union officer who served as an unofficial liaison between the county's unions and the chamber board reportedly ended his involvement with the chamber. Ironically, Capital Cities' editor and publisher held a seat on the chamber's board of directors at the time the *Citizens' Voice* joined the chamber.

In sum, because of local community support, the strikers have been able to secure both subscribers and advertisers. The *Citizens' Voice*'s demonstrable support among the community grass roots has convinced most actual and potential opponents of the strike that the best way to remain at peace with local society is to do business with the *Citizens' Voice,* while avoiding the appearance of being too intimately connected with the *Times Leader.* To do otherwise would be to risk massive, collective retribution. Although some businesses and organizations have managed to take all of the punishment the *Citizens' Voice* and its supporters can give and still remain economically viable, most have chosen to avoid such risks. They have preferred to set aside their objections to the strikers' paper and do business with it rather than face its wrath and that of its community supporters or lose contact with its readers.

Social movement theory and research provide a way for understanding why the community responded as rapidly as it did to the strikers' call for help. Charles Tilly (1978) and J. Craig Jenkins (1983) indicate that a population's "mobilization potential" (Jenkins, 1983:538) is influenced by its preexisting solidarity and collective identity. Other things being equal, a population with a large number of solidarity groups and a strong sense of collective identity has a higher degree of mobilization potential that does a population in which solidarity groups are weak or few in number and the sense of collective identity is weakly developed.

The *Citizens' Voice* has drawn its greatest support in Luzerne County's densely populated urban core—the Wyoming Valley and the towns just north and south of it. This is the former mining region. It is an area where there are vital multiple and overlapping solidarity groups based in families, neighborhoods and towns, civic and fraternal associations, churches and parish organizations, ethnic associations, trade unions, and informal social networks, including those centered on local taverns. These organizations and social networks were formed and shaped in interaction with the coal industry. They came to life as defensive institutions and have had a long history of mobilization on behalf of labor's cause, allowing the mine workers, as well as other labor organizations, to rely on communitywide collective action as a mainstay in their repertoire of contention with employers and their allies.

Unlike other cities where once vital traditions of community-based collective action on behalf of labor have virtually collapsed (see Cumbler, 1979), in Luzerne County community traditions of collective action, mutual self-help, solidarity, and communal responsibility and the capacity and will to act collectively have survived the demise of the original circumstances (the nature of anthracite mining and the workers' various responses to the industry) that brought them into being. The traditions, capacities, and will to act collectively have survived, first, because by the time the United Mine Workers disappeared these qualities already had become institutionalized in other organizations, especially other trade unions. They became part of the ongoing trade union culture of the region. Second, there was a continuing need for solidarity, even if only on the level of the extended family, as a means of self-defense and survival in a chronically depressed economy characterized by pandemic unemployment and underemployment. Third, local institutions and the culture of cooperation were revitalized, strengthened, and extended by the flood of 1972 (Wolensky, 1984), when old social structures were needed and a large number of new organizations were created to cope with the disaster. Fourth, the traditions of collective action have survived because they have been incorporated into people's interpretive, moral horizon. Engaging in collective action to protect oneself and to help others is a moral imperative that defines what is expected of a person as a member of the community. To act otherwise is to place oneself outside and against the community and to expose oneself to its rancor.

Because of the long common history shared by the various individuals, groups, and organizations in the former mining zone, these people have developed a strong collective consciousness and identity. They seem to see themselves as a distinct, unique people bound together by history, by shared contemporary circumstances and experiences, and by common future prospects and possibilities. This collective consciousness and identity transcend the particularities of religion, ethnicity, status, and, sometimes, class.

Their collective identity translates into and expresses itself in a strong sense of local patriotism, if not chauvinism, which the *Citizens' Voice* repeatedly called on in framing its attacks on Capital Cities. The company was depicted as the alien, outside intruder bent on destroying local culture. At the same time, the *Citizens' Voice* portrayed itself as a paper "100% produced by Valley Residents," as one of its early billboards read.

The portrayal of Capital Cities as an enemy of local culture supplied the strikers with the collective grievance around which they could rally the community grass roots and helped transform the strike from an economic dispute between two parties into a communitywide moral crusade. Capital Cities has never fully understood or appreciated that the strike quickly became a contest between two visions of how an enterprise ought to operate: one grounded in notions of "moral economy" (Hobsbawm, 1984) that, in classical sociological terms, was based on a logic of "value rationality" and the other the company's desire to organize its operations according to principles of "purposive rationality" (Weber, 1947), in which profit requirements were paramount in determining organizational structure and operations.

This lack of understanding is best illustrated in the company's response to the newspaper unions' claim that they were striking over the issue of "human dignity." Richard Connor, who at the time was editor and publisher of the *Times Leader,* was quoted as having said: "I don't know what human dignity is. . . . If you find out let me know. All we want is to be able to manage a paper without restrictive union policies and absurd contract language" (Woodmansee, 1978:28).

But though Connor might not have understood what the strikers meant by "human dignity," their supporters in the community knew that it meant that a business had no right to put profit ahead of all other considerations, especially what popular opinion regarded as its fundamental obligations to its workers, which included their rights to organize unions, to bargain collectively, to maintain and defend what they had won at the bargaining table, and to be secure in their jobs. To the local community such values had precedence over, or, at the very least, equal standing with, a company's decisions about appropriate levels of return, and all companies had the obligation to consider them when setting their profit targets. For a business to argue, as Capital Cities allegedly did, that such worker rights and values either had no place in determining profit levels or were subordinate to a company's right to manage its property so as to get the levels of profit it deemed reasonable flew in the face of the principles of the region's moral economy and was perceived as a threat to all of the region's workers and reason enough for many to oppose the *Times Leader.*

Confronting a community with a high potential for mobilization, grounded in preexisting solidarities and collective identity, demonstrating a capacity to act collectively, and having supplied the community grass roots with a collective grievance that was connected to both its material and moral interests, the strikers were able to engage in "bloc recruitment" (Oberschall, 1973:125), which some theorists (Jenkins, 1983:538; Snow, Zurcher, and Eckland-Olson, 1980) see as the most efficient means of mobilizing support. Groups, organizations, neighborhoods, towns, trade unions, and associational networks went over en masse to the strikers' side, with very little need for extensive, individually tailored organizing work on the part of the newspaper unions. Had the strikers been forced to engage in individualized organizing work, it probably would not have affected the ultimate extent of their support, but it certainly would have slowed down their mobilization efforts, and it would have given Capital Cities and its supporters more time to develop strategies to counteract their efforts. As it was, people moved so quickly that Capital Cities and its community supporters were continually kept off balance and always were in a reactive rather than proactive position. This was especially the case with the carriers.

In the early phases of the strike, contrary to what might be predicted from Olson's (1968) theory, the strikers were able to mobilize significant support, even though they controlled few selective material incentives. As in several other cases (Wilson, 1973; Gamson and Fireman, 1979; Moe, 1980), the newspaper unions were able to gain support by relying on "collective incentives of group solidarity and commitment to moral purpose," the phrase Jenkins (1983:537) uses to summarize the results of the studies cited above.

Had large numbers of the county's grass roots not possessed preexisting solidarities and a common moral purpose, the strikers would not have been able to achieve what they did. It was only after they had secured overwhelming public support that they could use community commitment to their cause to generate material incentives to maintain the backing of key actors and groups and to neutralize the opposition of others.

With community support, the *Citizens' Voice* was able to offer a number of selective material incentives to maintain the commitment of its affinity groups. For example, the newspaper carriers received raises, and they have far larger routes than they would have had if they had stayed with the *Times Leader,* assuming that the strike had been as successful as it was if the carriers had stayed with Capital Cities.

Local politicians who have supported the *Citizens' Voice* invariably have received favorable press coverage from the strikers' paper. The only exceptions have been politicians who have gotten in serious trouble with the law, and even then it is not always certain that the *Citizens' Voice* will abandon them. The paper stood by the region's long-term congressman, Daniel J. Flood, throughout his federal trial and continued to give him favorable publicity even after he resigned from office and pleaded guilty to charges that, as one local political wag

put it, "amounted to parking his bicycle crooked." By sticking
with Flood beyond a point at which they had repaid their
debts to him, the strikers showed other politicians and the
community that they were not about to abandon their friends
and supporters, no matter how much trouble they had.

The county's unions got everything they could have hoped
for from the strike and more. The *Citizens' Voice* has proven
itself to be an articulate and adamant defender and promoter
of labor's cause. Periodically it runs prounion articles and editorials, and it has endorsed every strike in the region, even
when doing so has created problems with its other constituencies. For example, the *Citizens' Voice* lost considerable support among Catholic clergy in the county when it backed a
teachers' strike at Wilkes-Barre's Catholic high school and,
later, when it supported a strike against the city's Catholic
hospital. The *Citizens' Voice* also has alienated some local
politicians by the unequivocal support it has given to strikes
by public school teachers.

The community grass roots never became organized into a
formally constituted social movement organization that
worked on behalf of the *Citizens' Voice,* so the paper could
offer its rank-and-file supporters no direct material benefits
for helping its cause, other than to supply them with the com-
munity-oriented news they preferred. The grass roots' major
reward was the opportunity to participate in an ongoing movement that both defended and glorified its history, culture, and
social practices. But seemingly, that has been reward enough.
Capital Cities has been unable to make many inroads into the
Citizens' Voice's base of support in Wilkes-Barre, the Wyoming Valley, and the other former mining towns in the county.

Capital Cities has struggled to have its fight with the *Citizens' Voice* defined purely as *market competition* between
two newspapers. Despite the substantial improvements the
company has made in the *Times Leader*'s graphics, the introduction of new features, more extensive coverage of state and
national news, daily columns by local reporters, the introduction of a community news section, and general improvements

in editing and reporting, all of which have made the *Times Leader* a far better paper than it once was and a paper that in many respects is technically superior to the *Citizens' Voice*, the latter's circulation has been maintained. The *Times Leader*'s circulation gains evidently have been achieved by expanding into new markets and by increasing its vending machine and newsstand sales, especially on Tuesdays, when it loads the paper with coupons.

Capital Cities also has tried to improve its public image. It sponsors charity events, encourages its employees to become active in public affairs, and once sponsored a job fair for unemployed workers in the county to show that it is a "good corporate citizen" of the community and not the moral leper that local unions contend it is. For the *Citizens' Voice*'s supporters, these efforts have proven to be too little, too late. They have not helped the *Times Leader* improve its reputation in the eyes of its opponents. As long as the *Citizens' Voice* continues to exist, Capital Cities has little chance of ever recovering those lost subscribers.

According to some of its journalists, the *Times Leader*, in order to survive, has introduced a variety of cost-cutting measures. It allegedly reduced the amount of the paper devoted to news rather than advertising, gave journalists compensatory time rather than overtime pay, cut back on various supplies, kept positions vacant to save money while passing the additional work on to others, and the like. These actions, according to at least two journalists with whom I spoke at the paper, led to increasing morale problems.

Even though Capital Cities, by its own admission, lost at least $20 million in Wilkes-Barre during the strike's first two years and reportedly has had continuing losses of approximately $2 million a year since that time, the company still does not think it is time to cut its losses and abandon the Wilkes-Barre market. Thomas Murphy reportedly once told his Wilkes-Barre employees that he would be willing to sell any of the company's properties if the price was right *except* the *Times Leader*. Murphy also is alleged to have once responded to the question of why he was determined to stay in Wilkes-Barre, in the face of all that had happened there, by saying that one should never anger an Irishman who has money, suggesting that continuing to publish the *Times Leader* had become a matter of personal pride to him and the company rather than a question of profits and losses.

The strikers were able to secure mass popular support and to use it to accomplish what they have because Wilkes-Barre, the Wyoming Valley, and the other towns in the mining zone were prepared structurally and ideologically, both by history and present circumstances, to respond to the newspaper unions' moral appeal for help. An extremely high "mobilization potential" (Tilly, 1978; Jenkins, 1983) alone, however, does not explain the genesis of the popular movement and its continued commitment to the *Citizens' Voice.* One also has to consider Capital Cities' behavior. The company followed a model of struggle with its Wilkes-Barre unions that had worked well in other settings. In Pontiac, it brought in guards and used a fence in anticipation of a strike and possible violence. The pressmen and the Newspaper Guild struck, and there was sporadic violence, but Capital Cities easily prevailed. It hired replacements, continued publishing, and decertified the unions. Eventually the strikers drifted away, never to be heard from again.

In Wilkes-Barre the outcome was different. Capital Cities' "repertoire of contention" (Tilly, 1979) was ill-suited for the region. People in Wilkes-Barre had seen such forms of contention before, and they responded as they believed appropriate. They used mass collective action to defend the unions and punish Capital Cities, the same response that once was used against the coal companies. In the process, the community's grass roots helped inflict enough damage on the company to keep it from making the *Times Leader* a profitable operation, reducing the value of the property, should Capital Cities ever decide to sell it, to almost zero.

The final factor explaining the community response and its success was the local newspaper unions. They were well organized; had high levels of internal solidarity; had an adequate flow of resources from the national office of the Newspaper Guild and the International Printing and Graphics Communications Union (the merged pressmen's and stereotypers' union); knew how to frame an appeal for support and how to use Capital Cities' behavior to discredit the company in the community's eyes; and had extensive organic connections with a broad range of local organizations and social networks, so that once the community moved to their side they could work directly with various organizations and groups, especially their affinity groups, to maintain commitment to their cause. If Tilly (1978) is correct, the most important of these connections were those with the local state. Well ensconced within local political structures and processes, the newspaper unions were able to organize the community and act against Capital Cities with virtual impunity, a luxury few social movements have, except during times of severe political crises, when state structures either are on the verge of collapsing or already have collapsed (Skocpol, 1979).

Had it not been for all these factors operating in conjunction, the newspaper unions would have been easily defeated by resource-rich Capital Cities. Instead, the unions have been able to carry on one of the longest and most successful strike newspaper operations in the industry's history, and they appear willing and able to continue doing so for the indefinite future.

6

Conclusion

_____

The Wilkes-Barre Strike and the Newspaper Industry

The 1970s were turbulent times for the newspaper industry. Daily newspapers experienced escalating production and distribution costs, stagnant or declining sales, and intensified competition for advertising dollars. Seeing no immediate end to their problems, many owners of smaller independent papers began withdrawing capital from the industry. As often happens in a sector plunging into crisis, circumstances producing losses for some create profit opportunities for others (Braudel, 1984). In the newspaper industry, those who profited were the giant communications conglomerates, which rapidly gobbled up at record-breaking prices all papers that came on the market. As prices soared, more independent owners were encouraged to put their papers up for sale. The end result has been increased consolidation and concentration in an industry that heretofore, at least in the United States, had been highly decentralized and owner-managed (Bagdikian, 1983).

One reason why the media conglomerates were interested in buying as many properties as possible was the tax code. In addition to the normal tax benefits from an acquisition, provisions of the tax code allowed media companies to escape some of their tax obligation by setting aside money for the express purpose of buying additional properties (Bagdikian, 1983).

But potential and actual tax gains do not completely explain the conglomerates' behavior. They made their moves because they also recognized that most newspapers could be made into extremely profitable ventures if labor costs were reduced and productivity increased. Such goals were within easy reach of publishers who could afford to install modern equipment and who had the strength and will either to subordinate or sweep aside the unions and impose new labor processes. When Capital Cities bought the Wilkes-Barre Publishing Company, half of the job had already been done. The paper had the most modern technical systems. The only obstacles to enhanced profitability were the union contracts and informal craft work practices.

Capital Cities arrived in Wilkes-Barre confident that it could subordinate and, should it prove necessary, eliminate the unions. After all, publishers had unions on the run from one end of the country to another. Workers daring to resist publishers' demands for wage and benefit concessions, work rule modifications, and changes in staffing patterns were being defeated and in some cases annihilated. And Capital Cities had just proven its mettle against the Newspaper Guild and pressmen in Pontiac, a union city, and had subordinated the printers in Fort Worth.

But the tactics that had proven successful in other places did not work in Wilkes-Barre. Capital Cities seriously underestimated the local unions' resolve and their capacity for resistance. In addition, it made a serious miscalculation about the community's response.

In Wilkes-Barre the newspaper unions were able to mount a successful resistance in the face of overwhelming odds. Whereas in most other cities newspaper interunion solidarity had been difficult to achieve and maintain (Raskin, 1982), in Wilkes-Barre the newspaper unions managed to build and maintain a united front. That the Wilkes-Barre newspaper unions behaved differently from those in other cities is partly a function of the social milieu within which these unions had been formed and continued to function. As already shown, pan-worker solidarity has been part of the area's trade union culture since the days of the Miners' and Laborers' Benevolent Association, the Knights of Labor, and the United Mine Workers. But the general labor history of the area is only one factor that explains the solidarity of the newspaper unions. These unions had their own long history of cooperation. Over the years, they supported each other even when it was not in their short-term economic interest to do so. Because of their traditions of mutual support and trust, the Wilkes-Barre newspaper unions built cooperative relationships seldom seen at other U.S. newspapers. And it was precisely such mutual trust that enabled the unions to agree to coordinate their bargaining so that no one union would sign a contract until all had reached agreements with the company.

Interunion cooperation was helped along by Capital Cities. The company took a hard line with all of the unions. Had the company adopted a divide-and-conquer strategy by signing some of the contracts without demanding major concessions, the alliance between the newspaper unions might have been severely tested. But Capital Cities chose not to do this. It took a high-risk gamble, only to find that, as a prominent city journalist connected neither to the *Times Leader* nor the *Citizens' Voice* observed: "You can't run a nonunion newspaper in this city. Maybe in another generation it would be possible, but not now. Unions are just too strong and people believe in them too much to let that happen."

One would assume that newspaper locals in other cities and the industry's internationals would have learned a valuable lesson about the need for interunion cooperation and solidarity from the experience of the Wilkes-Barre locals. But evidently they have not. Newspaper unions in other cities and the internationals show no more sign of being able to unite now, even in the short run, than they did before 1978. Persisting local and national divisions, conflicts, often petty jurisdictional rivalries, and outright betrayals of one union by another have weakened the unions' collective capacities to defend their contracts at the very moment when publishers are being strengthened through consolidation of the industry under the control of giant conglomerates. The guild's proposal to merge with the ITU never materialized, and a proposed merger between the ITU and the teamsters was defeated by the ITU rank and file in a bitterly contested referendum. In part, the referendum lost because teamster drivers were crossing picket lines to pick up and deliver papers during a major strike by other newspaper unions.

Just as the internationals and other locals have failed to reproduce the solidarity of the Wilkes-Barre strikers, they have failed to reproduce their militance. Of course, Wilkes-Barre has a unique historical and sociopolitical character, and newspaper unions in other cities lacking that character cannot be expected to reproduce the interunion cooperation and the militance exhibited by the Wilkes-Barre newspaper locals.

The lack of militance in other cities should be no more surprising than the inability of the industry's unions to achieve the same unity of purpose, strategy, and tactics found in Wilkes-Barre. It has been a long time since the ITU has had to engage in militant resistance (Wallace and Kalleburg, 1982). It occupied such a critical role in the production process that publishers acceded to most of its contract demands to buy labor peace. But at the same time, the publishers were financing research and development projects that eventually would decimate the union, so that it has come to be in danger of losing its independent existence.

Similarly, on a national level the guild has been beset by a host of problems. In 1982, it had only 206 contracts, 12 fewer than in 1972. Of the more than 200,000 workers eligible for guild membership, the union represented approximately 31,500. Outside of the top papers, the guild has been unable to negotiate contracts in which the top minimum wage equaled what the Federal Bureau of Labor Statistics projected to be needed to provide a family with a "modest, but adequate standard of living" in 1982 (Raskin, 1982).

In addition, the guild has been losing membership through newspaper closings, consolidations, and decertification elections. As if its problems with publishers were not enough, the guild also is being pressured by other unions that have begun organizing newspaper workers (Raskin, 1982). That these unions could succeed where the guild never made inroads further attests to the guild's weakened state.

Wilkes-Barre's Local 120 has maintained its strength, despite the decline of the international, for a variety of reasons. First, Local 120 has benefited from the sociopolitical context in which it was formed. Local 120 both was produced by and helped produce the region's trade union culture. Throughout its history it has held a leading role in the county's trade union movement. It has been among the most politically astute and active of the county's unions.

Ever since the Wilkes-Barre Newspaper Guild was formed in the 1930s, it has sided with those forces within the international that wanted to see the guild become a "real" trade union, rather than a professional association. It has been able to maintain this orientation, which is one of the foundations for its strength, because of the social context in which it operated, the personal and biographical characteristics of its membership, and its contracts, which prevented the company from hiring journalists who might have different beliefs about what a union of journalists should be or even whether such an organization ought to exist. The social context set the immediate tone for the fledgling Wilkes-Barre Newspaper Guild. According to all accounts, its first members were totally committed to trade unionism as a social movement and a way of life. This is not surprising given the close organizational relationships, through the CIO, that the local Newspaper Guild and its members had with the county's United Mine Workers.

Many of the journalists came from, and continue to come from, working-class or lower-middle-class families, and they had extensive personal contacts with trade unionism as a culture and a social practice even before they took their jobs with the Wilkes-Barre Publishing Company. Few of the journalists had any formal education beyond high school when they began their careers at the publishing company, and few have any ambition to be upwardly mobile on journalism's national job market. They are totally tied to the local job market. And they believe that whatever rewards come their way will be obtained through the union, rather than through personal mobility. Finally, because of the social context and the journalists' personal experiences, Wilkes-Barre's guild reporters and editors see no incompatibility between their status as white-collar workers and membership in a militant trade union. In Wilkes-Barre no white-collar worker who belongs to a union is likely to suffer loss of status because of that membership. Nor is a white-collar worker who strikes likely to find his or her status compromised. There have been a large number of teachers' strikes over the past dozen or so years, and there has been one major hospital strike, which included the nursing staff.

The guild's contract with the Wilkes-Barre Publishing Company guaranteed that this social type would be reproduced on the paper from one generation to the next and would not be displaced as retirements led to new hirings. The desire to create and control mobility opportunities for its own members is only part of the reason behind the contract provisions restricting the publisher's hiring and promotion rights. In part, the guild also wanted prohibitions against the employment of "outsiders," that is, people who received their jobs without coming up through the ranks of the paper's apprenticeship system but, rather, received appointments because of educational background or experience obtained elsewhere, so as to protect their brand of trade unionism at the paper. Based on their experiences in the political life of the international, Local 120's leaders saw the typical college-educated journalist as a possible threat to unionism as practiced at the Wilkes-Barre Publishing Company. They recognized that if the college-trained journalist supported unionism, he or she was likely to prefer an organization more akin to the American Federation of Television and Radio Artists (AFTRA) or the Screen Actors' Guild than a trade union. Although these unions negotiate contracts for their members, the contracts typically only set minimal wages, salaries, benefits, and working conditions. Individual members are free to negotiate personal contracts that exceed the standards specified in the union contracts. Under such conditions, it is difficult to build, let alone maintain, member discipline, collective commitment, solidarity, and militance.

The Wilkes-Barre guild also has managed to maintain its militance, solidarity, and strength because of the high quality of its local leadership. Some of its officers and members have gone on to important positions, including the presidency, in the international. This has assured the local of a continuing flow of resources from the international whenever necessary.

The local guild leaders also have been successful in maintaining rank-and-file support because time and again they have proven their mettle in battles not only with their employer but also with recalcitrant members and with factions inside of the international who have different philosophies about the purpose of the Newspaper Guild. The local's leaders seldom hesitate in taking disciplinary action against those they believe threaten the union's cause, no matter how seemingly slight the infraction might appear to be. For example, it imposed a heavy fine on a *Sunday Independent* reporter who filed a story on a professional sports event that he attended in New York on his day off. The *Sunday Independent* published the story with the reporter's authorization, but it did not pay the reporter for a day's work. To the union, the reporter had knowingly committed a flagrant violation: he had given away his work without charge and thus had to be punished. Capital Cities likes to cite this incident as an example of the Wilkes-Barre Guild's willingness to "violate" individual rights to serve its own ends; union members see it as a reasonable action taken in defense of principle: no one works without compensation.

Local 120 is no stranger to the International Newspaper Guild's internal political conflicts. The Wilkes-Barre guild's militance and success have enabled it to become a leading spokesman within the international not only for those who want to continue the union's trade union orientation but also for guild locals at small and midsize papers across the United States. Often this stance has brought the local into conflict with "professionalizers" and representatives of locals at larger metropolitan dailies.

Finally, Local 120 has maintained its militant orientation because the philosophy worked: before the strike, guild members were well paid, had good working conditions and fringe benefits, and, for all intents and purposes, were guaranteed jobs for life. In an economy such as Luzerne County's, what more could one ask from a job?

The unions representing pressmen and stereotypers merged at the national level in 1973 to form the International Printing and Graphics Communications Union. The national merger came about not so much because of the impact of technology on pressmen as because of its effect on stereotypers. Photocomposition and offset printing had all but eliminated the need for stereotypers as an independent craft in the newspaper industry. At the Wilkes-Barre Publishing Company, the stereotyper craft designation had been preserved and workers continued to be employed as stereotypers, even though they no longer performed most of the tasks historically associated with this craft's role in newspaper production.

But even though technological changes have not been as extensive or as detrimental for pressmen as for printers and stereotypers, publishers still have tried to take advantage of the new technologies to get concessions from the union. The pressmen responded by striking, and met several serious defeats before the Wilkes-Barre strike, the biggest of which was at the *Washington Post* in 1975. Capital Cities defeated the pressmen in the 1977 Pontiac strike. The pressmen suffered a partial defeat in New York in August 1978, when they had to accept reductions in the pressroom work force, reductions in overtime, and changes in the staffing provisions of their contract (Zimbalist, 1979).

Although new presses reduce the number of workers needed and have lessened the skill requirements for the job (see Zimbalist, 1979:116), pressroom jobs are still available, even though several cities have had to close their union rolls to outsiders. In the Wilkes-Barre area, at the time of the strike there were, and continue to be, both union and nonunion jobs available for pressmen in book, magazine, and other publishing operations.

The integration of pressmen and stereotypers had not been completely accomplished in Wilkes-Barre by the time the strike began in 1978. Divisions between the two groups obstructed complete integration. Each has its own local, and pressmen and stereotypers have separate representation on the Unity Council. In part, these divisions contributed to the union's delay in signing its last contract with the former owners, so that when Capital Cities purchased the company, stereotypers and pressmen were working under contract extensions.

The pressmen estimate that the strike against Capital Cities cost each of them more than $2,000 in lost back wages. It had been customary at the pre–Capital Cities *Times Leader* for unions to agree to work under a contract extension while negotiations continued. Once an agreement was reached, workers would be paid a lump sum to make up the difference between what they would have been getting had the new contract gone into effect immediately after the old one expired. The publishers did not mind doing this because they could invest the money that would have been paid out in wages and make a tidy profit during the protracted negotiations.

As a result of events in other cities, the Wilkes-Barre pressmen knew they would have a hard time negotiating with Capital Cities, and they were prepared for the worst. The pressmen in Wilkes-Barre were not about to agree to any concessions. They were willing to strike to defend their contract. And even if they should get the contract they wanted, they were willing to strike, or to stay out of work, to help defend the contracts of the other unions. The guild and the ITU knew that even though the pressmen seldom initiated labor actions at the Wilkes-Barre Publishing Company, their union was sufficiently committed to the principles and practices of union solidarity and sufficiently militant that it would not sell out the other unions and continue working while others were on strike. The guild and ITU were confident of the pressmen because all groups came from the same trade union culture and because in the past the pressmen and stereotypers had always honored picket lines.

The Wilkes-Barre strike showed the industry's internationals that militant action and pan-union solidarity can work to inflict heavy financial losses on a publisher, but it also clearly demonstrated that labor's traditional weapon, the strike, is no longer effective in counteracting employers' aggression in the newspaper industry. There are a number of reasons for this loss of effectiveness. First, because of the new production technologies employers no longer need to depend on skilled labor. Thus a walkout by skilled workers no longer forces a paper to stop publishing. Newspapers can continue to be produced by supervisors and replacements, as Capital Cities showed in Wilkes-Barre. Second, strikes have become less effective because of changes in the nature of ownership in the industry. Strikes have far less impact on a conglomerate than they do on an individual or family capitalist. Few individual publishers could afford to absorb the continuing losses the unions have inflicted on the *Times Leader.* An individual capitalist would have either gone bankrupt or sued for peace. Capital Cities has not had to do either.

The roughly $30 million it has lost has had no visible effect on the company. Since the strike began, Capital Cities' other operations have continued to make handsome profits, the price of the company's stock has continued rising, and the company has continued purchasing new properties to add to its empire, including the American Broadcasting Company. This expansion has been possible, despite the strike in Wilkes-Barre, because of the growing mismatch between the organizational structure of unions in the newspaper industry and the industry's newly emerging structures of ownership.

Newspaper unions developed during a time when the industry was dominated by independent, local capitalists, and they were designed for the express purpose of counterbalancing owners' power on a case-by-case basis. There was no need to have national collective bargaining agreements with various chains, such as the UAW has with the various automobile companies, or industrywide agreements between unions and a large number of small producers, such as the United Mine Workers and the teamsters have with the bituminous coal operators and with trucking firms. Newspaper unions thus have no effective power to check the operation of a conglomerate's other profit centers when a local is on strike. These other centers continue operating. Nor do local unions have much power to stop national corporations from advertising in chains' struck papers. Because Capital Cities was able to bring its losses at the *Times Leader* under control and to succeed financially in its other operations, it has been able to continue operating in Wilkes-Barre, much to the frustration and puzzlement of the newspaper unions.

The Wilkes-Barre locals have not been the only ones to experience such frustration. Across the country newspapers are publishing while one or more of their unions are on strike. This has been the case in Pontiac, Michigan, Madison, Wisconsin, Washington, D.C., and Chicago, to name but a few instances. Publishers have been able to continue operations because the unions no longer have a monopoly over a scarce commodity—skilled labor. Publishers can simply transfer workers from their other operations or they can turn to Southern Production Program, Inc., headquartered in Oklahoma City, which provides "emergency" training to strikebreakers. It is funded by publishers throughout the country (Zimbalist, 1979). I could not determine whether Capital Cities is a member of the organization or whether it sent any of its people there in preparation for the Wilkes-Barre strike. But it probably did not have to avail itself of such a program because it could bring into Wilkes-Barre nonunion workers from its other operations. Before the strike, Capital Cities rotated employees into

Wilkes-Barre to familiarize them with the paper's equipment. They were taught how to operate it on weekends by local workers, several of whom stayed with the company once the strike began.

Because of the current situation, publishers suspend operations during a strike less for reasons of necessity than habit, a sense of propriety, or some other reason such as public pressure. The one union that still seems able to stop production is the teamsters. If they refuse to pick up and deliver the papers, a publisher has little recourse except to try to contract with a nonunion trucking firm that is willing to risk the teamsters' wrath. The Wilkes-Barre Publishing Company employed no truck drivers. It contracted for this service.

Until newspaper unions develop new organizational forms and new forms of conflict, they will continue to be at the mercy of corporate publishers who follow a strategy of fighting their unions ad seriatim in the hope that eventually the unions either will be pacified or eradicated from the chain. As of yet, there is no sign that the internationals have learned how to cope with the new corporate employers, other than to reach an accommodation at any cost. For the unions to develop new strategies to address the imbalance of power between local unions and corporate employers would require a rethinking of their organizational structure and the form of their bargaining process and agreements and also greater efforts at organizing nonunion workers. Any new organizing efforts must avoid the fratricidal competition, conflict, and raiding now taking place among the various unions active in trying to organize newspaper workers (Raskin, 1982). Until the newspaper unions can overcome these obstacles, it is unlikely that they will achieve decisive victories in struggles with the media conglomerates. The best that can be hoped for is a standoff such as happened in Wilkes-Barre.

With a little imagination and a bit more courage, however, the international newspaper unions might have been able to help prevent such a stalemate. It would have been interesting to see how Capital Cities, or any other conglomerate, would respond to a mixture of local and national pressure. The internationals and the AFL-CIO could have implemented a program of disinvestment from companies owning shares in or doing business with Capital Cities. Although there are legal limitations on certain disinvestment strategies, the unions might have been able to demonstrate that their disinvestment was not for political reasons, which is subject to legal challenge, but for the financial health of their portfolios, on grounds that Capital Cities' labor policy was costing the company money and could have a negative effect on the value of its stock and the stock of institutions associated with it. Even if disinvestment raised legal problems, however, the unions might still have been able to direct new deposits and investments away from companies that held Capital Cities' shares. Unions have hundreds of millions of dollars in bank accounts, pension funds, insurance purchases and investments, and the like that they could have tried to use to squeeze Capital Cities (or any other company refusing to deal with its own unions) until it was willing to reach an accommodation with the Wilkes-Barre unions. Like any conglomerate, Capital Cities' economic health depends on its access to capital, without which it cannot make investments that result in growing profits. And without the ability to achieve higher rates of profit than other enterprises with which it competes for capital it would lose its relative and even, perhaps, its absolute attractiveness as an investment. Faced with such difficulties, the company *might* have decided to try to negotiate contracts that the unions found more reasonable or, failing that, to abandon the Wilkes-Barre market altogether, leaving it to the *Citizens' Voice* or to some other company that was willing to negotiate an agreement with the unions.

There is a good deal of debate in trade union circles about the wisdom and effectiveness of strategies that put direct financial pressures on corporate investors. Union leaders have not always been enthusiastic supporters of such actions, as can be seen in the failure of many to support the grass-roots campaign in western Pennsylvania to block corporate disinvestment in and around the Monongahela River valley and in the more recent strike against the Hormel meatpacking company by a Minnesota local. Some opponents of the so-called "corporate strategy," which places pressures on investors, claim that it is far too radical and, therefore, is counterproductive; others claim that it is too politically and economically risky. Those who support such a strategy, on the other hand, dismiss the charge of radicalism and argue that such a strategy is the only effective way to complement a strike when one is dealing with diversified corporate employers, who can move production from place to place so as to avoid serious disruptions from a strike or who can choose either to suspend production so as to outlast the unions or to go on producing without them.

All of this, of course, is idle speculation. The international newspaper unions and the AFL-CIO unions did not take concerted action against Capital Cities' investors, nor have they taken such action in subsequent strikes in the newspaper industry. Because they are wedded to a traditional repertoire of contention, the unions have given Capital Cities enough leeway so that it can continue operating in Wilkes-Barre as long as it chooses to do so, for the local unions can inflict no more damage on the company than they already have.

The Wilkes-Barre strike would have been an ideal occasion for testing the effectiveness of a national strategy designed to put pressures on national advertisers and Capital Cities' investors. The international unions did not have to worry about the strike failing because of local circumstances: the Wilkes-Barre unions were united, the rank and file was committed, and the strikers had the backing of the local community. Moreover, the target was perfect for the project. Capital Cities was a glamorous corporate purveyor of information, and a major defeat of such a company would have sent shivers down the spine of every publisher in the country, including the conglomerates.

But the international unions, by their failure to use their financial muscle and that of their allies in the AFL-CIO, allowed Capital Cities to slip off the hook. As a result, both the company and the locals can legitimately claim partial victories. The unions can take solace because the workers were able to start a newspaper and maintain it as a viable economic enterprise, thereby preserving jobs and preventing Capital Cities from running the *Times Leader* as a profitable investment. The company and other publishers can gain comfort because Capital Cities has been able to continue operating in Wilkes-Barre in the face of resistance from locals nationally renowned for their militance and strength and supported by the community. Such a feat could not help but give heart to publishers who faced unions with lower levels of resolve and militance and much less community backing. Had the international unions used the financial weapon, their recent history might not have been a succession of surrenders and defeats, punctuated with an occasional partial victory. As more newspapers fall to conglomerate ownership, the old forms of struggle carried out by relatively autonomous, occupationally specific unions will prove increasingly unable to protect workers' contracts. Until newspaper unions adopt new forms of contention such as integrated unions, firmwide organizing and bargaining, and the use of corporate strategies during strikes, matters are not likely to get any better for them in the future.

The Strike and the Rank and File

The rank-and-file workers, like the unions, have experienced mixed results from the strike. All strikers who desired to do so have been employed but at considerable cost: many have had to give up their craft positions and accept other jobs at the *Citizens' Voice,* and all the craft and editorial workers have had to accept wage and benefit reductions, including suspension of payments into their pension funds, which has hurt most of the workers who are retirement age. No contributions have been made to their pension plans since 1978, so they are getting only the minimum amounts based on years of service to that date. But because the local economy provides few jobs, let alone jobs that pay well and offer good benefits, the majority of the rank and file believe that these sacrifices have been well worth the payoff of stable employment since 1978.

Even those who would not have lost their jobs had the union and the company reached agreement believe that they are better off working at the *Citizens' Voice* than they would have been had they stayed at the *Times Leader*. They claim, for example, that the company's job standards are so high that few people can successfully meet them. To illustrate their case, the strikers point to the high turnover rate among employees at the *Times Leader*, which was almost unheard-of under the former owners. In its fourth-year anniversary issue, October 6, 1982, the *Citizens' Voice* ran a story headlined "Strikebreakers Don't Last Long." The article claimed:

> The turnover of employees at the *Times Leader* over the last four years has been nothing short of phenomenal.
>
> Some departments have experienced a turnover of 300 percent or more.
>
> Many strikebreakers hired to replace striking employees have themselves been fired, some for odd reasons.
>
> That in itself is ironic since one of the key strike issues has been job security; the strikers wanted language that would give employees a chance to grieve and arbitrate an unfair dismissal.
>
> Following is a list, as complete as possible of people who have been fired, have quit or who have been "urged to leave the *Times Leader* over the last four years." (*Citizens' Voice*, October 6, 1982:B14)

The list contained the names of more than eighty men and women who had worked for the *Times Leader* since the strike began but no longer were with the paper. Some of the people listed were Capital Cities personnel who had been transferred to the *Times Leader* for temporary strike duty and had returned to their home papers after the company hired permanent replacements, although that fact was never mentioned in the article. Others listed were Capital Cities executives who, after serving at the *Times Leader*, were rotated to other corporate positions. And still others had been hired by the company and later left, not always of their own volition.

Times Leader officials acknowledge that in the first few years after the strike they did have a high turnover rate. They attribute it, in part, to problems in recruiting and retaining journalists who were willing to work under strike conditions and to the professional ambitions and successes of others, who took better jobs at more prestigious papers. But even at present, under more settled conditions, the *Times Leader* continues to have a higher turnover than it did under its former owners and than does the *Citizens' Voice.*

The *Citizens' Voice* and its supporters do not accept such explanations for the high turnover and point to two firings from the *Times Leader* to make their case about the "real" reasons for the personnel changes. They cite the example of a woman who was fired from her reporting job after she placed an advertisement in both the *Citizens' Voice* and the *Times Leader* for a small business she and her mother ran at a local resort. The other involves Bernie Gallagher, who had been a reporter for the *Times Leader* and went on strike with the guild in 1978. In 1980 he returned to the *Times Leader* as sports editor, replacing Larry Stephenson, who allegedly was fired. In turn, Gallagher allegedly was fired by Capital Cities. He gave the following explanation of his dismissal to the *Sunday Independent*'s sports editor: "I got in at a time when the *Leader* couldn't get a local story. . . . Because of the strike situation and the fact that the majority of the reporters at the *Leader* were from out of town, they needed a local guy to get the scoop for them and someone who had local contacts" (Don Zimmerman, *Sunday Independent*, February 27, 1983). He stated further that it was Capital Cities' style to replace expensive journalists, such as himself, whenever possible, with younger, less experienced, and cheaper workers.

Regardless of how correct the strikers are in claiming that the *Times Leader* has an abnormally high turnover rate or in attributing turnover to excessive performance requirements or to a desire by Capital Cities to have as cheap a work force as possible, it probably is true that few of the strikers could or would have wanted to adjust to Capital Cities' production demands, which were far greater than had once been the norm at the *Times Leader* and are currently in effect at the *Citizens' Voice*.

Capital Cities does not believe its production demands are any more unreasonable than those of any other well-managed paper in the United States. Nevertheless, the company reportedly had tried to help its staff cope with the stress of meeting company production requirements under strike conditions by bringing in professionals to run stress management workshops for the employees. The company, however, is not willing to lower its production requirements to eliminate or minimize objective stressors.

In addition to protecting their employment, the strikers have gained in other respects. First, the rank and file have far more opportunities to participate in effective decision making at the *Citizens' Voice* than they ever had at the *Times Leader*. The paper is governed and managed by workers, who have "partial participation" rights, as Carol Pateman (1970) uses that term, at the highest levels of the enterprise. Thus the workers have a far greater say in shaping their own labor process and their destiny than they ever had at the *Times Leader*, before or after Capital Cities' takeover.

Second, the workers do not appear to have gained much shop floor control over that contained in their old contracts with the *Times Leader*. But shop floor control at the *Citizens' Voice* far exceeds that presently permitted at the *Times Leader*. Third, should the *Citizens' Voice* be transformed into a directly worker-owned enterprise, even if only an ESOP, the rank and file will be able to acquire equity in a potentially very valuable piece of property, which could become even more valuable should Capital Cities pull out of the local market. Fourth, the strikers have gained tremendous psychological satisfaction from having taken control of the local newspaper market away from a company as rich and prestigious as Capital Cities. In the face of seemingly overwhelming odds against them, they have not only survived but have thrived.

Thus, even though the rank and file may not have forced Capital Cities to give them the contracts they wanted or to withdraw from the Wilkes-Barre market, it is clear that the strike has achieved at least one of the ends which William A. Gamson (1975) sees as the mark of a successful social movement: it has delivered to its members some of the most important benefits they were seeking—jobs have been protected and the workers have been able to preserve their human dignity.

The Strike and the Local Community

When asking Wilkes-Barre businessmen, managers, and professionals about the strike, one is apt to hear that the conflict between Capital Cities and its unions "tore the community apart," "split the community," or some such phrase. Such statements contain a grain of truth, but they fail to recognize that the division of the community into pro-*Citizens' Voice* and pro-*Times Leader* factions occurred along old social, cultural, political, economic, and geographical fault lines, which originated in the mining era.

By the 1960s, a casual observer might have thought that the divisions that had been characteristic of the mining era had disappeared and the old contenders for power, organized labor and the business elite (along with their respective allies), had achieved a new community consensus based on a shared interest in achieving economic growth. During this time, labor, capital, and the local state cooperated on several fronts to attract new investors to the region. In addition, the frequency, duration, and magnitude of strikes in the county began to approximate statewide averages (see U.S. Department of Labor, *Analysis of Work Stoppages,* 1940–80).

Cooperation, however, appears to have been predicated on the national prosperity that had resulted in Wilkes-Barre and Luzerne County making important economic gains rather than on any great change in local attitudes or an elimination of old cleavages in local society. When prosperity ended, so, too, did the spirit of cooperation. Good times had lasted for too short a period and had affected too few people for there to have been any massive changes in community attitudes or for the social divisions to have been transcended.

As a result, when the strike came, the alignments of various parts of the community were similar to those of the mining era. On one side stood Capital Cities, the local business elite, most parts of the middle classes, and a small number of working-class households; on the other were the striking newspaper unions, other trade unions, the largest part of the county's working classes, probably a smaller part of the local middle classes, and some small businesses.

Citizens' Voice supporters seldom mention how the strike divided the community. Rather, they say the strike brought the "community together," "united people," and rekindled popular "militance," a word used by one of the county's labor leaders in describing public reaction. In other words, from the vantage point of the newspaper unions' supporters and allies, the strike was not the tragedy that Capital Cities' backers claimed it was. Instead, it was positive, insofar as it helped renew the bonds of grass-roots solidarity and reawaken a willingness to fight to defend local working-class political, economic, cultural, and social interests.

In assessing the overall effects of the community response, the speed and intensity of which surprised both Capital Cities and the strikers, there is no doubt that the *Citizens' Voice* owes its continuing success primarily to the unflagging support it has received from the community grass roots. The community, however, has realized little material gain from having supported the strike. The local economy continues to deteriorate, the upper class and its allies are continuing to pressure politicians to cut back expenditures on social programs, and the local infrastructure has continued to decay, despite the massive infusion of capital from federal and state governments following the 1972 flood (Wolensky, 1983, 1984).

There are several reasons why the community as a whole achieved no substantial political and economic gains as a result of its mobilization on behalf of the *Citizens' Voice*. First, the popular movement that came into being was a reactive, defensive protest movement. Since 1978, the movement has remained tied to the specific cause of protecting the strikers and their paper. It never moved beyond this particular "limit situation," the "initial grievances around which self-determined action may occur" (Gaventa, 1980:208–9), to a more general, offensive action against the centers of economic power in the county. The popular movement has been content with merely trying to defend a specific group of workers and the autonomy and integrity of local culture, history, and social practice from a perceived attack by a hostile corporate power. Thus confined to these objectives, the dialectical process of critical reflection, action, and deepening awareness, which Paulo Friere (1972:68) considers essential to the form of mobilization and politicization he subsumes under the concept of "conscientization," never took hold within the popular movement organized on behalf of the strike.

The purely defensive and reactive nature of the movement, if anything, has led to a strengthening of local institutions against all forms of criticism and change, however correct the commentary and necessary the change. Even legitimate critical commentary about some of the less desirable features of local life, such as political corruption, economic and political domination by a handful of finance capitalists, machine politics, and nondemocratic trade unions, came to be looked upon as a betrayal of local society.

Second, because of the supportive response the strikers received from politicians, government officials, and parts of the middle and upper classes, the conflict between Capital Cities and the community rank and file never fused the issues in the strike with the multiple problems the region's residents face in trying to live a meaningful life in a chronically depressed urban economy. Because the issues that gave rise to the strike were never explicitly linked to the region's other economic problems, configurations of power and dominance in the local political economy have emerged unscathed from the turmoil surrounding the conflict between Capital Cities and its unions.

Third, it was not just the response of local elites that confined the impact of a mobilized community to a clearly delimited arena of conflict. The *Citizens' Voice* itself has been partly responsible for this outcome. The paper's leadership has not aspired to anything beyond creating an organ for the defense of the strikers, trade unionism, and the abstract principles and practices of local life. It has never put forward an agenda for either grand or specific changes in the local political economy, nor has it ever been tempted to become an advocate for the special interests of one or more of its constituent groups, save for the trade unions and the politicians who support the unions' agenda. Such policies probably have been important factors in helping the paper to succeed, as research on other social movements suggests (see Jenkins, 1983). From the *Citizens' Voice*'s perspective, to become involved in such causes would serve no purpose other than possibly to create needless splits in its support network. But there was more to it. The *Citizens' Voice* was not about to sponsor a challenge to a system of power in which it and two of its major affinity groups (the trade unions and the Democratic party) played major roles.

The community mobilized around very specific *defensive* goals. These goals were not directed toward introducing major changes in the local political economy but only toward protecting the strikers, punishing Capital Cities, and defending the contours, relations, and practices of local social life and culture. Because it lacked an agenda for change, confined itself to only one target, and never emancipated itself from established centers of local power, the popular movement accomplished little in improving conditions of life in the Wilkes-Barre area.

A Final Look—Who Won?

If one could construct an overall balance sheet of gains and losses in the Wilkes-Barre strike, it would show that no one has clearly won or lost. If Capital Cities and other publishers were to measure the strike against the hope that the company could have delivered a paralyzing blow to the industry's unions by defeating locals nationally renowned for their militance, they must be disappointed by the strike's outcome. Capital Cities not only has been unable to defeat the local unions, but it has lost millions in simply trying to maintain a stalemate. Yet the publishers can draw some satisfaction because Capital Cities has been able to keep its Wilkes-Barre operation afloat without accommodating itself to the unions.

The newspaper unions can be pleased that they have shown publishers just how costly trying to rid their papers of unions can be and that workers, under the right conditions, can start and maintain a profitable, competitive newspaper. Even this success, however, contains a threat. In 1982 a reporter told me that the greatest danger he saw for the strike was that people eventually might begin to view the struggle between the *Citizens' Voice* and the *Times Leader* as normal competition between two businesses, and if this should happen, the strikers would lose their moral advantage. He already was beginning to see signs of such an attitude. If it does become commonplace, it will have emerged not merely because people have come to accept the *Times Leader*'s definition of the situation but also because of the behavior of the *Citizens' Voice*. By 1986 many of the strikers were describing the paper as a "normal" business. More than one used words to the effect that their enterprise was "a business just like any other paper." About the only visible reminder of the *Citizens' Voice*'s peculiar origins is the annual anniversary issue, but whether that is sufficient to sustain moral backing is an open question.

Events in Wilkes-Barre also have demonstrated to the newspaper unions that their old organizational forms and traditional weapon, the strike, are no longer adequate for disciplining publishers in the face of new production technologies, consolidation of the industry into giant conglomerates, and the availability of large pools of surplus labor. By remaining fragmented into occupationally specific organizations, by bargaining only at the local level, and by relying on the strike as the primary means for defending their interests, the unions can hope only to punish a conglomerate but not to defeat it in struggles over labor policy, wages, and the like.

As with the unions and the company, the results of the strike for the community are ambiguous. The community has been able to achieve its specific goals of protecting the strikers and defending certain principles and practices of local social life and culture by participating in an old ritual of mass struggle that many had thought would no longer be seen in the region. Undoubtedly, this has helped the community grass roots recover its own heritage, strengthened its subjectivity, and heightened its solidarity.

In addition, the strike has shown the community grass roots, especially workers, that the old repertoire of contention built up during the mining era still can be an effective means of self-defense. For example, the strike demonstrated that militant unions with high levels of solidarity are still capable of protecting their members; that a union still can count on assistance from other labor organizations in the county; that the community rank and file still has the structural and cultural potential to mobilize; and that the community will engage in collective activity on behalf of beleaguered workers when called upon to do so, especially when the appeal for help is framed in such a way that it taps into local historical sensibilities, principles of moral economy, and community patriotism. It has also shown that the support of public officials is vital so that there will be little likelihood of police repression, especially when tactics exceed the normal, institutionalized routines of contemporary industrial conflict; and, finally, it has shown local workers that when all else fails it is possible, under certain conditions, to take production into their own hands and establish a viable worker self-managed enterprise.

But despite all these positive signs, the strike was a missed opportunity for both the county's trade unions and the community grass roots. For the trade unions the strike, along with the general community mobilization, was a chance to build a sustained, active trade union social movement that not only could have advanced the cause of workers already organized but also could have been used as a springboard for launching new organizing drives in the rapidly growing service and retail sectors of the local economy. It also provided the unions with a chance to forge *continuing* alliances with other organized community dissidents, especially groups that are struggling against problems growing out of contradictions of urban life (Castells, 1983). For the unions to have accomplished this they would have had to move beyond the confines of unionism pure and simple, with its myopic focus on contracts and other principles of business unionism (see Aronowitz, 1983), toward a greater concern for general social issues. They did not do so.

Remaining confined to their narrow political and economic agendas, the local unions were not able to take a leading role in moving the community grass roots toward developing and implementing a program or programs for progressive social change. And because few, if any, other groups in the county had the same legitimacy and contacts with the grass roots as the unions, once the community rank and file accomplished the limited goals of protecting the *Citizens' Voice* and punishing Capital Cities, it returned to "quiescence" (Gaventa, 1980) and allowed existing local centers of economic and political domination and hegemony (Gramsci, 1971) to continue functioning much as they always have.

Afterword

This study grew out of a personal and professional interest in the Wyoming Valley and Luzerne County. On a personal level, I am a native of the area, was educated there, and have family still residing in the county. On a professional level, in the summer of 1978 I was in Luzerne County collecting data for a social history of anthracite miners, their families, and their communities. This was just after Capital Cities assumed control of the *Times Leader* but before the strike began. Already, however, rumors were circulating suggesting that the company and the unions were likely to have a hard time reaching agreement on new contracts. For example, I talked with a pressman who told me about the difficulties his union was likely to face in getting an acceptable contract with the paper. Because of my other research concerns and the relative commonness of strikes at the paper, I did not pay much attention to what was happening.

Once the strike began, however, it appeared that it was not going to be a normal labor action, and I began collecting newspaper clippings dealing with events surrounding the walkout. In December 1978, I returned to the region and began collecting information on what had happened. Through interviews and conversations with residents and key informants in the county labor movement, public officials and politicians, and people in the local media and by reading local and national newspaper accounts of the strike I started trying to make sense of what had happened at the publishing company.

Between December 1978 and the end of 1981, I made several more trips to the region, each time with the intention of collecting more data for the social history. Soon, however, I found that I was spending more time collecting information on the strike than on my original project. I spent a good deal of time reading back issues of the *Citizens' Voice* and the *Times Leader* to catch up on what had happened since my last trip to the area and talking with everyone I could about their impressions of events and their reactions to the strike.

In 1982, I finally got the chance to spend an extended period of time in the region thanks to funding from the University of Louisville's College of Arts and Sciences and its Office of Graduate Programs and Research. This financial support enabled me to make seven trips to Luzerne County between January and August 1982 to collect data on the strike. The duration of each trip was from one to three weeks. Since 1982, I have made five more visits to the region, the last in December 1986.

Before January 1982, I had not spoken with officials at either paper. On my first trip into the region in 1982, I decided I would begin my interviewing by first approaching the strikers. Mainly because of my personal predilections and my local contacts, I felt that I would have no difficulty in getting interviews with the strikers. At the same time, because of my own political convictions and personal biases I wanted to put off as long as possible what I thought would be the distasteful task of interviewing anyone at the *Times Leader*.

My first contact with the union leadership was with the Unity Council's official spokesman, who was a guild reporter. We discussed the background of the strike, the issues that had spawned it, and the current status of the conflict between the *Times Leader* and the *Citizens' Voice*. During the course of the interview, it became clear to me that although he was willing to provide me with rich and detailed information on what he wanted me to know, there were certain subjects about which he would not speak. He was especially noncommunicative about the internal structure and operations of the workers' paper. He saw no useful purpose for my knowing how the paper operated, despite my attempts to explain why a sociologist would be interested in finding out such information.

During the course of the entire study, he was the only member of the Unity Council, with one exception, who granted me an in-depth interview. Whenever I approached other members, they always told me that if I wanted any information about the strike I would have to get it from their official spokesperson because the members of the Unity Council had pledged not to discuss the strike with outsiders.

I began to resent the refusal of the leaders to talk with me and their directing me to someone who, at the time, I thought was merely their public relations expert. Later, however, I was glad that I had gotten the opportunity to interview this person because I was told by sources both inside the *Citizens' Voice* and outside the paper that he was the "real power" on the Unity Council, even though he had no formal position on the body other than being an ex officio member.

When I first began trying to get information about the strikers' paper, I asked for an opportunity to attend Unity Council meetings. Each time I made the request I was rebuffed. In hindsight, it seems that my field work coincided with an internal struggle for power at the *Citizens' Voice,* which involved personality clashes as well as substantive issues about work rules, labor discipline, and work quality. A key figure in the struggle reportedly was the *Citizens' Voice*'s spokesman. I was told that he and his supporters represented a tendency within the paper that wanted to see more labor discipline, increased productivity, and higher-quality work. Allegedly they were being resisted by some of the "old guard," who wanted to preserve as free and relaxed an environment as they knew at the pre–Capital Cities *Times Leader.*

Because of the internal turmoil at the strikers' paper, it is understandable that the leaders did not want to give a stranger access to its inner workings. They clearly feared that if word leaked to Capital Cities about internal conflicts the company would be able to take advantage of the tensions within the paper to split the strikers' ranks. Also at the time, the paper was fighting a $20-million lawsuit Capital Cities had filed and was battling the government over its tax status. The lawsuit was for damages that the company claimed it suffered because of alleged contract violations. According to Capital Cities, its contracts with the local unions prohibited the workers from engaging in any business that competed with the publishing company. This suit was still working its way through the courts in 1986. In April of that year, the strikers won another round when a federal judge ruled in their favor. But if Capital Cities chooses to appeal the decision, it should be several more years before the matter is finally settled. Just as the law-suit remains unresolved, so, too, does the paper's tax status. The Internal Revenue Service is still trying to have the strikers' compensation defined as wages, rather than as strike benefits. Feeling pressed on all sides, it is little wonder that the strike leaders were hesitant about being fully cooperative with someone they did not know.

It was not only members of the Unity Council who refused to talk with me. So, too, did almost all of the Newspaper Guild members, be they reporters or white-collar workers. With only a few exceptions, most of the information I could get about how the guild had reacted to the strike came from secondhand sources, including a reporter and a manager at the *Sunday Independent.*

The reporter freely answered all the questions I asked him, gave me useful tips on who to talk with to get additional infor-mation, and confirmed, corrected, or denied information that I checked out with him. The information he gave me always proved accurate when checked against other sources' reports and, similarly, when I checked information that I knew to be valid with him, he always gave me a truthful answer.

I also was able to interview third parties who had firsthand knowledge of what was happening in the guild and who, therefore, were able to give me good information on how the strike was affecting reporters and what the reporters' attitudes were about Capital Cities and the strike. When I was in Wilkes-Barre in April 1986, I found a marked difference in guild members' attitudes. They were far more willing to talk about what the strike has meant to them personally and about the status and even the organizational structure of the *Citizens' Voice*. This change of attitude was partly related to increased confidence that the *Citizens' Voice* was not going to be defeated by Capital Cities.

I also interviewed journalists in other media in the region, including journalists from each of the region's television stations, several radio stations, and the publisher of the *Sunday Independent*. Among other things, these sources provided useful information on how the strike had affected both sets of reporters, the relations between the *Citizens' Voice* and the *Times Leader*, and the ways in which news gathering has been affected by the battle between the two papers.

Within the *Citizens' Voice* initially I received the most cooperation from the craft workers. I was able to talk with a number of printers, pressmen, and stereotypers. They showed none of the recalcitrance of the guild members. Not only were they willing to talk, they often went out of their way to grant me interviews. I supplemented the meetings I had with striking craft workers by interviewing members of their unions who worked at different businesses in the city, which added to the information the strikers gave me.

It was not until I felt that I had gathered most of the data I needed about the *Citizens' Voice* that I began conducting interviews with *Times Leader* workers. Part of my rationale for proceeding in this manner was that I believed that if the strikers found out that I was talking to Capital Cities at the same time that I was collecting data from them, they would give me no more access to information. I knew that there would be no way to hide the fact that I was interviewing Capital Cities' workers and officials. Even though no one at either paper talked with anyone from the other, a surprising amount

of information flowed back and forth between the *Citizens'*
Voice and the *Times Leader.* Neither paper could keep much
hidden from the other. Each had detailed information about
the other. I never was able to determine whether the intelligence gathering was simply the result of loose talk between
workers who had remained friends, even though they had
chosen to take different sides during the conflict, or whether
the two papers were operating formal and/or informal industrial espionage operations against each other. Regardless of
how the information was acquired, the result was that each
side was well informed about what the other was doing, despite formal protestations that they were unconcerned with
the details of their competitor's operations. The *Citizens'*
Voice seemed to have had far more detailed information about
what was happening at the *Times Leader* than the *Times*
Leader had about the *Citizens' Voice.* The *Citizens' Voice* always seemed to know well in advance what its competitor
was planning to do, and this helped its leaders plan their own
actions.

When I first began interviewing people from Capital Cities,
I arranged to do it away from the company's premises. I could
not bring myself to cross the picket line. Finally, when I had
no other choice, I did cross the line and conduct some interviews on the company's property. But I must admit I was one
of those people who timed his entry into the building. I entered the building when the picket had his back turned and
was at the far end of the block. Had he turned to confront me,
I probably would have fled in panic and shame.

Initially I had thought that I would encounter substantial
resistance from Capital Cities in carrying out interviews with
its exployees. I was wrong. Everyone I approached at the
Times Leader was extremely cooperative with the project. No
one refused me an interview and, except for the matter of circulation figures, all of my respondents were open and spoke
with a great deal of candor on any and all topics. This is not to
say that some were not suspicious about my motives. The
wife of one Capital Cities local executive asked me a number

of questions about my background before we started talking about the strike. She wanted to know whether I had any friends or family members who were members of one of the striking unions (the answer was no) and whether any members of my family had ever been coal miners. To her these were the two best indicators of whether I could be trusted as a neutral party. She was the only *Times Leader* person who showed *overt* signs of suspicion about my motives for gathering information on the strike. As with some of the *Citizens' Voice* respondents, I interviewed some of the *Times Leader* workers at their homes, where I had the chance to talk not only with them but also with their families.

In most cases I found the *Times Leader* people easier to interview than the *Citizens' Voice* workers. I concluded that one of the principal reasons for this was that the *Times Leader*'s management, journalists, and I shared a common "professional-managerial" culture. As a result, they had a clearer understanding of what a sociologist did and why I was doing the study than did anyone at the *Citizens' Voice.*

In addition to interviewing people at both papers, I also interviewed a host of other local actors, including spouses of workers on both sides, newspaper carriers for both papers, parents of carriers on both sides, politicians, government officials, police officers in both the city and suburbs, court officials and attorneys, the executive director of the local Chamber of Commerce, several clergymen, community activists, faculty at local colleges, workers at other media outlets in the region, small merchants and big businessmen, managers of enterprises, other academics and researchers who were working on various projects dealing with the region, postal workers, rank-and-file union members who did not work at either paper, and leaders of other unions not immediately involved in the strike, as well as dozens of people who had no other interest in the strike than that they subscribed to one paper or the other. At every available opportunity, I tried to engage people from the area in conversations about the strike to get their impressions of what had happened and how they viewed the events.

In all, I conducted more than three hundred hours of interviews with upward of one hundred people. As in any study of this nature, the people with whom I spoke cannot be considered to be a representative sample of the strikers, the employees of Capital Cities, or the community. Rather, they are a self-selected group, who, for one reason or another, were willing to give me their impressions of what had taken place and how they felt about it. Although the bulk of these interviews were conducted between January and August 1982, data were collected through December 1986. All interviews were open-ended and semistructured. Some were as short as ten or fifteen minutes and others lasted several hours. Interviews were conducted in a variety of settings. I spoke with people in their homes, in restaurants and taverns, on street corners, on buses, in offices, and on shop floors. A few were done over the telephone.

When I first began to plan this study, I had developed an elaborate survey methodology to gather data from the *Times Leader*, the *Citizens' Voice*, and the community. Being unable to get funding for such a project, I was forced to switch to far less expensive and systematic methods of data collection. Because of the way data were collected, this study, like others of the same genre, has serious limitations with regard to questions of internal and external validity.

I would not presume to tell the reader that I have done anything novel to overcome these problems, because I did not. My goal was simply to learn as much about what had happened as I could, try to portray this from the perspective of those who experienced the events, and, finally, connect these experiences, when appropriate, with other studies of similar happenings.

There is one further caveat that I would like to offer. I did not go to Wilkes-Barre as a tabula rasa. I went there as a former resident, as someone whose family once had been involved in mining, as someone with family living there, and as someone who was entirely sympathetic with the cause of the strikers and their allies.

In addition to carrying this personal baggage, I went into the field with preexisting theoretical and philosophical orientations about the nature of that particular community and American society in general. I feel that I have a special obligation to let readers know what these orientations are so that they may more intelligently assess the materials I have presented. Stated as simply and, I hope, as clearly as possible, I approached the study from a framework of class analysis. By this I mean that American society, first and foremost, is a class society and that we can learn more about how it is organized, its laws of motion, its divisions of interest, the operation of its institutions, and its possibilities for and limits of change by using this framework than we can by using any other method available to a social scientist.

I would like to think that this narrative is objective, in the sense that it is faithful to the experiences of the people who lived through the events, and that it is fair to all concerned. I think that the greatest mistake a reader of my account could make is to accept the moral judgments of the participants on either side of the strike and conclude that it was after all a battle between "good" and "evil." It was not. Both the *Citizens' Voice* and the *Times Leader* have their fair share of rogues, scoundrels, and blackguards. They are a minority on each side. For the most part, the men and women who have been fighting each other since 1978 are decent folk of sound character. They are not villains but people acting out of deeply felt convictions or economic need.

I would like the reader to reflect on this seemingly banal observation for a moment. Recall, if you will, how each side has explained the behavior of the other. Capital Cities blames the entire strike on power-hungry union leaders, who were willing to sacrifice their members' long-term interests to protect their own positions. It saw the rank and file as weak and powerless men and women, who recognized that Capital Cities was right in its demands but were too afraid to speak out on their own behalf. The strikers and their community supporters took an equally negative view of Capital Cities. They saw it as a company owned and managed by ruthless, greedy, and evil people who would stop at nothing to get their way so that they could maximize their profits. If the situation were really so simple, there would be grounds for hoping that at some point in the future, if and when different leaders come to power in the unions and in the company, amends could be made and there could be a reconciliation in which the proverbial lion and lamb would lie together in peace (I leave it to the reader to decide which side is which).

To accept such an explanation for what transpired, however, is to miss the central point of this study. And that is that the conflict between the unions and Capital Cities grew out of a special set of historical circumstances confronting publishers and the unions in the mid-1970s. The social structure of accumulation within which each side had prospered since the end of World War II had come unglued. As a result, Capital Cities demanded concessions from its unions and was willing to annihilate them if it did not get the concessions it wanted—not because its stockholders, executives, managers, and employees are greedy, evil people of poor character, but because of the economic rationality of capitalism. If management wanted to attain levels of profit that would allow the company to survive and expand as it had in the past, it had to make war on its unions. If it did not, then firms against which it competed to attract investment capital would grow while it stagnated. To stagnate in a competitive market economy is to die.

Likewise, the unions fought as hard as they did because they had no alternative. To accept Capital Cities' contract proposals would not only have meant the possible loss of a hundred or more jobs, which, though not a pleasant prospect anywhere, would have been especially traumatic in an economy such as Luzerne County's, but it also would have meant the death of trade unionism as it had come to be practiced at the Wilkes-Barre Publishing Company. The community responded as it did because the largest part of the grass roots still held to the notions of moral economy that once had animated the mine workers, and they still were committed to the principles of collective responsibility, mutual self-help, solidarity, and collective action in defense of one's own people and their interests.

Therefore, should the unions have understood Capital Cities' predicament; should they have had the "good sense" to make the concessions that would have passed complete control over the labor process to management; and should the workers have been willing to increase their productivity? Should the community have stood on the sidelines and watched the newspaper unions be defeated, if not dismantled? And, in a parallel question, should the community have been willing to put aside its past and its present commitment to trade unionism as a way of life and as an ideal so as to facilitate new investment in the region?

Social science cannot answer such questions. Only the people affected by the decisions have the right to make the choices. In Wilkes-Barre the unions and the community made the choice to stand and fight in defense of their principles and what they defined as their rights. Capital Cities made the same choice. There matters still stand.

References

Abrecht, Stephen, and Michael Locker, eds. 1981. *CDE Stock Ownership Directory.* New York: Corporate Data Exchange.

Anderson, John. 1978. "New Management Needed." In *Violence in the Valley.* Wilkes-Barre, Pa: Wilkes-Barre Publishing Co.

Apple, Michael W. 1979. *Ideology and Curriculum.* London: Routledge & Kegan Paul.

Aronowitz, Stanley. 1973. *False Promises.* New York: McGraw-Hill.

———. 1983. *Working Class Hero: A New Strategy for Labor.* New York: Pilgrim Press.

Ashton, Patrick J. 1984. "Urbanization and the Dynamics of Suburban Development under Capitalism." In William K. Tabb and Larry Sawers, eds., *Marxism and the Metropolis,* pp. 54–81. 2d ed. New York: Oxford University Press.

Aurand, Harold W. 1971. *From the Molly Maguires to the United Mine Workers: The Social Ecology of an Industrial Union.* Philadelphia: Temple University Press.

Bagdikian, Ben H. 1983. *The Media Monopoly.* Boston: Beacon Press.

Becker, Howard S. 1963. *Outsiders.* New York: Free Press.

Bernstein, Paul. 1976. *Workplace Democratization.* Kent, Ohio: Kent State University Press.

Bimba, Anthony. 1932. *Molly Maguires.* New York: International Publishers.

Block, Fred. 1977. "The Ruling Class Does Not Rule: Notes on the Marxist Theory of the State." *Socialist Revolution* 33 (May–June): 6–28.

Bluestone, Barry, and Bennett Harrison. 1982. *The Deindustrialization of America.* New York: Basic Books.

Blumberg, Paul. 1968. *Industrial Democracy.* London: Constable.

Bonacich, Edna. 1980. "Class Approaches to Ethnicity and Race." *Insurgent Sociologist* 10 (Fall): 9–25.

Bowles, Samuel, and Herbert Gintis. 1976. *Schooling in Capitalist America.* New York: Basic Books.

Braudel, Fernand. 1984. *The Perspective of the World: Civilization and Capitalism, 15th–18th Century.* Vol. 3. Translated by Sian Reynolds. New York: Harper & Row.

Braverman, Harry. 1974. *Labor and Monopoly Capital: The Degradation of Work in the Twentieth Century.* New York: Monthly Review Press.

Brecher, Jeremy. 1972. *Strike!* Boston: South End Press.

Brownstein, Ronald, and Nina Easton. 1983. *Reagan's Ruling Class.* New York: Pantheon.

Burawoy, Michael. 1979. *Manufacturing Consent.* Chicago: University of Chicago Press.

Capital Cities Communications, Inc. 1981. *Annual Report.* New York: Capital Cities Communications, Inc.

Carroll, Jackson W., Douglas W. Johnson, and Martin E. Marty. 1979. *Religion in America, 1950 to the Present.* San Francisco: Harper & Row.

Castells, Manuel. 1983. *The City and the Grassroots.* Berkeley and Los Angeles: University of California Press.

Coleman, J. Walter. 1936. *The Molly Maguire Riots: Industrial Conflict in the Pennsylvania Coal Region.* New York: Arno.

Committee on Economic Growth. 1985. "Union/Non-Union Employment Greater Wilkes-Barre Area as of October 1985." Unpublished survey results.

Corbin, David Allen. 1981. *Life, Work, and Rebellion in the Coal Fields: The Southern West Virginia Miners, 1880–1922.* Urbana: University of Illinois Press.

Cox, Oliver Cromwell. 1948. *Caste, Class, and Race.* New York: Doubleday.

Cumbler, John T. 1979. *Working Class Community in Industrial America: Work, Leisure, and Struggle in Two Industrial Cities, 1880–1930.* Westport, Conn.: Greenwood Press.

Cummings, Scott. 1980. "Collectivism: The Unique Legacy of Immigrant Economic Development." In Scott Cummings, ed.,

Self-Help in Urban America: Patterns of Minority Economic Development, pp. 5–29. Port Washington, N.Y.: Kennikat.

Dahrendorf, Ralph. 1959. *Class and Class Conflict in Industrial Society.* Stanford: Stanford Univerisity Press.

Davies, Carl T. 1978a. "TLEN Staffers Question 'Security Moves.'" *Wyoming Valley Observer*, August 20, p. 1.

———. 1978b. "When the Big Fish Swallows the Little Fish: Chain Ownership Portends Change for W-B Daily." *Wyoming Valley Observer*, August 20, p. 3.

Davies, Edward J. 1983. "Class and Power in the Anthracite Region: The Control of Political Leadership in Wilkes-Barre, Pennsylvania, 1845–1885." *Journal of Urban History* 9 (May): 291–334.

Domhoff, G. William. 1983. *Who Rules America: A View for the 80's.* Englewood Cliffs, N.J.: Prentice-Hall.

Domowitch, Paul. 1978. "People Are Falling for It—Hometown Bay's View." In *Violence in the Valley*, Wilkes-Barre, Pa: Wilkes-Barre Publishing Co.

Editor and Publisher. 1981. *The International Yearbook.* Harold B. Mers, Director, Yearbook Staff. New York: Editor and Publisher.

Ernst, Morris L. 1937. *Anthracite Coal Commission Report.* Harrisburg: Commonwealth of Pennsylvania.

Folsom, Burton W. 1981. *Urban Capitalists: Entrepreneurs and City Growth in Pennsylvania's Lackawanna and Lehigh Regions, 1800–1920.* Baltimore: Johns Hopkins University Press.

Forbes. 1986. *The Forbes 500s Annual Directory.* April.

Friere, Paulo. 1972. *The Pedagogy of the Oppressed.* Harmondsworth: Penguin.

Gadamer, Hans-Georg. 1982. *Truth and Method.* London: Sheed and Ward.

Gamson, William A. 1975. *The Strategy of Social Protest.* Homewood, Ill.: Dorsey.

Gamson, William A., and Bruce Fireman. 1979. "Utilitarian Logic in the Resource Mobilization Perspective." In M. N. Zald and J. M. McCarthy, eds., *The Dynamics of Social Movements*, pp. 8–44. Cambridge, Mass.: Winthrop.

Gans, Herbert. 1979. *Deciding What's News.* New York: Vintage.

Gaventa, John. 1980. *Power and Powerlessness: Quiescence and Rebellion in an Appalachian Valley.* Urbana: University of Illinois Press.

Gordon, David M., Richard Edwards, and Michael Reich. 1982. *Seg-*

mented Work, Divided Workers: The Historical Transformation of Labor in the United States.* New York: Cambridge University Press.

Gouldner, Alvin W. 1976. *The Dialectic of Ideology and Technology: The Origins, Grammar, and Future of Ideology.* New York: Seabury.

Gramsci, Antonio. 1971. *Selections from the Prison Notebooks of Antonio Gramsci.* Edited and translated by Quinton Hare and Geoffrey Nowell-Smith. London: Lawrence and Wisehart.

Greene, Victor. 1968. *Slavic Community on Strike.* South Bend: University of Notre Dame Press.

Hobsbawm, Eric. 1959. *Primitive Rebels.* New York: Norton.

―――. 1984. *Workers: Worlds of Labor.* New York: Pantheon.

Janowitz, Morris. 1967. *Community Press in an Urban Setting.* 2d ed. Chicago: University of Chicago Press.

Jenkins, J. Craig. 1983. "Resource Mobilization Theory and the Study of Social Movements." In Ralph Turner and James F. Short, eds., *Annual Review of Sociology,* pp. 527–53. Palo Alto, Calif.: Annual Reviews, Inc.

Keil, Thomas J. 1982. "Capital Organization and Ethnic Exploitation: Consequences for Miner Solidarity and Protest (1850–1870)." *Journal of Political and Military Sociology* 10 (Fall): 237–55.

―――. 1984. "Mobilizing Adolescent Workers' Support for an American Newspaper Strike: Results from a Case Study." *Organization Studies* 5, no. 4, 327–43.

―――. 1987. "Business, Labor, and the Local State: Contesting Control over the Local Economic Development Agenda." In Scott Cummings, ed., *Corporate Elites and Urban Development.* Albany: State University of New York Press.

Lauck, W. J., and Edgar Sydenstriker. 1917. *Conditions of Labor in American Industries.* New York: Arno.

Lewis, Arthur H. 1964. *Lament for the Molly Maguires.* New York: Harcourt Brace Jovanovich.

McCarthy, J. M., and M. N. Zald. 1973. *The Trend of Social Movements.* Morristown, N. J.: General Learning.

―――. 1977. "Resource Mobilization and Social Movements." *American Journal of Sociology* 82 (May): 1212–41.

Miller, Donald L., and Richard E. Sharpless. 1985. *The Kingdom of*

Coal: Work, Enterprise, and Ethnic Communities in the Mine Fields. Philadelphia: University of Pennsylvania Press.

Mire, Joseph. 1975. "Trade Unions and Worker Participation in Management." In Louis E. Davis and Albert B. Cherns, eds., *The Quality of Working Life,* 1: 416–38. New York: Free Press.

Moe, T. M. 1980. *The Organization of Interests.* Chicago: University of Chicago Press.

Molotch, Harvey. 1976. "The City as a Growth Machine." *American Journal of Sociology* 82 (September): 309–32.

Montgomery, David. 1979. *Workers' Control in America.* Cambridge: Cambridge University Press.

Moody's. 1982. *Bank and Finance Manual.* New York: Moody's Investor Services.

Mulder, Mauk. 1971. "Power Equalization through Participation?" *Administrative Science Quarterly* 16 (March): 31–39.

Northeast Pennylvania Business Journal. 1986. "Who'll Buy All the Hamburgers?" 1 (April):4.

Novak, Michael. 1978. *The Guns of Lattimer.* New York: Basic Books.

Oberschall, Anthony. 1973. *Social Conflict and Social Movements.* Englewood Cliffs, N.J.: Prentice-Hall.

Offe, Claus. 1985. "Two Logics of Collective Action." In John Keane, ed., *Disorganized Capitalism: Contemporary Transformations of Work and Politics,* pp. 171–220. Cambridge, Mass.: MIT Press.

Olson, Mancur. 1968. *The Logic of Collective Action.* New York: Schocken.

Oppenheimer, Martin. 1974. "The Sub-Proletariat: Dark Skins and Dirty Work." *Insurgent Sociologist* 4 (Winter): 6–20.

Pateman, Carol. 1970. *Participation and Democratic Theory.* Cambridge: Cambridge University Press.

Pennsylvania Bureau of Statistics and Planning. 1974. *Pennsylvania Abstract.* Harrisburg: Pennsylvania Bureau of Statistics and Planning.

Pennsylvania Department of Environmental Resources. 1981. *Report on Mining Activities.* Harrisburg.

Pennsylvania Manual. 1978–79. *The Pennsylvania Manual.* Vol. 104. Harrisburg: Department of General Services, Commonwealth of Pennsylvania.

Raskin, A. H. 1982. "The Once and Future Newspaper Guild." *Co-*

lumbia Journalism Review, September–October, pp. 26–34.

Reich, Michael. 1977. "The Economics of Racism." In David M. Gordon, ed. *Problems in Political Economy,* pp. 183–87. 2d ed. Lexington, Mass.: D. C. Heath.

Ricci, David. 1971. *Community Power and Democratic Theory: The Logic of Political Analysis.* New York: Random House.

Ricoeur, Paul. 1969. *The Symbolism of Evil.* Boston: Beacon Press.

_____. 1984. *Time and Narrative.* Vol. 1. Translated by Kathleen McLaughlin and David Pellaur. Chicago: University of Chicago Press.

Roberts, Peter. 1901. *Anthracite Coal Industry.* New York: Macmillan.

Rothschild, Joyce and J. Allen Whitt. 1986. *The Cooperative Workplace: Potentials, Dilemmas, and Organizational Democracy and Participation.* Cambridge: Cambridge University Press.

Rothschild-Whitt, Joyce. 1979. "The Collective Organization: An Alternative to Rational-Bureaucratic Models." *American Sociological Review* 44 (August): 509–27.

Russell, Raymond, Arthur Hochner, and Stewart E. Perry. 1979. "Participation, Influence, and Worker Ownership." *Industrial Relations* 18 (Fall): 330–41.

Schudson, Michael. 1978. *Discovering the News.* New York: Basic Books.

Schur, Edwin M. 1971. *Labeling Deviant Behavior.* New York: Harper & Row.

Schwartz, Michael. 1976. *Radical Protest and Social Structure: The Southern Farmers' Alliance and Cotton Tenancy, 1880–1890.* New York: Academic Press.

Skocpol, Theda. 1979. *States and Social Revolutions.* New York: Cambridge University Press.

Snow, David A., Louis A. Zurcher, and Sheldon Eckland-Olson. 1980. "Social Networks and Social Movements." *American Sociological Review* 45 (October): 787–801.

Stolarik, Mark. 1980. "A Place for Everyone: Slovak Fraternal-Benefit Societies." In Scott Cummings, ed., *Self-Help in Urban America: Patterns of Minority Economic Development,* pp. 130–44. Port Washington, N.Y.: Kennikat.

Szymanski, Albert. 1974. "Race, Sex, and the U.S. Working Class." *Social Problems* 21 (June): 706–25.

Teulings, Ad. 1982. "Interlocking Interests and Collaboration with the Enemy: Corporate Behavior in the Second World War." *Organization Studies* No. 12: 99–118.

Tillock, Harriet, and Denton E. Morrison. 1979. "Group Size and Contributions to Collective Action." In Louis Kriesberg, ed., *Research on Social Movements, Conflict, and Change* 2:131–58. Greenwich, Conn.: JAI Press.

Tilly, Charles. 1978. *From Mobilization to Revolution.* Reading, Mass.: Addison-Wesley.

———. 1979. "Repertoires of Contention in America and Britain, 1750–1830." In Mayer N. Zald and John D. McCarthy, eds., *The Dynamics of Social Movements*, pp. 126–55. Cambridge, Mass.: Winthrop.

U.S. Bureau of the Census. 1810. *Third Census of the United States.* Washington, D.C.: U.S. Government Printing Office.

———. 1850. *Seventh Census of the United States.* Washington, D.C.: U.S. Government Printing Office.

———. 1900. *Twelfth Census of the United States.* Washington, D.C.: U.S. Government Printing Office.

———. 1980. *Census of Population and Housing: Northeast Pennsylvania Standard Metropolitan Statistical Area.* Washington, D.C.: U.S. Government Printing Office.

U.S. Department of Labor. 1940–78. *Analysis of Work Stoppages.* Washington, D.C.: Bureau of Labor Statistics, U.S. Department of Labor.

von Halle, Ernst. 1895. *Trusts or Industrial Combinations in the United States.* New York: Macmillan.

Wackenhut. 1982. *Annual Report.* Coral Gables, Fla.: Wackenhut.

Wallace, Michael, and Arne L. Kalleburg. 1982. "Industrial Transformation and the Decline of Crafts: The Decomposition of Skill in the Printing Industry." *American Sociological Review* 47 (June): 307–24.

Wardell, Mark L., and Robert L. Johnston. 1983. "Intra-Class Conflict and Platforms of Collective Action." Paper presented at Annual Meeting, Southern Sociological Society, Atlanta. April 6–9.

Weber, Max. 1947. *The Theory of Social and Economic Organization.* Translated by A. M. Henderson and Talcott Parsons. New York: Oxford University Press.

Wilson, James Q. 1973. *Political Organizations.* New York: Basic Books.

Wolensky, Robert P. 1983. "Power Structure and Group Mobilization

Following Disaster: A Case Study." *Social Science Quarterly* 64 (March): 96–110.

_____. 1984. *Power, Policy, and Disaster: The Political Organizational Impact of a Major Flood.* Final Report, NSF Grant No. CEE 8113529. Stevens Point, Wisc.: University of Wisconsin–Stevens Point, Center for the Small City.

Wolfe, Alan. 1977. *The Limits of Legitimacy: Political Contradictions of Contemporary Capitalism.* New York: Free Press.

Woodmansee, Lee. 1978. "Strike!" *Mainstream* 1 (December): 6–8, 17, 18, 28.

Wright, Erik Olin. 1978. *Class, Crisis, and the State.* London: NLB.

Yancey, William L., Eugene P. Erikson, and Richard N. Juliani. 1976. "Emergent Ethnicity: A Review and Reformulation." *American Sociological Review* 41 (June): 391–403.

Yearly, Clifton K., Jr. 1961. *Enterprise and Anthracite: Economics and Democracy in Schuylkill County, 1820–1875.* Baltimore: Johns Hopkins Press.

Zimbalist, Andrew. 1979. "Technology and the Labor Process in the Printing Industry. In Andrew Zimbalist, ed., *Case Studies in the Labor Process,* pp. 103–26. New York: Monthly Review Press.

Zimmerman, Don. 1983. Article on firing of Bernie Gallagher. *Wilkes-Barre Sunday Independent,* February 27.

Zurcher, Louis A., and David A. Snow, 1981. "Collective Behavior: Social Movements." In Ralph Turner and Morris Rosenberg, eds., *Social Psychology,* pp. 447–82. New York: Basic Books.

Index

249